"We can't all be as charismatic as Alexander the Great or Madonna, but with Cabane's help, we can sure get close!"

—Marshall Goldsmith, author of *Mojo*

"Charisma is not a gift, it's a tool. Cabane makes a big promise with this book and delivers on it."     —Seth Godin, author of *We Are All Weird*

"Cabane has done a masterful job of pulling together scientific findings and personal insights to present a coherent and compelling view of charisma. This book is engaging, clear, and chock-full of wisdom, practical recommendations, and uncommonly good sense."

—Stephen M. Kosslyn, director, Stanford University Center for Advanced Study in the Behavioral Sciences

"Olivia Fox Cabane demystifies charisma by exposing the science behind it. She clearly shows how, like every other aspect of leadership, charisma can and must be intentionally developed and through focused work can actually be increased. Used with integrity, the ideas in this book can provide a critical advantage for people looking to make a positive impact in the world."     —Evan Wittenberg, chief talent officer, Hewlett-Packard

"Cabane's masterful work puts within reach the skills we teach at the Marine Corps War College. This book will hone your charismatic talents to fully become the extraordinary person you are. In fact, this is more than a book—it's a self-transformation tool."

—Dr. Tammy S. Schultz, director, National Security and Joint Warfare, U.S. Marine Corps War College

"Some people seem to have been born with charisma, and others ask, 'Why wasn't I?' Olivia Fox Cabane has mastered the art of teaching charisma and answers, 'Why not everyone?' In this book, readers will find answers and techniques that help them create their own personal magnetism."

—Michael Feuer, cofounder, OfficeMax

"The Charisma Myth exposes the elements of that mystical appeal and power we sometimes envy in others. Olivia gives us wonderfully actionable insights to help anyone increase their effectiveness and enhance their influence."

—Randy Komisar, author of *The Monk and the Riddle* and *Getting to Plan B*

"Practical and groundbreaking: Cabane combines a compelling analysis and breakdown of the key elements of charisma, with practical and easy-to-understand advice and exercises for developing one's own charisma. Highly recommended to anyone seeking an easily approachable and engaging guide to developing their own charismatic skills."     —*Blog Business World*

PORTFOLIO / PENGUIN

# THE CHARISMA MYTH

Olivia Fox Cabane has lectured at Harvard, Yale, Stanford, MIT, and the United Nations. She is a frequent keynote speaker and executive coach to the leadership of Fortune 500 companies. From a base of thorough behavioral science, Cabane extracts the most practical tools for business, giving her clients techniques she originally developed for Harvard and MIT. She has been featured in media such as *Forbes*, *The New York Times*, *BusinessWeek*, and *The Wall Street Journal*.

# The Charisma Myth

How Anyone Can
Master the Art and Science
of Personal Magnetism

## Olivia Fox Cabane

**Portfolio • Penguin**

PORTFOLIO/PENGUIN
Published by the Penguin Group
Penguin Group (USA) Inc., 375 Hudson Street,
New York, New York 10014, USA

USA | Canada | UK | Ireland | Australia | New Zealand | India | South Africa | China
Penguin Books Ltd, Registered Offices: 80 Strand, London WC2R 0RL, England
For more information about the Penguin Group visit penguin.com

First published in the United States of America by Portfolio/Penguin,
a member of Penguin Group (USA) Inc. 2012
This paperback edition published 2013

THE LIBRARY OF CONGRESS HAS CATALOGED THE HARDCOVER EDITION AS FOLLOWS:
Cabane, Olivia Fox.
The charisma myth : how anyone can master the art and science of personal magnetism / Olivia Fox Cabane.
p. cm.
Includes bibliographical references and index.
ISBN 978-1-59184-456-3 (hc.)
ISBN 978-1-59184-594-2 (pbk.)
1. Charisma (Personality trait) I. Title.
BF698.35.C45C33 2012
158.2—dc23
2011043729

Printed in the United States of America
15  17  19  20  18  16  14

Set in Adobe Caslon Pro
Designed by Designed by Elyse Strongin and Neuwirth & Associates

While the author has made every effort to provide accurate telephone numbers, Internet addresses, and other
contact information at the time of publication, neither the publisher nor the author assumes any responsibility
for errors or for changes that occur after publication. Further, publisher does not have any control over and does
not assume any responsibility for author or third-party Web sites or their content.

# Contents

# Introduction

MARILYN MONROE WANTED to prove a point.

It was a sunny summer day in New York City, 1955. With a magazine editor and a photographer in tow, Marilyn walked down into Grand Central Terminal. Though it was the middle of a busy workday and the platform was packed with people, not a single person noticed her as she stood waiting for the subway. As the photographer's camera clicked, she boarded the train and rode along quietly in a corner of the car. Nobody recognized her.

Marilyn wanted to show that just by deciding to, she could be either glamorous Marilyn Monroe or plain Norma Jean Baker. On the subway, she was Norma Jean. But when she resurfaced onto the busy New York sidewalks, she decided to turn into Marilyn. She looked around and teasingly asked her photographer: "Do you want to see *her*?" There were no grand gestures—she just "fluffed up her hair, and struck a pose."

With this simple shift, she suddenly became magnetic. An aura of magic seemed to ripple out from her, and everything stopped. Time stood still, as did the people around her, who blinked in amazement as they suddenly recognized the star standing in their midst. In an instant Marilyn was engulfed by fans, and "it took several shoving, scary minutes" for the photographer to help her to escape the growing crowd.[1]

Charisma has always been an intriguing and controversial topic. When I tell people at conferences or cocktail parties that I "teach charisma," they immediately perk up and often exclaim, "But I thought it was something that you either have or don't." Some see it as an unfair advantage, others are eager to learn, *everyone* is fascinated. And they are right to be so. Charismatic people impact the world, whether they're starting new projects, new companies, or new empires.

Have you ever wondered what it would feel like to be as magnetic as Bill Clinton or as captivating as Steve Jobs was? Whether you think you already have some charisma and would like to take it to the next level or you've been wishing for a bit of that magic but think that you just aren't the charismatic type, I have good news: charisma is a skill that you can learn and practice.

## What Will Charisma Do for You?

Imagine what your life would be like if you knew that the moment you entered a room, people would immediately take notice, want to hear what you have to say, and be eager to earn your approval.

For charismatic people, this is a way of life. Everyone is impacted by their presence. People are magnetically drawn to them and feel strangely compelled to help them in any way they can. Charismatic people seem to lead charmed lives: they have more romantic options, they make more money, and they experience less stress.

Charisma gets people to like you, trust you, and want to be led by you. It can determine whether you're seen as a follower or a leader, whether your ideas get adopted, and how effectively your projects are implemented. Like it or not, charisma can make the world go round—it makes people *want* to do what you want them to do.

Charisma is, of course, critical in business. Whether you're applying for a new job or want to advance within your organization, it will help you achieve your goal. Multiple concurring studies indicate that charismatic people receive higher performance ratings and are viewed as more effective by their superiors and subordinates.[2]

If you're a leader, or aspire to be one, charisma matters. It gives you a competitive advantage in attracting and retaining the very best talent. It makes people want to work with you, your team, and your company. Research shows that those following charismatic leaders perform better, experience their work as more meaningful, and have more trust in their leaders than those following effective but noncharismatic leaders.[3]

As Wharton School business professor Robert House notes, charismatic leaders "cause followers to become highly committed to the leader's mission, to make significant personal sacrifices, and to perform above and beyond the call of duty."[4]

Charisma is what enables one successful salesman to sell five times more than his colleagues in the same region. It's the difference between entrepreneurs who have investors banging on their doors and those who have to beg the bank for a loan.

The power of charisma is equally valuable outside of the business environment. It's useful for the stay-at-home mom who needs to influence her children, their teachers, or other community members. It can be an invaluable tool for high school students who'd like to ace their college interviews or are running for leadership roles in student organizations. It can help individuals become more popular with their peers and feel more confident in social situations. Charismatic physicians are better liked by patients and are in greater demand, and their patients are more likely to adhere to the medical treatments they prescribe. They're also less likely to be sued when things go wrong. Charisma matters even in research and academia: charismatic individuals are more likely to get published, to attract research funding from industry grants, or to teach the most desirable courses. The professor who is always surrounded by admiring students after lectures— that's charisma, too.

## It's Not Magic, It's Learned Behaviors

Contrary to popular belief, people are not simply born charismatic—innately magnetic from birth. If charisma were an inherent attribute, charismatic people would always be captivating, and that's just not the case. Even for the most engaging superstar, charisma can be present one moment and absent the next. Marilyn Monroe could "turn off" her charisma like flipping a switch and go completely unnoticed. To turn her charisma back on, she simply changed her body language.

As extensive research in recent years has shown, charisma is the result of specific nonverbal behaviors,[5] not an inherent or magical personal quality. This is one of the reasons why charisma levels fluctuate: its presence depends on whether or not someone is exhibiting these behaviors.

Have you ever had the experience of feeling totally confident, master of a situation? A moment when people seemed impressed by you—even just one moment of the people around you going "Wow!" We don't necessarily think of these experiences as charisma, or consider ourselves charismatic, because we assume that charismatic people are magnetic every instant of every day. They aren't.

One of the reasons charisma is mistakenly held to be innate is that, like many other social skills, charismatic behaviors are generally learned early in life. In fact, people usually don't consciously realize they are learning them. They're just trying new behaviors, seeing the results, and refining them. Eventually, the behaviors become instinctive.

Countless well-known charismatic figures worked hard to gain their charisma, increasing it step by step. But because we come to know them at the peak of their charisma, it can be hard to believe these superstars weren't always so impressive.

Former Apple CEO Steve Jobs, considered one of the most charismatic CEOs of the decade, did not start out that way. In fact, if you watch his earliest presentations, you'll see that he came across as bashful and awkward, veering from overly dramatic to downright nerdy. Jobs progressively increased his level of charisma over the years, and you can see the gradual improvement in his public appearances.

Charisma has come under the scrutiny of sociologists, psychologists, and cognitive and behavioral scientists. It has been studied in multiple ways, from clinical laboratory experiments and cross-sectional and longitudinal survey research to qualitative interpretative analysis. The subjects of these studies have been presidents, military leaders, students of all ages, and business executives from low-level managers to CEOs. Thanks to such research, we now understand charisma as a set of behaviors.

## What Does Charismatic Behavior Look Like?

When we first meet someone, we instinctively assess whether that person is a potential friend or foe and whether they have the power to enact those intentions. Power and intentions are what we're aiming to assess. "Could you move mountains for me? And would you care to do so?" To answer the first question, we try to assess how much power he or she has. To answer the second question, we try to assess how much he or she likes us. When you meet a charismatic person, you get the impression that they have a lot of power and they like you a lot.

The equation that produces charisma is actually fairly simple. All you have to do is give the impression that you possess both high power and high warmth, since charismatic behaviors project a combination of these two qualities. "Fight or flight?" is the power question. "Friend or foe?" is the warmth question.

A final dimension underlies both of these qualities: presence. When people describe their experience of seeing charisma in action, whether they met Colin Powell, Condoleezza Rice, or the Dalai Lama, they often mention the individual's extraordinary "presence."

Presence is the single most requested aspect of charisma when I'm coaching executives. They want to increase their *executive presence* or *boardroom presence*. And they're right to focus on it: presence turns out to be the real core component of charisma, the foundation upon which all else is built. When you're with a charismatic master—take Bill Clinton, for example—you not only feel his power and a sense of warm engagement, you also feel that he's completely here with you, in this moment. Present.

## Practical Magic

Charisma has been turned into an applied science. What this book does is translate the science into practical, immediately applicable tools, with measurable results. You'll learn charisma in a methodical, systematic way, with practical exercises immediately useful in the real world. And, unlike those of us who learned by trial and error, you won't have to waste any time figuring out what works and what doesn't. *You* can go straight to the tried-and-true tools that really do enhance charisma.

Becoming more charismatic does involve work—work that is sometimes hard, uncomfortable, and even daunting. But it's also incredibly rewarding, both in terms of how you will relate to yourself and how others will relate to you. It involves managing your mental ecosystem, understanding and attending to your own needs, as well as knowing which behaviors inspire others to see you as charismatic and learning how to project them.

This book will guide you through that process. It will give you concrete tools for projecting the three crucial aspects of charisma: presence, power, and warmth. As you use them, you will experience an increased sense of personal magnetism—and if it was already strongly present, you'll gain finer control over that charismatic power. You'll learn how to harness it and how to skillfully wield it. You'll also learn how to choose the right kind of charisma for your personality and your goals in any situation.

You'll get an inside peek at what goes on in the minds—and bodies—of charismatic people. I'll give you insights into what the CEOs I coach wrestle with behind closed doors.

What you'll find here is practical magic: unique knowledge, drawn from a variety of sciences, revealing what charisma really is and how it works. You'll get both the insights and the techniques you need to apply this knowledge. The world will become your lab, and every time you meet someone, you'll get an opportunity to experiment.

Once you've mastered the basics, you'll be ready to learn how to be charismatic even in difficult situations, for instance when you're having a career-changing conversation, dealing with a difficult person, or delivering a presentation. And once you know how to access charisma at will, you'll get the insider secrets to living life as a charismatic person.

You'll learn how to become more influential, more persuasive, and more inspiring. You'll learn how to exude charisma—the ability to move through a room and have people go, "Wow, who's *that*?"

# 1

## Charisma Demystified

IN THE TORRID London summer of 1886, William Gladstone was up against Benjamin Disraeli for the post of prime minister of the United Kingdom. This was the Victorian era, so whoever won was going to rule half the world. In the very last week before the election, both men happened to take the same young woman out to dinner. Naturally, the press asked her what impressions the rivals had made. She said, "After dining with Mr. Gladstone, I thought he was the cleverest person in England. But after dining with Mr. Disraeli, I thought *I* was the cleverest person in England."

Guess who won the election? It was the man who made *others* feel intelligent, impressive, and fascinating: Benjamin Disraeli.

Consciously or not, charismatic individuals choose specific behaviors that make other people feel a certain way. These behaviors can be learned and perfected by anyone. In fact, in controlled laboratory experiments, researchers were able to raise and lower people's levels of charisma as if they were turning a dial.[1]

Contrary to commonly held charisma myths, you don't have to be naturally outgoing, you don't have to be physically attractive, and you won't have to change your personality. No matter where you're starting from, you can significantly increase your personal charisma and reap the rewards both in business and in daily life.

The most common charisma myth is that you have to be naturally boisterous or outgoing to be charismatic. One of the most interesting research findings is that you can be a very charismatic introvert. In Western society, we place such emphasis on the skills and abilities of extroverts that introverts can end up feeling defective and uncool. But introversion is not a terminal handicap. In fact, as we'll see, it can be a strong advantage for certain forms of charisma.

It is also a myth that you have to be attractive to be charismatic. Countless charismatic figures were far from fitting classic standards of beauty. Churchill was not generally considered handsome and certainly not known for his sex appeal. And yet he was one of history's most influential and powerful leaders.

Yes, good looks do confer some advantage. But it's very possible to be charismatic without a striking face or figure. In fact, charisma itself will make you more attractive. When instructed to exhibit specific charismatic behaviors in controlled experiments, participants' levels of attractiveness were rated significantly higher than before.[2]

Last but not least, you won't have to change your personality. In order to become more charismatic, you don't have to force yourself into one particular personality style or do something that is against your nature.

Instead, you will learn some new skills.

Through charisma training you will learn how to adopt a charismatic posture, how to warm up your eye contact, and how to modulate your voice in ways that make people pay attention. Three quick tips to gain an instant charisma boost in conversation:

- Lower the intonation of your voice at the end of your sentences.
- Reduce how quickly and how often you nod.
- Pause for two full seconds before you speak.

As you can see, these are simple tweaks, not deep value changes. Your personality will stay the same as long as you want it to.

Will these new skills and behaviors feel odd at first? They may. But, then, so did brushing your teeth when you first learned how, though now (I hope) it's become a habit you perform each day without thinking. Like many new skills, charismatic behaviors might feel awkward at first, but with practice they will become second nature, like walking, talking, or driving. This book is your step-by-step guide to acquiring these behaviors and making them your own.

We understand that proficiency at chess, singing, or hitting a fastball requires conscious practice. Charisma is a skill that can also be developed through conscious practice, and because we're interacting with people all the time, we get to use our charisma tools on a daily basis.

I know that a person's charisma level can be changed through conscious practice because I've helped countless clients increase theirs in this way. Interviewing people close to my clients before and after our work together confirmed that they were able to change how people perceived them. I've also taught these charisma tools at both the undergraduate and graduate levels, after UC Berkeley's business school asked me to create a complete curriculum for charisma and leadership.

If you follow the instructions in this book, you *will* increase your level of charisma. And once these practices become second nature, they keep operating in the background without your needing to give them any thought—and you'll keep reaping their rewards from then onward.

## How This Will Work for You

I've reverse-engineered the science of charisma by learning the behavioral and cognitive science behind it and striving to extract the most practical tools and techniques. This book helps you put the science into practice so that you can accelerate your learning curve.

I am offering you the tools that will give you the highest return on your investment and the best, most effective techniques from a broad range of disciplines—from behavioral, cognitive, and neuroscience to meditation; from peak-performance athletic conditioning to Hollywood Method acting.

I'll give you the science when it's relevant (or fun, or fascinating), and, more important, I'll give you the practical tools. My goal with this book is to give you techniques you can immediately apply to gain both the skills and the self-confidence that lead to outstanding performance.

When I'm asked how soon my coaching produces results, I answer: In one session, you'll feel the difference. In two sessions, others will see the difference. In three sessions, you'll have a whole new presence.

However, just reading this book won't yield its full benefits. You would be shortchanging yourself if you avoided any of the exercises, as odd or even uncomfortable as they may feel at times. To be successful, you have to be willing to put in the effort of applying what you read. When an exercise asks you to close your eyes and imagine a scene, really close your eyes and do it. When I ask you to write out a scenario, grab a piece of paper and a pen that writes.

This is the very challenge I bring into the office of every executive who's ever hired me. There is no substitute for doing the exercises. Skimming through them with the earnest intention of completing them "another day" is not enough, nor is doing only the exercises that seem easy or interesting. If I ask you to do something, it's for a good reason, and it will have a real impact on your level of charisma.

Some of the techniques you'll learn here will give you results immediately, such as learning how to be charismatic when presenting to audiences small or large. Others will take weeks to fully unfold. Some might be surprising, like learning how your toes can help maximize your charisma potential.

When I asked one of my clients what advice he would give others about to start this work, he said: "Tell them that: even though it can seem intimidating at first, and you'll be taken out of your comfort zone, it's worth it." Commit, and do your homework.

# 2

# The Charismatic Behaviors

Presence, Power, and Warmth

CHARISMATIC BEHAVIOR CAN be broken down into three core elements: presence, power, and warmth. These elements depend both on our conscious behaviors and on factors we don't consciously control. People pick up on messages we often don't even realize we're sending through small changes in our body language. In this chapter, we'll explore how these signals can be influenced. In order to be charismatic, we need to choose mental states that make our body language, words, and behaviors flow together and express the three core elements of charisma. Since presence is the foundation for everything else, that's where we'll start.

## Presence

Have you ever felt, in the middle of a conversation, as if only half of your mind were present while the other half was busy doing something else? Do you think the other person noticed?

If you're not fully present in an interaction, there's a good chance that your eyes will glaze over or that your facial reactions will be a split-second delayed. Since the human mind can read facial expressions in as little as seventeen milliseconds,[1] the person you're speaking with will likely notice even the tiniest delays in your reactions.

We may think that we can fake presence. We may think that we can fake listening. We believe that as long as we seem attentive, it's okay to let our brains churn on other things. But we're wrong. When we're not fully present in an interaction, people will see it. Our body language sends a clear message that other people read and react to, at least on a subconscious level.

You've surely had the experience of talking to someone who wasn't really listening. Maybe they seemed to be just "going through the motions" of listening to you so you wouldn't be offended. Somehow, they didn't seem to be paying full attention. How did you feel then? Brushed off? Annoyed? Just plain bad? As a student in one of my Harvard lectures told me: "It happened recently when I was talking to someone—I felt she wasn't really present. I felt resentful, inferior to whatever was more important to her than our conversation."

Not only can the lack of presence be visible, it can also be perceived as inauthentic, which has even worse emotional consequences. When you're perceived as disingenuous, it's virtually impossible to generate trust, rapport, or loyalty. And it's impossible to be charismatic.

Presence is a learnable skill. Like any other ability (from painting to playing the piano), you can increase it with practice and patience. Being present means simply having a moment-to-moment awareness of what's happening. It means paying attention to what's going on rather than being caught up in your own thoughts.

Now that you know the cost of lacking presence, try the exercise on the next page to test yourself, see how present you can be, and learn three simple techniques to immediately boost your charisma in personal interactions.

## Putting It into Practice: Presence

Here are a few techniques for remaining present, adapted from mindfulness disciplines. All you need is a reasonably quiet place where you can close your eyes (whether standing or sitting) for just one minute and a way to keep track of time.

Set the timer for one minute. Close your eyes and try to focus on one of the following three things: the sounds around you, your breathing, or the sensations in your toes.

1. Sounds: Scan your environment for sound. As a meditation teacher told me, "Imagine that your ears are satellite dishes, passively and objectively registering sounds."

2. Your breath: Focus on your breath and the sensations it creates in your nostrils or stomach as it goes in and out. Pay attention to one breath at a time, but try to notice *everything* about this one breath. Imagine that your breath is someone you want to give your full attention to.

3. Your toes: Focus your attention on the sensations in your toes. This forces your mind to sweep through your body, helping you to get into the physical sensations of the moment.

So how did that go? Did you find your mind constantly wandering even though you were trying your best to be present? As you've noticed, staying fully present isn't always easy. There are two main reasons for this.

First, our brains are wired to pay attention to novel stimuli, whether they be sights, smells, or sounds. We're wired to be distracted, to have our attention grabbed by any new stimulus: It could be important! It could eat us! This tendency was key to our ancestors' survival. Imagine two tribesmen hunting through the plains, searching the horizon for signs of the antelope that could feed their family. Something flickers in the distance. The tribesman whose attention wasn't immediately caught? He's not our ancestor.

The second reason is that our society encourages distraction. The constant influx of stimulation we receive worsens our natural tendencies. This can eventually lead us into a state of *continuous partial attention,* in which we never give our full attention to any single thing. We're always partially distracted.

So if you often find it hard to be fully present, don't beat yourself up. This is entirely normal. Presence is hard for almost all of us. A 2,250-person study coauthored by Harvard psychologist Daniel Gilbert estimated that nearly half of the average person's time was spent "mind wandering."[2] Even meditation masters can find their minds wandering during their practice. In fact, this is a common subject of jokes during intensive meditation retreats (yes, there are such things as meditation jokes).

The good news is that even a minor increase in your capacity for presence can have a major effect on those around you. Because so few of us are ever fully present, if you can manage even a few moments of full presence from time to time, you'll make quite an impact.

The very next time you're in a conversation, try to regularly check whether your mind is fully engaged or whether it is wandering elsewhere (including preparing your next sentence). Aim to bring yourself back to the present moment as often as you can by focusing on your breath or your toes for just a second, and then get back to focusing on the other person.

One of my clients, after trying this exercise for the first time, reported: "I found myself relaxing, smiling, and others suddenly noticed me and smiled back without my saying a word."

Don't be discouraged if you feel that you didn't fully succeed in the one-minute exercise above. You actually did gain a charisma boost right then and there simply by practicing presence. And because you've already gained the mindset shift (awareness of the importance of presence and the cost of the lack of it), you're now already ahead of the game. If you were to stop right here and read nothing further, it would be well worth it.

Here's how this could play out for you in a practical, everyday setting. Let's say a colleague walks into your office, wanting your opinion on some matter. You have only a few minutes to spare before your next meeting, and you're worried that this might take more time than you have.

If you let your mind continue churning away while he's talking to you, not only will you feel anxious and have a hard time concentrating, you'll also give the impression that you're restless and not fully present. Your colleague might conclude that you don't care enough about him or his problem to really pay attention.

If instead you remember to use one of the quick fixes—focusing for just a second on your breath or your toes—this will instantly bring you back to the present moment. This full presence will show in your eyes and your face, and will be seen by the person who's talking to you. By giving them just a few moments of full presence, they will feel respected and listened to. When you're fully present, it shows in your body language in a highly charisma-enhancing way.

Being charismatic does not depend on how much time you have but on how fully present you are in each interaction. The ability to be fully present makes you stand out from the crowd; it makes you memorable. When you're fully present, even a five-minute conversation can create a "wow" effect, as well as an emotional connection. The people you're with feel that they have your full attention and that they are the most important thing in the world to you at that moment.

One client told me that he frequently upset people when he was under pressure or dealing with multiple requests. If someone came to see him, while they talked his mind would wander back to whatever he had been working on, and as a result that person felt brushed off and unimportant.

After putting some of these focus exercises to work, he reported, "I learned how valuable it was to give them my full attention even for just a few moments, and the techniques helped me stay present in that moment. As a result, people left my office feeling cared for, special." This, he told me, was one of the most valuable lessons he'd learned from all our work together.

Increasing your ability to be present not only improves your body language, listening skills, and mental focus, it could even enhance your ability to enjoy life. Too often when a special moment arrives, such as a celebration or even a few minutes of quality time with a loved one, our mind is running in six different directions.

Meditation teacher Tara Brach has made the practice of *being present* a lifetime study. Here's how she puts it: "In most moments we have a continuous internal commentary on what is happening and what we should do next. We might greet a friend with a hug, but the warmth of our greeting becomes blurred by our computations about how long to embrace or what we're going to say when we're done. We rush through the motions, not fully present." Being present enables you to fully notice and drink in the good moments.

You've just gained three instant fixes to use during interactions, and through practice, they can become second nature. Remember that every time you bring yourself back to full presence, you reap major rewards: you become more impactful, more memorable, and come across as more grounded. You're laying the foundation for a charismatic presence.

Now that you know what presence is, why it matters to charisma, and how to get it, let's look at the other two crucial charisma qualities: power and warmth.

## Power and Warmth

Being seen as powerful means being perceived as able to affect the world around us, whether through influence on or authority over others, large amounts of money, expertise, intelligence, sheer physical strength, or high social status. We look for clues of power in someone's appearance, in others' reaction to this person, and, most of all, in the person's body language.

Warmth, simply put, is goodwill toward others. Warmth tells us whether or not people will want to use whatever power they have in our favor. Being seen as warm means being perceived as any of the following: benevolent, altruistic, caring, or willing to impact our world in a positive way. Warmth is assessed almost entirely through body language and behavior; it's evaluated more directly than power.

How do we gauge power and warmth? Imagine that you're meeting someone for the first time. In most instances you don't have the benefit of an extensive background check, interviews with friends or relatives, or even the time to wait and observe their behavior. So in most instances you have to make a quick guess.

Throughout our interactions, we instinctively look for clues with which to evaluate warmth or power, and then we adjust our assumptions accordingly. Expensive clothing leads us to *assume* wealth, friendly body language leads us to *assume* good intentions, a confident posture leads us to *assume* the person has something to be confident about. In essence, people will tend to accept whatever you project.

Just by increasing your projection of power or your projection of warmth, you increase your level of charisma. But when you can project both power and warmth together, you really maximize your personal charisma potential.

Today, there are many ways to be perceived as powerful, from displaying intelligence (think Bill Gates) to displaying kindness (think the Dalai Lama). But in the earliest days of human history, one form of power was predominant: brute force. Yes, intelligence was valuable, but much less than it is today—it's hard to imagine Bill Gates faring well in the jungle. Few of those who gained positions of power through raw strength and aggression would have also exhibited much warmth. The combination of power and warmth would have been very rare and very, very precious: a powerful person who also viewed us kindly could mean the difference between life and death in critical moments. Figuring out who might want to help us and who has the power to do so has always been critical to our survival.

That's why our reaction to power and warmth is wired so deep. We react to these qualities as we do to fat and sugar. Our ancestors survived by having a strong positive reaction to fat and sugar—they aided our survival and were scarce in our original environment. Though they're abundant today, our instinct remains. The same holds true for charisma: though the combination of warmth and power is far easier for people to attain today, it still plays powerfully on our instincts. From lab experiments to neuroimaging, research has consistently shown that they are the two dimensions we evaluate first and foremost in assessing other people.[3]

Both power and warmth are necessary conditions for charisma.

Someone who is powerful but not warm can be impressive, but isn't necessarily perceived as charismatic and can come across as arrogant, cold, or standoffish. Someone who possesses warmth without power can be likable, but isn't necessarily perceived as charismatic and can come across as overeager, subservient, or desperate to please.

William Gladstone projected power during the 1886 elections. A high-status individual of strong political weight and powerful connections, known for keen intelligence and deep knowledge, he impressed his young dinner companion with his power, but lacked the warmth to make her feel special.

Disraeli was also projecting power. He, too, had a history of political power, impressive wit, and keen intelligence. But Disraeli's genius was his ability to make whomever he was speaking with feel intelligent and fascinating. He projected presence and warmth in addition to power and was handsomely rewarded for it.

Though other approaches to charisma are possible, the combination of presence, power, and warmth is one of the most effective frameworks to help maximize your full charisma potential.

## Charismatic Body Language

After extensive studies, the MIT Media Lab concluded that it could predict the outcome of negotiations, telephone sales calls, and business plan pitches with 87 percent accuracy simply by analyzing participants' body language, without listening to a single word of content.[4]

Though this may sound incredible—how could words carry so little weight compared to the body language of the person delivering them?—it actually makes sense. In the scope of human evolution, language is a relatively recent invention. But we've been interacting well before this through nonverbal modes of communication. As a result, nonverbal communication is hardwired into our brains, much deeper than the more recent language-processing abilities. This is why nonverbal communication has a far greater impact.

For charisma, your body language matters far more than your words do. No matter how powerful your message or how skillfully crafted your pitch, if your body language is wrong, you won't be charismatic. On the other hand, with the right body language you can be charismatic without saying a word. Projecting presence, power, and warmth through your body language is often all you need to be perceived as charismatic.

## Charisma Begins in the Mind

While you were reading the last paragraph, were you aware that your eyelids were regularly fluttering in front of your eyes?

No? Yet they were blinking at precise intervals.

Did you notice the weight of your tongue in your mouth?

Or the position of your toes?

Have you forgotten your eyelids again?

Without our realizing it, our bodies send out thousands of signals every minute. Just like our breath and heartbeat, these signals are part of the millions of bodily functions controlled not by our conscious mind but by our subconscious mind. There is far too much body language for us to control consciously.

This has two consequences. First, because we can't consciously control all of our body language, we can't just broadcast charismatic body language at will. To get all the signals right, we'd need to simultaneously control thousands of elements, from minute vocal fluctuations to the precise degree and kind of tension around our eyes. It's practically impossible. We can't micromanage charismatic body language. On the other hand, since our subconscious is responsible for most of our nonverbal signals, if we could direct our subconscious appropriately, then the issue would be solved. (Hint: we can, and you'll learn how.)

The second consequence is that our body language expresses our mental state whether we like it or not. Our facial expressions, voice, posture, and all the other components of body language reflect our mental and emotional condition every second. Because we don't control this flow consciously, whatever is in our head will show up in our body language.

Even if we control the main expression on our face or the way we hold our arms, legs, or head, if our internal state is different from what we're aiming to portray, sooner or later what's called a *microexpression* will flash across our face. These split-second microexpressions may be fleeting, but they will be caught by observers (remember, people can read your face in as little as seventeen milliseconds). And if there's an incongruence between our main expression and that microexpression, people will feel it on a subconscious level: their gut will tell them something's not quite right.*

Have you ever sensed the difference between a real smile and a fake one? There is a clear, visible difference between a *social smile* and a *true smile*. A true smile brings into play two groups of facial muscles—one lifts the corners of the mouth and the other affects the area around the eyes. In a genuine smile, while the outer corners of the mouth lift, the inner corners of the eyebrows soften and fall down. In a fake smile, only the mouth-corner muscle (the zygomatic major) is used. The smile does not reach the eyes, or at least not in the same way a real smile would,[6] and people can spot the difference.

Because what's in your mind shows up in your body and because people will catch even the briefest microexpression, to be effective, *charismatic behaviors must originate in your mind.*

If your internal state is anticharismatic, no amount of effort and willpower can make up for it. Sooner or later, some of your underlying thoughts and feelings will show through. On the other hand, if your internal state *is* charismatic, then the right body language will flow forth effortlessly. Thus, the first step in learning charisma—and what the first part of this book is all about—is developing the various mental states that produce charismatic body language and behaviors.

We will start by gaining some insight into charismatic mental states—what they are, how to best access them, and how to fully integrate them so they become effortless. Only afterward will we start practicing external charismatic behaviors. Learning these skills in the reverse order could lead to embarrassing results. Imagine that you're giving an important presentation. You're doing well, using all the great new tools you've learned, being incredibly charismatic. And

---

* In fact, Stanford researchers conducted experiments showing that when people try to hide their real feelings, they provoke a threat-response arousal in others.[5]

then suddenly, someone says something that rattles your mental focus and shakes your emotional confidence. You become flustered, and all your newly acquired skills fly out the window.

Striving to acquire external charisma skills without learning how to handle your internal world is like adding pretty balconies to a house with a weak foundation. It's a nice touch, but at the first earthquake everything falls apart. If your internal state is in turmoil, it's hard to remember, let alone use, the new skills you've just learned. Charismatic internal skills, which help you manage your internal state, form the necessary foundation upon which to build your charismatic external skills.

When companies hire me to help them improve performance—to help their executives become more persuasive, more influential, more inspiring—they often tell me that their people possess solid *technical* skills. Technical skills are raw brainpower, what we use to understand the instructions for assembling furniture. What these executives are lacking, I'm told, are social skills—and so people arrive expecting surface lessons in social graces and business etiquette.

But what these executives need first and foremost are personal, *internal* skills. Individuals with strong internal skills are aware of what exactly is happening inside them and know how to handle it. They can recognize when their self-confidence has taken a hit and have the tools to get back to a confident state so that their body language remains charismatic.

Here's a self-rating diagram I often draw for the people I coach, from young associates to CEOs, asking them to evaluate themselves and their subordinates. Take a moment to rate your technical, external, and internal skills in the table below.

|        | TECHNICAL SKILLS | EXTERNAL SKILLS | INTERNAL SKILLS |
|--------|------------------|-----------------|-----------------|
| High   |                  |                 |                 |
| Medium |                  |                 |                 |
| Low    |                  |                 |                 |

I often see brilliant engineers described by others, and by themselves, as possessing high technical, medium external, and low internal skills. CEOs tend to self-report medium technical and internal skills but high external skills. And highly charismatic people often rate themselves low in technical skills but high in external and internal skills.

While charismatic people may report fewer technical skills than their peers, their internal and external skills give them a far greater advantage overall. The internal skills necessary for charisma include both the awareness of your internal state and the tools to effectively manage it. Chinese philosopher Lao Tzu reportedly said: "To know others is knowledge. To know oneself is wisdom."

## What Your Mind Believes, Your Body Manifests

Knowing your internal world starts with one key insight upon which all charisma is built: your mind can't tell fact from fiction. This is the one dimension of your internal world that can help you get into the right charismatic mental state at will, and almost instantly.

Have you ever felt your heart pounding during a horror movie? Consciously, you know it's just a movie. You realize you are watching actors who are delighted to pretend they're being murdered in exchange for a nice paycheck. Yet your brain sees blood and guts on the screen, so it sends you straight into fight-or-flight mode, releasing adrenaline into your system. Here's how it works in practice:

Think of your favorite piece of music.

Now imagine dragging your fingernails across a chalkboard.

Now imagine plunging your hand into a bucket of sand and feeling the grains crunch between your fingers.

And now taste the difference between lemon and lime—which is more sour?

There was no sand; there was no lemon. And yet, in response to a set of completely imaginary events, your mind produced very real physical reactions. Because your brain cannot distinguish imagination from reality, imaginary situations cause your brain to send your body the same commands as it would for a real situation. Whatever your mind believes, your body will manifest. Just by getting into a charismatic mental state, your body will manifest a charismatic body language.

In medicine, the mind's powerfully positive effect on the body is known as the *placebo effect*. A placebo is a simulated medical procedure: patients given "pretend" pills are told they're receiving real ones; or people are told they've received a medical intervention when in fact nothing has been done. In a surprising number of cases, patients given these inert treatments still experience a real improvement in their medical condition.

The placebo effect was discovered during World War I when medicine stores had run out and doctors found they could sometimes still ease their patients' suffering by telling them that they had administered pain-relieving treatments. It became widely acknowledged during the 1950s as the medical community began running controlled clinical studies. Through much of human history, most of medicine was in fact pure placebo: doctors would prescribe potions or interventions that we now know to be fundamentally ineffective. Yet people's conditions still often improved, thanks to the mind's impressive ability to affect the body.

The placebo effect can sometimes be remarkably powerful. Ellen Langer, a Harvard University professor of psychology, gathered a group of elderly patients in a nursing-home-like environment and surrounded them with the decor, clothing, food, and music that was popular when they were in their twenties. In the following weeks, physical exams showed tighter skin, better eyesight, increased muscle strength, and even higher bone density than before.

The placebo effect is the basis for many of the best charisma-enhancing techniques, and we'll refer to it often throughout the book. In fact, this is probably something you already do naturally, and many of the practices will make intuitive sense to you. In the following chapters, we'll fine-tune this skill and make more powerful the internal processes you already use.

The mind-over-body effect also has a corresponding downside, called the *nocebo effect*.[7] In this case, the mind creates toxic consequences in the body in reaction to completely fictional causes.

Both the placebo effect and the nocebo effect play a critical role in our ability to unleash our full charisma potential. Due to the fact that whatever is in our mind affects our body, and because our mind has trouble distinguishing imagination from reality, whatever we imagine can have an impact on our body language and, thus, on our levels of charisma. Our imagination can dramatically enhance or inhibit our charisma, depending on its content.

You've just gained the foundation for many of the most powerful internal charisma tools, and we'll refer to it often.

### KEY TAKEAWAYS

- Charisma has three essential components: presence, power, and warmth.
- Being present—paying attention to what's going on rather than being caught up in your thoughts—can yield immense rewards. When you exhibit presence, those around you feel listened to, respected, and valued.
- Because your body language telegraphs your internal state to those around you, in order to be charismatic—to exhibit presence, power, and warmth—you must display charismatic body language.
- Because your mind can't tell the difference between imagination and reality, by creating a charismatic internal state your body language will authentically display charisma.
- In terms of achieving charisma, your internal state is critical. Get the internal state right, and the right charismatic behaviors and body language will pour forth automatically.

# 3

## The Obstacles to Presence, Power, and Warmth

MICHELANGELO INSISTED THAT he never *created* his glorious statues—he simply *revealed* them. His only talent, he said, was in looking at the block of marble and discerning the statue within. All he then needed was the skill to chip away the excess, letting the statue emerge. That is what this chapter will help you do: identify the obstacles that are holding back your charismatic self.

As you now know, your mental state is critical to your ability to project charismatic body language. However, there are a number of things that can—and often do—get in the way of having the right mental state to project presence, power, or warmth. Increasing your charisma requires first knowing which internal obstacles are currently inhibiting your personal charisma potential. In this chapter we'll take a look at the different kinds of physical and mental discomfort that can stand in the way of your charismatic self.

## Physical Discomfort

It was a $4 million deal, and it was nearly lost because of a black wool suit.

On a hot, sunny day in Manhattan, traffic is humming and people are rushing along the busy streets. Sitting at the terrace of a restaurant, wearing his very best black wool suit, Tom is studying the menu. Across the table, studying his own menu, is Paul, CEO of a company Tom has been courting for months. As they make their choices, the waiter jots down their orders, whisks the menus off the table, and departs.

For months, Tom and his team have obsessively run the numbers and tested all possible scenarios. They know for sure that their system would save Paul both time and money. But for Paul, this would be a big gamble. Implementing a new system company-wide could go catastrophically wrong. What if it stops working on Christmas morning, when stores need to be operating flawlessly? Would Tom and his team be there for him if a crisis hits?

Paul has decided to give Tom one final shot at convincing him. For Tom, this could be a turning point in his career. He's confident that his system is solid and that he and his team can deliver. It's now up to him to communicate this complete confidence to Paul.

When Paul asks about crisis situations, Tom has a ready answer. But as he details contingency plans, he starts fidgeting with his suit, running his fingers inside the rim of his collar, and Paul can see Tom's eyes narrowing. *Is that tension in his eyes?* Paul wonders. Tom's expression looks tight and uncomfortable, and Paul starts to get a bad gut feeling. *What's going on?*

Paul was right in seeing tension in Tom's eyes and face, but that tension had nothing to do with the business matter at hand. Wearing a black woolen suit on a hot, sunny day, Tom was simply feeling *physically* uncomfortable.

What if you had been in Tom's place? Even without the itchy suit, imagine being on a sunny terrace in the middle of an important conversation, and suddenly the sun starts hitting your eyes. When human eyes are hit by sunlight, they automatically tighten or narrow in reaction. Our eye muscles react in the exact same way to this kind of external stimuli as they do to internal stimuli. To the outside world, your face will show the same reaction to discomfort from the sun as it would to feelings of anger or disapproval. This reaction will be seen by the person facing you, and he or she may not know about your physical discomfort. All they know is that they've been speaking with you. It would be natural to misinterpret your tension as a reaction to what they've just said.

In fact, that's probably exactly what will happen, because most of us tend to interpret events—whether they're personal or impersonal—as relating to us. Traffic on the way to an important meeting can lead us to wonder, *Why did this have to happen to* me *today?*

Any physical discomfort that affects your visible, external state— your body language—even slightly may affect how charismatic you are perceived to be. When interacting with someone, assume that he or she will feel (at least on a subconscious level) that whatever you do relates to him or to her.

Physical discomfort doesn't just affect your external state; it also affects your internal state. Some forms of it, such as hunger, can impair your performance in multiple ways. You may already know that you think less clearly when you're hungry, or at least less clearly about anything that isn't food-related. Numerous studies confirm that low blood glucose levels lead to impaired attention as well as to difficulties regulating emotions and behavior.[1] This means that you might have a harder time getting into the specific mental state required for the charismatic behavior you would like to exhibit.

Counteracting charisma-impairing physical discomfort is simple:

1. Prevent
2. Recognize
3. Remedy or explain

The first, and optimal, step is to plan ahead to prevent the discomfort from occurring. The classic adage "An ounce of prevention is worth a pound of cure" holds true here. As much as you can, plan ahead to ensure you're physically comfortable. Keeping this in mind as you make your choices every day is a simple way to make charisma easier to attain.

When you're choosing a location for a meeting, take comfort into consideration. Ask yourself what the temperature and noise level will be like. Ensure that you'll be well fed; don't let yourself (or your guests if you're hosting) get too hungry. Think about your energy level, and the energy level of the people with whom you'll be interacting. Is the meeting very early or very late? Signs of fatigue can easily show up in people's body language as lack of enthusiasm.

Be sure to choose clothing that will make you neither too hot nor too cold. Avoid clothing that is itchy, ill fitting, or in any way distracting. Though you may not realize it, any physical distraction will use up part of your mental focus and impair your performance. It's particularly important to ensure that your clothing is loose enough for you to breathe well and fully (this means you can take deep belly breaths, not shallow chest breaths). How well you breathe affects how much oxygen gets to your brain, and therefore how well you perform mentally.

Admittedly, people may gain valuable confidence, and therefore charisma, from feeling that they look impressive even if their clothing is not comfortable. It's really up to you to decide: is the discomfort worth the gain in confidence? Ideally, you should wear clothing that makes you feel both comfortable and highly confident in your appearance. Make sure you're not sacrificing comfort in small ways that might actually be holding you back. You're looking to get every advantage you can, right?

One young man told me his eyes are so sensitive to sunlight that even when he explains the real cause of his facial tension, the people he's with often seem to doubt his explanation. On a gut level, they still feel there's a problem between them. His solution is to assess the room before sitting down to make sure he won't be facing the sun or to ask to change positions as soon as the sun becomes a problem. Because he is aware of this problem, he can take action before it affects the way he's perceived.

Awareness is the second step in dealing with physical discomfort.

Check in with your face from time to time; notice if it is tense. This is where the ability to stay present will help you yet again: the more present you are, the better your chances of noticing if your body language is showing tension.

The third step is to take action. If you realize that something has created tension in your face, *do something about it*. Before others misinterpret it, try to remedy both the discomfort as well as the misinterpretation.

Let's go back to that conversation on the terrace, when the sun was in Tom's eyes. Now you know that he shouldn't try to ignore his discomfort. Instead, he could act to explain and remedy the situation. When it's his turn to speak, he could pause for a second, hold up a hand (the visual cue helps), and say something like: "Would you mind if we move just a bit? My eyes are having a hard time with the sunlight."

When the physical discomfort can't be alleviated, it's even more important to prevent other people from taking your tension personally. Take a moment to explain that you're in discomfort due to a particular issue. For instance, if you're feeling irritated by constant nearby construction noise, explain the problem. Giving voice to something will generally allow both of you to move on from it.

## Mental Discomfort

Though it originates entirely in the mind, psychological discomfort can play out through our bodies as well as through our minds. It affects both how we feel and how we're perceived. Mental discomfort can result from anxiety, dissatisfaction, self-criticism, or self-doubt, all of which are forms of internal negativity, and each of which can handicap our personal charisma potential.

Knowing how to skillfully handle mental discomfort is even more important than knowing how to handle physical discomfort. This is both one of the most challenging sections of the book and one of the most important. It may be difficult to process, but I promise you will benefit in the end. In fact, you'll be much more powerful. You will have gained insights to put you ahead of the game, and you will have laid a foundation of understanding upon which the next sections will build. So brace yourself, take a deep breath, and read on.

## Anxiety Caused by Uncertainty

Have you ever had the awful feeling that you're just waiting for the other shoe to drop, and finding sometimes that you'd rather hear bad news than be left in suspense? Let's say you've recently become romantically involved with someone, and all of a sudden they stop returning your calls. Your brain goes into all sorts of possible explanations, obsessing about why they've gone silent. Haven't you ever felt that you'd rather get a definite "It's over" than never know the cause of their silence? Even though the answer would be a rejection, *at least then you'd know.*

For many of us, a state of doubt or uncertainty is an uncomfortable place to be. Robert Leahy, director of the American Institute for Cognitive Therapy, says his patients often report they would rather receive a negative diagnosis than be left in suspense, even though the uncertainty would still allow hope of a positive outcome.

Our inability to tolerate uncertainty carries multiple costs. It can cause us to make premature decisions. It can handicap us in negotiations, leading us to reveal more than we should as we scramble to fill the silence, unable to bear the uncertainty of not knowing what the other person is thinking. And most important, it can lead us to feel anxious. Anxiety is a serious drawback to charisma. First, it impacts our internal state: quite obviously, it's hard to be fully present while you're feeling anxious. Anxiety can also lower our confidence. Anxiety, low presence, and low confidence can show up directly in our body language, as well as reduce our ability to emanate warmth.

Yet if there's one thing that's certain, it's that uncertainty isn't going away. Considering the ever-increasing pace of business and technological advances as well as unforeseeable economic upheavals, uncertainty and ambiguity will be an increasingly present factor of our daily lives. Those who are better at handling it will gain a distinctive advantage over others.

Imagine you're dealing with a difficult situation whose outcome is uncertain. You envision a variety of ways it could play out, and you strategize how to best deal with each. So far, so good. Once you've thought through each scenario, the rational, reasonable, logical thing to do would be to put the situation out of your mind and go about your day until action is actually required.

But how many of us have felt our minds going over the different outcomes again and again, rehashing the various plans we've made, replaying possible scenarios, mentally rehearsing the upcoming conversations not just once or twice but ad nauseam?

In the weeks leading up to his meeting with Paul, Tom's mind started spinning out different possibilities. First, he imagined a positive outcome and explored all the ramifications this would have. He thought about whom he'd want to call, and in what order, to bring them into the project. But what if the answer was negative? His mind started to unfold the sequence of actions that would follow: how he would explain the verdict to his boss, how he would tell his team, and so on.

For the next three days, Tom realized both scenarios kept popping up in his mind, his brain replaying the strategies he'd planned for each eventuality. As he drove to work, he caught himself rehearsing the conversation he'd have with his boss to explain the rejection. During work, he would suddenly realize he'd been aimlessly staring out the window, daydreaming about how he'd announce the win to his team. Tom knew he was ignoring other pressing matters. He tried to stop thinking about the situation, but his mind just kept returning to the possibilities again and again.

The reason Tom couldn't let go is that our minds are fundamentally uncomfortable with uncertainty. The minute our brain registers ambiguity, it flashes an error signal. Uncertainty registers as a tension: something that must be corrected before we can feel comfortable again.

Our natural discomfort with uncertainty is yet another legacy of our survival instincts. We tend to be more comfortable with what is familiar, which obviously hasn't killed us yet, than with what is unknown or uncertain, which could turn out to be dangerous.

It's worth learning how to handle uncertainty, not just because it increases charisma but also because the ability to be comfortable with uncertainty and ambiguity turns out to be one of the strongest predictors of success in business. This is what Adam Berman, the executive director of UC Berkeley's Business School Center for Innovation, concluded after tracking his MBA students in their career progression.

Very few business schools specifically teach students how to handle uncertainty. On the other hand, psychologists have been helping people increase their skills in this arena for decades, creating and refining tools for just this purpose. When Berman asked me to create a program to help business executives better navigate and embrace uncertainty, he suggested we examine the tools psychologists had devised and see which ones might be applicable within a business context. I've since tailored this toolkit for many companies in a wide variety of industries, and its effectiveness holds.

The single most effective technique I've found to alleviate the discomfort of uncertainty is the responsibility transfer.[2] In uncertain situations, what we really want to know is that things are somehow going to work out fine. If we could be certain that things will work out—that everything will be taken care of—the uncertainty would produce much less anxiety. Take a moment to try the exercise in the box below. If you'd rather have my voice guide you from start to finish, go to the Charisma Myth Web site: http://www.CharismaMyth .com/transfer.

---

### Putting It into Practice: Responsibility Transfer

1. Sit comfortably or lie down, relax, and close your eyes.

2. Take two or three deep breaths. As you inhale, imagine drawing clean air toward the top of your head. As you exhale, let that air whoosh through you, washing away all worries and concerns.

3. Pick an entity—God, Fate, the Universe, whatever may best suit your beliefs—that you could imagine as benevolent.

4. Imagine lifting the weight of *everything* you're concerned about—this meeting, this interaction, this day—off your shoulders and placing it on the shoulders of whichever entity you've chosen. They're in charge now.

5. Visually lift everything off your shoulders and feel the difference as you are now no longer responsible for the outcome of any of these things. Everything is taken care of. You can sit back, relax, and enjoy whatever good you can find along the way.

The next time you feel yourself considering alternative outcomes to a situation, pay close attention. If your brain is going around in circles, obsessing about possible outcomes, try a responsibility transfer to alleviate some of the anxiety. Consider that there might be an all-powerful entity—the Universe, God, Fate—and entrust it with all the worries on your mind.

So how did that work for you? Did you feel a physical reaction? After doing the responsibility transfer, many clients report feeling lighter, or their chests opening up and expanding. If you didn't feel any physical reaction or mental relief, it may simply mean that uncertainty was not creating anxiety for you. If you did feel something happen, fantastic: you've just performed a responsibility transfer.

Over time, many of my clients have found themselves returning to this technique so often, it becomes instinctive. With each practice, it becomes easier to visualize, to transfer their everyday worries and cares, and to enjoy the physiological effects of the transfer.

The reason this technique works is that when presented with a scenario, our brain's first reaction is to consider it as possible.

William Bosl, research scientist at the Harvard-MIT Health Sciences and Technology Program, explains the implications of a recent functional MRI study on belief, disbelief, and uncertainty as follows:[3]

"Our brains are wired first to understand, then to believe, and last to disbelieve. Since disbelief requires additional cognitive effort, we get the physiological effects first. And, though this belief may last only a brief moment, it's enough to produce an emotional and physical reassurance, which can change our thought patterns as well as help alleviate the uncomfortable feelings."[4] Our physiology responds to visuals well before cognitive disbelief kicks in. In addition, visuals short-circuit our cognitive circuits and go straight to our brain's emotional levels.

The responsibility transfer does not actually dispel uncertainty (the outcome remains uncertain). Instead, it makes the uncertainty less uncomfortable. This distinction matters. People will go to great lengths to get rid of the anxiety produced by uncertainty, from making premature decisions to forcing bad outcomes to numbing their anxiety with mind-altering substances of various kinds. However, the responsibility transfer works without trying to negate uncertainty. Instead, it helps you to be less affected by it, drawing you out of the negative mental and physical states that often accompany a position of not knowing. The outcome of your situation may still be uncertain, but you're no longer so anxious about it.

By presenting your mind with the possibility that responsibility has been transferred, you're putting to good use the wonderful placebo effect—the brain's inability to distinguish between imagination and reality. As we'll see in later chapters, the placebo effect works even when we know we're self-deceiving, perhaps thanks to this natural cognitive delay in disbelief.[5]

One of my clients used this technique just before stepping on stage to give a key presentation. It had the potential to be a turning point in his career, and he'd been feeling tense for a week. In the hour leading up to his big moment, his anxiety rose and his stomach started churning. When the CEO turned to him and said, "All right, Patrick, you're up next," he felt his stress level skyrocket. He could feel the tension in his shoulders, in his face, in his eyes.

He knew how damaging stressed-out body language could be to his presentation. So he stepped out of the room, found a quiet corner, closed his eyes, and for just three minutes imagined transferring responsibility for both his performance and how the presentation was received onto the shoulders of a benevolent entity. He told me that he felt an instant relief sweep through his body from head to toe. And his presentation was a major triumph.

Personally, I've chosen to believe in a benevolent Universe, which has a grand master plan for me (and for everything else). I've found this belief to suit me best; it helps me see anything that's happening as part of this plan. When I realize that my anxiety level is rising, I often perform a quick visualization to transfer responsibility. It's amazing to feel the instant sense of relief and the warmth, calm, and serenity rising. I feel my whole body relax, and it's as if my whole being starts to glow.

## Dissatisfaction Caused by Comparison

Imagine that it's Friday night, and you're at a large dinner party with people sitting at multiple tables. The conversation at your table is rather dull, in sore contrast to the last party you attended, which was great fun. To make matters worse, the table next to you erupts with laughter. Wouldn't it be natural to think, *I wish I were at that other table. They're having a much better time . . . ?*

Human beings are by nature driven to compare. Whenever we have an experience, we tend to compare it to our past experiences, to others' experiences, or to our ideal image of what the experience should be. This tendency becomes even more acute when we're presented with several options and want to make the best possible choice, seeking to optimize the outcome.

Each stage of this cycle impairs our charisma. The very act of comparing and evaluating hinders our ability to be fully present. Trying to optimize both impairs our presence and creates anxiety due to the pressure of finding the best possible choice. And a negative evaluation can easily put us in a negative mental state, such as dissatisfaction, envy, or resentment.

Because this tendency to compare is wired very deeply in our brains, trying to fight it can take a lot of effort. Instead, notice when you're making comparisons and use the responsibility transfer technique to alleviate any internal discomfort it may have caused.

## Self-Criticism

Imagine that you're on your way to an important job interview. As the hour of the interview approaches, your internal critical voice attacks you with self-doubt, bringing up memories of past failures, past humiliations, and inadequacies. Anxiety rises, and if you don't know how to skillfully handle the physical effects of your internal critic's attack, your performance will suffer. (Don't worry, you'll gain all the tools you need to handle episodes like this in chapter 4.)

Few things impact people's performance more than how they feel about themselves. Athletes will tell you that a bad mental state will affect their performance no matter how well prepared they are physically. Psychological negativity can have real physical consequences.

When our internal voice starts criticizing us, lashing out, it can feel like we're under attack. Because our brain doesn't distinguish between imagination and reality, these internal attacks are perceived by our mind just as a real, physical attack would be, and they can generate an automatic physical reaction known as the *threat response* or *fight-or-flight response*.

The effects of this activation are well-known. Just as a zebra reacts to the stress of being chased by a lion, the human body shoots adrenaline and cortisol (stress hormones) through its veins, and directs all its resources toward crucial functions: elevated heart and breathing rates, muscle reaction, vision acuity, and so forth. The body is no longer concerned with living ten more years, but with surviving ten more minutes. It shuts down nonurgent functions such as muscle repair, digestion, and the immune system,[6] as well as "superfluous" functions such as cognitive reasoning. In other words, because it's not critical to survival, intelligent thinking gets shut down.

David Rock, founder of the NeuroLeadership Institute, explains that "the threat response impairs analytic thinking, creative insight, and problem solving."[7] This kind of negativity doesn't just affect our actual performance, it also affects how others perceive us.

Let's say you're in a conversation. You say something, and immediately think, *Oh, that was a stupid thing to say.* What's going to happen to your face? You may wince at the thought and your expression may tense. As we've discussed, because we can't control our body language, any negativity in our mind will eventually show up on our face.

No matter how brief that negative expression, the person facing you is going to spot it. And all they know is that while you were looking at them and listening to them, a negative expression crossed your face. Naturally they'll assume that expression was a reaction to them—what they said or did, or what you thought about them. This is how internal negativity affects your body language, and thus your charisma, in addition to your performance.

Self-criticism is one of the most common obstacles to great performance in any field. It's often called the *silent killer* of business, because so many executives suffer from it, yet so few dare to speak out about it. I've heard a variety of people, from junior associates to the most senior executives, privately admit that much of their workday was consumed by negativity, their inner critics constantly pointing out their failings, or predicting disappointing outcomes for their projects and initiatives. In some cases, they (and I) were amazed that they got anything done at all, considering that, as one executive reported, "Eighty percent of my day is spent fighting my inner critic."

### Self-Doubt

Self-doubt, simply put, is lack of confidence in our own ability to achieve something: we doubt our capacity to do it or our capacity to learn how to do it. Worse, it is the fear that there is something essential that we lack, something necessary but unattainable, and that *we are just not good enough.* In one of the manifestations of self-doubt, known as the *impostor syndrome,* competent people feel they don't really know what they're doing and are just waiting for someone to expose them as a fraud. Since the impostor syndrome was first identified by Georgia State University professors in 1978, we've learned that more than 70 percent of the population has experienced this feeling at one time or another.[8] Today, we finally have effective tools to handle it (see chapter 4). But already, just knowing the universality of such feelings can help us neutralize their effect and reduce their power.

Interestingly, the impostor syndrome is worst among high performers. When I speak about it at Harvard, Yale, Stanford, and MIT, the room goes so silent you could hear a pin drop. And I see the students breathe a sigh of relief as they realize this feeling has a name and they are not alone in experiencing it.

Every year, the incoming class at Stanford Business School is asked: "How many of you in here feel that you are the one mistake that the admissions committee made?" Every year, two-thirds of the class immediately raises their hands. When I mention this in speeches, people express astonishment. How could Stanford students, some of the best and brightest in the country, who've succeeded through an exhaustive admissions process and have a long track record of solid accomplishments behind them, feel that somehow they don't belong?

And yet this feeling is one you'll hear echoed at every stage of success. Michael Uslan, producer of every modern *Batman* movie, still gets that feeling occasionally when he's in the studio. "I still have this background feeling that one of the security guards might come in and throw me out," he told me.

For some, it has been a direct corollary of career progression—with greater responsibility comes greater internal doubt as the cost of failure gets higher and higher. Bob Lurie, managing partner for the Monitor Group, told me that he, too, knows what this feels like. "For the first six or seven years of my career, I was the poster child for the impostor syndrome. I was convinced that if I got into a room with senior executives, they would immediately figure out I was a fraud."

We've seen the effects of anxiety, dissatisfaction, self-criticism, and self-doubt. Where does all this negativity come from? The difficult feelings we experience are a natural by-product of one of our most useful survival mechanisms. Negativity exists to spur you to action, to either resolve the problem or get out of the situation. Feelings like fear or anxiety are designed to get you to do something. They're uncomfortable because they're "designed" to be uncomfortable.

There are times when the discomfort of full-blown fear is highly appropriate. If we were in life-threatening physical danger, then we would surely appreciate our body focusing all of its resources toward ensuring our short-term survival. However, in today's world, few situations merit a full fight-or-flight response. In these cases, our instinctive reactions actually work against us.

Have you ever become paralyzed in the middle of an exam or had the experience of stage fright? Like a deer in headlights, you freeze, your heart races, your palms get sweaty. You're desperately trying to remember what you'd planned to say or do, but your mind is blank. Your higher cognitive functions have shut down.

Sometimes, under the effect of stress, the mind thinks we're in a fight-or-flight situation, declares a state of emergency, and shuts down what it deems to be superfluous functions. Unfortunately, that means the body is reducing our cognitive abilities just when we need them most. Though it may be hard to remember this in the midst of an anxiety attack, rest assured that this reaction is an entirely normal, natural one that was intended for your well-being.

Of course, some degree of self-doubt can be helpful in spurring us to action. For instance, the impostor syndrome can be a great motivating tool, getting us to work harder than anyone else. But at what cost? Considering that this kind of internal negativity impairs our body language, and thus our interactions, not to mention our ability to actually enjoy life, might it not be better to learn how to handle the impostor syndrome and be motivated instead by confidence in our abilities and the joy of accomplishment?

Knowing how to handle the impostor syndrome and the inner critic is essential to unleashing your charisma potential. With practice, by using techniques such as the ones you'll learn in the next chapter, you can achieve some distance from internal negativity, and even get to a place where the inner critic's voice evokes in you only a smile or a chuckle. I promise.

So far you've gained key insights about internal negativity, how to recognize it, and how it plays out in your mind and in your body. In the next chapter, you'll acquire the tools to put these insights into practice.

## KEY TAKEAWAYS

- Any internal discomfort—either physical or mental—can impair how you feel, how you perform, and how others perceive you.
- Physical tension caused by something as simple as the sun in your eyes produces the same changes in body language as a more serious discomfort, like anxiety or irritation.
- Prevention is optimal: plan ahead to ensure comfort in clothing, location, and timing.
- Aim to stay aware of any physical sensation of discomfort. If physical discomfort arises during an interaction, act promptly to alleviate or explain it.
- Use techniques such as the responsibility transfer to reduce the feelings of anxiety, uncertainty, and dissatisfaction that play out in your body language and inhibit your charisma.
- Understand that mental negativity such as anxiety, dissatisfaction, self-criticism, or self-doubt is normal and something that everyone experiences.

# 4

## Overcoming the Obstacles

YOU'VE ALREADY ACQUIRED important insights about the way physical and mental discomfort can handicap your personal charisma potential. In this chapter, you'll gain the tools to put these insights into practice, surmount the obstacles, and successfully handle almost any internal discomfort. No matter what difficult feelings arise—self-doubt, impatience, annoyance, irritation—you'll be able to confidently handle them.

Skillfully handling any difficult experience is a three-step process: destigmatize discomfort, neutralize negativity, and rewrite reality. Let's get started.

### Step One: Destigmatize Discomfort

Destigmatizing an experience means reducing its power simply by understanding that it's normal, common, and nothing to be anxious about or ashamed of. Feeling internal discomfort and negativity is a natural part of life. Everyone experiences it.

We all feel the whole spectrum of emotions, no matter how good we are. Even Thich Nhat Hanh, a monk, lifelong practitioner of Buddhism, and the very symbol of enlightened peace in the world, once got so angry at someone, he wanted to stand up and slug him.

And yet somehow, in our culture, we've gotten into the habit of viewing any physical or mental discomfort as a sign of something gone awry, perhaps even the sign of something wrong within us. Even during unsettling life events—a major job change, a divorce, death of a loved one—when we accept a certain amount of sadness or discomfort, we often put a time limit on the acceptability of our feelings, after which point we believe that continuing to feel this way would be inappropriate.

This mindset is one of the main reasons that negative thoughts, emotions, and internal experiences are difficult to handle: we feel they "shouldn't" be happening. So not only do we feel bad, we then also feel bad *about* feeling bad.

To destigmatize, remind yourself that this internal discomfort, whatever it might be, is a normal part of the human experience and a by-product of one of our brain's survival mechanisms. It helps to think of others who have experienced what you're going through, especially if you can think of a person who is like you, but maybe just a step or two ahead—a person you both relate to and admire.

If you've just lost a key client, for instance, think of someone you know—a mentor you have a high regard for, or a colleague you respect—who suffered a similar setback. Imagine them going through this experience. Of course, hearing them tell you their tale of woe in person would be ideal, but even simply imagining them going through this experience and telling you about it can be very helpful. (Remember, your brain won't know the difference.)

Another way to destigmatize discomfort is to remind yourself that you're not alone in this experience. With about 7 billion people on the planet, I can absolutely guarantee you that not just one but scores of people are going through the same thing at this very moment. Rather than seeing it as one big emotion felt by one person, see a community of people struggling with it—one difficult burden shared by many. Rather than being *yours* alone to bear, see the issue as *the* depression, *the* shame, *the* sadness that is being felt by a multitude of people right now.

One of my clients told me that connecting himself to others in this way is helpful and gives him the same calming effect as the responsibility transfer. He likes to look around wherever he is and imagine thought bubbles streaming out of people's heads while they're going about their day. And he says, "It's relieving to realize that it's not 'wrong' to be thinking or feeling whatever it is that I'm thinking or feeling. That it's normal."

In both my personal experience and in coaching clients, I've found that simply adapting this new mindset and learning how to allieviate anxiety or shame can make internal turmoil much easier to bear.

You see, shame is the real killer. Of all the emotions that human beings can feel, it is one of the most toxic to health and happiness. Shame researcher Brené Brown defines it as "the fear of being unlovable: Shame is the intensely painful feeling or experience of believing that we are flawed and therefore unworthy of love and belonging."

Shame hits us so powerfully because it conveys a message about our fundamental acceptability as human beings. And in basic survival terms, if the tribe rejects you, you die. It *is* a life-and-death situation. The brain equates social needs with survival; being hungry and being ostracized activate similar neural responses.[1] Somewhere in the back of our minds is the fear of being so disapproved-of that we'd be excluded by those who matter to our survival.

Because it's easily triggered and fast to escalate, shame can quickly grow out of proportion and show up in ways that are not helpful to us. I've heard clients express a level of shame for having eaten a candy bar that would have been more appropriate for third-degree murder.

Chade-Meng Tan, Google's Jolly Good Fellow* and a devoted practitioner of mindfulness meditation, believes that the tendency to feel bad about feeling bad is especially true for good people. We start

---

* Yes, that's his official title. His subtitle, of course, reads "Which nobody can deny."

thinking, *If I'm a good person, why am I feeling this shame? Surely if I were really good I wouldn't feel this way.*

Knowing how to remove the stigma of shame from difficult emotions and experiences is absolutely critical to charisma. Often, it's not what we feel that is the most painful—it's our *shame* about feeling this way that really does the damage. Once we see this feeling as normal and even something to be expected, it becomes much easier to bear. As with any discomfort or difficult feeling, it is helpful to remember that shame is a standard part of the human experience, and that *everyone* feels it from time to time.

## Putting It into Practice: Destigmatizing Discomfort

The next time an uncomfortable emotion is bothering you, try this step-by-step guide to destigmatizing:

1. Remember that uncomfortable emotions are normal, natural, and simply a legacy of our survival instincts. We all experience them from time to time.

3. Dedramatize: this is a common part of human experience that happens every day.

4. Think of others who've gone through this before, especially people you admire.

5. See it as one burden shared by many. You are part of a community of human beings experiencing this one feeling at this very moment.

What you've just learned is how to destigmatize internal discomfort, which increases your resiliency to charisma-impairing negativity. Just by gaining these tools, you've raised your charisma level. These are important tools you'll be using repeatedly throughout the rest of the book.

## Step Two: Neutralize Negativity

Once you've destigmatized the experience, the next step in handling internal negativity is to neutralize negative thoughts. The best way to do this is to realize that your thoughts aren't necessarily accurate at all.

Do you remember Tom's and Paul's experience at the restaurant caused by the itchy black suit? Even when it seems clear that someone is reacting negatively to us, what we're seeing in their face might have nothing to do with us. What's going on that we can't see? Are they hungry, sick, or tired? Maybe they're in some kind of mental or physical discomfort that they're struggling to manage.

The next time you think you see coldness or reservation in someone's face while they're talking to you, try to remember that it could simply be the visible signs of their internal discomfort. You might be catching the surface tremors of an internal tempest, and there's a good chance that it has nothing to do with how they feel about you or what you've just said.

This reminder helps me on a regular basis. When I'm involved in a conversation and I catch a tone of annoyance or impatience in someone's voice, or when I see a fleeting negative expression cross their face, sometimes I still feel instinctively dismayed. It's hard not to assume that what I've just seen is a reaction to what I've just said. But right on the heels of this instinctive reaction comes the recognition that whatever I've seen may well be the sign of how they're feeling about themselves, an itchy wool suit, or something else entirely.

One of the main reasons we're so affected by our negative thoughts is that we think our mind has an accurate grasp on reality, and that its conclusions are generally valid. This, however, is a fallacy. Our mind's view of reality can be, and often is, completely distorted.

In one well-known study, Harvard researchers asked the participants to watch a short video in which two groups of people passed around a basketball. They were asked to count the number of passes made by one of the teams. Partway through the video, a woman walked onto the court wearing a full gorilla suit.

After watching the video, the participants were asked if they saw anything out of the ordinary take place. In most groups more than half missed the gorilla even though it had waved its arms at the camera![2]

Think you'd do better? You can try this out for yourself:

Right now, look around the room and notice everything that's blue.

Now keep your eyes glued to this page. Without lifting your eyes, think of everything in the room that is red.

Really. Bear with me. Give it your best try.

Now look around. Do you see a lot more red all of a sudden?

Why did this happen? We have a limited capacity for conscious attention, which constrains how much we can be aware of at any particular time. Of the millions of visual inputs our eyes take in every moment, we consciously perceive very few. The conscious awareness of absolutely everything around us would be overwhelming.

To deal with this, our brain filters for relevant information—either what it considers to be important or what we've consciously asked it to pay attention to. Through this process, our mind does not provide us with a complete, accurate representation of reality. Because it has to filter, it gives us an incomplete view, presenting only some elements and withholding all others.

Most of the time, the elements we're missing don't matter, and the picture we get is fairly close to reality. But sometimes our mind will present us with a seriously distorted view of reality. And the distortion often skews negative because the elements that our danger-focused brain deems important are usually the most negative ones. This tendency is called the *negativity bias,* and here's how it can play out in practice:

Mary is a young graphic designer who for the first time is leading a project for one of her firm's biggest clients. A few weeks after the project starts, she gets a call from Jim, her counterpart within the client. Jim tells her: "Listen, you know I'm your biggest fan. I've been raving about you and your brilliant work to everyone within earshot. But somehow, my boss doesn't get it. I guess he just wasn't impressed when you guys first met, and he hasn't gotten a chance to change his mind." Jim goes on to explain that he'd like Mary to be in charge of all of his company's design work, and that he thinks her work is so good, he's sure his boss will be wowed when he sees it again. Therefore, he'd like her to present her work at the company's next management meeting.

There are many positive elements Mary's mind could focus on. Her client says he's a big fan of hers, her work is "brilliant," and he wants her to handle all of his company's projects. Mary's mind *could* spend the next few hours reveling in her client's praises, but that's not how most minds work. Despite the high positive-to-negative ratio, what does Mary's mind focus on? The one negative element: the fact that Jim's boss hadn't been impressed with her when they first met. If Mary gets stuck focusing on the one negative in a very positive scenario, you can imagine how unfortunate this could be for her confidence level, and thus her charisma level, when pitching day comes around.

When your brain spins negative scenarios, remind yourself that you may not be getting an accurate perception of reality. Your brain might be following its negativity bias, playing up some elements more than others, or omitting some positives entirely.

Just like an optical illusion that tricks your eyes into seeing things that aren't real, your mind can experience thought illusions that make you feel certain an inaccurate thought is true.

Cognitive scientist Steven Hayes suggests that we see negative thoughts as graffiti on a wall. If you're walking down the street and you see graffiti, you may find it an ugly sight, but just because you see an ugly sight doesn't mean you're an ugly person.

Imagine strolling along the paths of your mind. Suddenly, you notice an unpleasant thought. See it as graffiti on the wall. That's all it is, graffiti—not a verdict on what kind of person you are.

You can also see thoughts as flickers of electricity crackling on the surface of your mind. Thoughts, in fact, have no tangible substance: they're just little electrical impulses sent from one part of your brain to another.

Understanding that my thoughts are not necessarily valid was a revelation for me. It took a lot of practice, but these days, neutralizing unhelpful negative thoughts often happens so fast that I take it for granted. It has become an automatic reflex that often kicks in as soon as I notice an unhelpful thought that could create internal negativity.

Some of my clients like to ask themselves, "What's the worst that can happen?" As Churchill said, failure is seldom fatal, and just realizing that even the worst-case scenario is survivable can bolster your confidence. Although for some people this can backfire—imagining the worst-case scenario increases their anxiety—it's worth a try to see whether it works for you.

## Putting It into Practice: Neutralizing Negativity

Use the techniques below anytime you'd like to lessen the effects of persistent negative thoughts. As you try each technique, pay attention to which ones work best for you and keep practicing them until they become instinctive. You may also discover some of your own that work just as well.

♦ Don't assume your thoughts are accurate. Just because your mind comes up with something doesn't necessarily mean it has any validity. Assume you're missing a lot of elements, many of which could be positive.

♦ See your thoughts as graffiti on a wall or as little electrical impulses flickering around your brain.

♦ Assign a label to your negative experience: self-criticism, anger, anxiety, etc. Just naming what you are thinking and feeling can help you neutralize it.

♦ Depersonalize the experience. Rather than saying "I'm feeling ashamed," try "There is shame being felt." Imagine that you're a scientist observing a phenomenon: "How interesting, there are self-critical thoughts arising."

♦ Imagine seeing yourself from afar. Zoom out so far, you can see planet Earth hanging in space. Then zoom in to see your continent, then your country, your city, and finally the room you're in. See your little self, electrical impulses whizzing across your brain. One little being having a particular experience at this particular moment.

♦ Imagine your mental chatter as coming from a radio; see if you can turn down the volume, or even just put the radio to the side and let it chatter away.

♦ Consider the worst-case outcome for your situation. Realize that whatever it is, you'll survive.

♦ Think of all the previous times when you felt just like this— that you wouldn't make it through—and yet clearly you did.

We're learning here to *neutralize* unhelpful thoughts. We want to avoid falling into the trap of arguing with them or trying to suppress them. This would only make matters worse. Consider this: if I ask you *not* to think of a white elephant—don't picture a white elephant at all, please!—what's the first thing your brain serves up? Right. Saying "No white elephants" leads to troops of white pachyderms marching through your mind.

Steven Hayes and his colleagues studied our tendency to dwell on the forbidden by asking participants in controlled research studies to spend just a few minutes *not* thinking of a yellow jeep. For many people, the forbidden thought arose immediately, and with increasing frequency. For others, even if they were able to suppress the thought for a short period of time, at some point they broke down and yellow-jeep thoughts rose dramatically. Participants reported thinking about yellow jeeps with some frequency for days and sometimes weeks afterward.

Because trying to suppress a self-critical thought only makes it more central to your thinking, it's a far better strategy to simply aim to neutralize it.

You've taken the first two steps in handling internal negativity: destigmatizing discomfort and neutralizing negativity. The third and final step will help you not just to lessen internal negativity but to actually *replace* it with a different internal reality.

## Step Three: Rewrite Reality

It's eight A.M. on a Monday morning and you're driving on the free-
way, en route to an important meeting. You'll be giving a thirty-
minute presentation that could change the course of your career.
You're focused and calm. All of a sudden, a large black car cuts in
front of you, swerving into your lane. With your heart pounding and
your hands gripping the steering wheel, you stomp on the brake. Not
only did this car cut in front of you without signaling, it's now speed-
ing up and slowing down erratically, nearly causing you to rear-end
it. And then it swerves out of your lane again, making the car to your
right screech its tires. What an idiot, reckless driver! Anger surges
through your veins.

What happened to your body during this incident? A fight-or-
flight response made your heartbeat accelerate, your muscles tighten,
and stress hormones flood your system. Now you're pumped up with
stress and anger. You know you need to get back into a charismatic
mental and physical state in time for your presentation, but you have
only a few minutes, and you can't get that idiot driver out of your
mind.

Once the fight-or-flight response is aroused, it's hard to quiet
down. Anger is a difficult emotion to flush out of your system—this
is why an unpleasant traffic encounter in the morning can stay on
your mind for hours and sometimes all day.

If you aimed to simply suppress the anger, you would pay a high
price. When people are induced into a negative emotional state and
then asked to *suppress* negative emotions, their internal negative experience often remains unchanged and they sustain elevated stress
responses in their brain and cardiovascular system.[3]

But what if you happened to learn that this apparently reckless
driver was actually a distraught mother whose baby was choking in
the backseat, and she was desperately trying to pull over into the
breakdown lane while reaching back to save her baby's life?

Would that immediately reduce your anger?

For most people, it would.

Deciding to change your belief about what happened (technically called *cognitive reappraisal*) effectively decreases the brain's stress levels. This came to light through research performed at Stanford using functional MRI machines. The researchers concluded that deciding to change beliefs was a far more effective and healthier solution than attempting to repress or ignore emotions.[4]

In most situations, we don't know for certain what motivates a person's actions, so we might as well choose the explanation that is most helpful to us and create a version of events that gets us into the specific mental state we need for charisma.

Though this suggestion may sound outlandish at first, choosing to rewrite your perception of reality is actually the rational and smart thing to do. It can help you get back into the right mental state to emanate charismatic body language and can improve your performance, too.

I first learned about the rewriting reality technique during a business school course,* and it has served me brilliantly in the years since. I always think of one night in Bogotá, when I got a direct experience of how powerful this technique could be.

It was four in the morning and I couldn't sleep. My mind was filled with apprehension. In a few hours I would be addressing the three hundred senior executives of a large multinational corporation. The CEO, who had asked me to address his top management, expected his people to come out of my session with both a mindset shift and a practical toolkit. I had ninety minutes to make them more confident, influential, persuasive, and inspiring. And all this, in Spanish. The pressure was high.

I had already tossed and turned for hours, paced around the soulless hotel room, and stared out the window at the blinking city lights, desperately trying to find sleep. I felt nauseated, exhausted, and emotionally spent. My mind was churning, and I dreaded the hours of insomnia I felt were ahead of me.

---

* Professor Srikumar Rao's class on happiness was one of the most popular courses ever offered at Columbia Business School. The admissions process for the course was grueling.

Suddenly, the rewriting reality exercise floated through my mind. Though it seemed far-fetched, I realized that at this point I'd tried everything else, and had nothing to lose by giving the technique a try. I sat down at the desk, pulled out pen and paper and asked myself: *What if this unfortunate, unpleasant experience is absolutely perfect just as it is—the insomnia, the nausea, the fact that this is happening the very night before a high-profile assignment? In what way can this turn out to be absolutely perfect for me?*

It took a few minutes, but eventually answers began to arise. And I wrote: "Maybe I'll somehow do well tomorrow and come to know that even sleep-deprived, and in a foreign language, I can still do all right. Maybe this knowledge will be key someday when I'm faced with an even more important assignment. And I'll be grateful for having had the uncomfortable experience I'm living through now."

At first, these statements felt like sheer delusion. But writing them down (you'll learn why this is important) opened up a little window of possibility in my mind. I continued to write all the possible upsides of this unfortunate experience. I made this new reality as detailed and sensory-rich as possible: describing what I said, what the audience looked like, when and how they nodded and laughed throughout my speech. As the list grew longer, I felt my anxiety subside. Eventually, my calm turned into drowsiness, and—hallelujah—I headed back to bed, albeit for less than an hour of sleep.

And you know what? Every bit of the slightly delusional, impossibly good version of reality that I'd dreamed up the night before came true. The speech went brilliantly, the audience of senior executives was enthusiastic, and the CEO was thrilled. Nowadays, whenever my mind starts to worry because things aren't quite perfect before an important speech, I remind myself: *Remember Bogotá.*

Since then, I've often used the rewriting reality technique to get into a better-performing mental state, and I now give it to all my coaching clients. Not only does it work for them, but I've met many other highly successful people over the years who've told me they use similar techniques. One charismatic entrepreneur told me: "I *decide* to interpret everything favorably toward myself. It's not just that I'm optimistic, I'm actually conveniently deluded."

Why does this work? Once again, we can thank the brain's tendency to accept imagination as reality. A study conducted by the Harvard Medical School suggests that deception may not be necessary for the placebo effect to take hold; it may work its wonders even when people know full well that they're taking a placebo. [5]

So when a difficult experience arises and risks impairing your charisma levels, rather than trying to suppress or ignore your internal difficulties, consider a few alternate versions of reality. Conjure a few different scenarios that would induce you into a more useful mental state.

Of course, the most useful alternate reality is not necessarily the most pleasant. When my publishers gave me a year to write the book you're now holding, I wanted to progress as efficiently as possible, avoiding the procrastination pitfalls that ensnare so many first-time authors. One author friend reminded me of a maxim called Parkinson's Law: "Work expands so as to fill the time available for its completion." He challenged me: "Rather than letting the writing process fill the entire year, try to write the entire book in one month. At the end of a month, what you have will certainly not be a finished book, but it'll be more than you would have without this self-imposed deadline."

This seemed sensible, so I decided to give it a try. I imagined—as vividly as possible, with sensory-rich details—that my publisher had somehow given me an insane one-month deadline to write the entire book. And I was amazed at how fast this completely imaginary deadline became emotionally real. I even felt a knot in the pit of my stomach, a physical reminder that the clock was ticking.

Was this pleasant? Definitely not. Effective? Absolutely. Within one month, I was able to send one-third of the rough draft to my editor. Though this was far less than a full book, it was indeed far more than I would have produced without the imaginary deadline.

The key questions are: Which mental state would be most useful in this situation? And which version of reality would help you get there? For charisma, you can use this technique whenever a situation threatens your level of warmth or confidence. For minor events, simply imagining an alternative explanation is often enough to reduce anger or impatience and generate compassion instead.

## Putting It into Practice: Rewriting Reality

Let's imagine that traffic is making you late for an important meeting and your anxiety level is on the rise. Ask yourself: What if this delay is a good thing? Repeat the question a few times, and watch how creative your mind can get with its answers. It might come up with explanations like these:

♦ This delay is going to save my life—had traffic been flowing normally, my path would have crossed that of an eighteen-wheel truck skidding across the intersection.

♦ The people with whom I'm due to meet are under a drastic deadline and are grateful for every minute I'm late, which allows them to work just a little bit longer.

♦ The Universe (or Fate or God), having my best interests at heart, does not want this meeting to happen. There's an even better direction things will take instead.

When you're dealing with a more serious situation, sit down and write out a new reality on a piece of paper. Writing accesses different parts of our brain[6] and affects our beliefs in ways that other modes of expression do not. The act of committing things to writing has been shown to be critical both in changing a person's mind[7] and in making imagined stories feel more real.[8] Write in the present tense: "The speech is going well . . ." Or, even better, in the past tense: "The speech was a complete triumph . . ."

One of my clients describes using the rewriting reality technique as follows: "A colleague sent me a rather sarcastic message. This immediately brought up a host of negative feelings, and I realized this was just getting me into a negative thought spiral. So I tried the rewriting reality tool. I imagined that this person was really lonely at the moment. They didn't know how to reach out, so they were trying the best they could to connect. This helped me stay in a positive mindset (good for me) and send a positive response (good for both of us!)."

There may be times when you need to be charismatic toward

someone you resent. As you can imagine, resentment is a very un-charismatic mental state that causes high negativity both in your mind and in your body language. In addition, it's *your* body that suffers the consequences of carrying around this negativity. To quote one of my favorite adages: "Resentment is like drinking poison and waiting for the other person to die."

No matter what the circumstances of your resentment, you can indeed prevent your internal discomfort from interfering with your charisma. But getting relief from resentment isn't easy. This is when rewriting your reality can be invaluable. The exercise below will give you one good way to alleviate resentment. You may find this to be simultaneously the most uncomfortable and the most rewarding of all the reality rewriting you do.

### Putting It into Practice: Getting Satisfaction

♦ Think of one person in your life who has aggrieved you.

♦ Take a blank page and write that person a letter saying anything and everything you wish you had ever told them. Really get into this—you have nothing to lose. Make sure you write it out by hand.

♦ When you've gotten absolutely everything off your mind and onto paper, put the letter aside.

♦ Take a fresh sheet and write their response just the way you wish they would respond. You might have them taking responsibility for their actions, acknowledging and apologizing for everything they've ever done that hurt you. You don't need to find any justification for their actions, just an acknowledgment and an apology. It's your imagination, so you get to decide exactly what you'd like to hear.

This exercise may feel alien, awkward, or unreal at first—that's the case for many people. And you may not feel an immediate internal shift. However, over the next few days you may be amazed to feel this "new reality" gradually taking hold. You may feel that you *did* get the closure you needed. To accelerate the process, simply reread the apology letter nightly for a few days. You'll appreciate the results.

One of my clients told me that persevering through this exercise lifted a ten-year burden off her shoulders more effectively than years of therapy. Another told me that his interactions with his business partner, which had become increasingly difficult, benefited greatly from this technique. He said:

> If I had the choice, I'd never see him again. But I was going to have to interact with him, and I knew that if I didn't find a way to alleviate the resentment, it would just stay in the back of my mind, eating away at my attention and impacting both my body language and my performance. So I did the getting satisfaction exercise. At first I didn't really notice a change, though it felt good to get things off my chest. But in the days that followed, I felt different when interacting with my part-ner. Though he still hadn't apologized for his behavior, the resentment was no longer eating away at my attention. Be-cause I really did get the apology I needed (even though I wrote it myself), I actually no longer felt I needed it from him, and this makes it far easier to interact. Though it won't mend the relationship, it's enough to make things work for now.

By using these two exercises, rewriting reality and getting satis-faction, you can choose your perception of the situation—one that allows you to be both effective and charismatic.

## Putting It All Together

Now that you've learned the three-step process to overcoming inter-nal obstacles to charisma, let's put it all together. The following real-life scenario will help you see the sequence in action. It includes instructions you can use anytime to destigmatize discomfort, neu-tralize negativity, and rewrite reality.

Up until now, it had been a good day. Michael had put the finishing touches on an exciting project, showed it to his team, and everyone was enthusiastic. As he walked back to his office, he was riding high. He noticed the blinking light on his answering machine, sat down, and pressed PLAY. It was his biggest client, John, sounding tense, and asking Michael to call back as soon as possible.

With those few words, Michael's stomach dropped. "I just had this visceral certainty that John was about to pull the plug. Terminate our engagement. I knew I was about to lose my biggest client. It felt so inevitable. I mean, I could *hear* the tension in John's voice."

Michael felt certain that something had gone wrong. But rather than reaching for the phone with dread filling his mind and affecting his voice, he stopped. *You know how to handle this,* he reassured himself. Then he followed this checklist:

1. Take a deep breath and shake out your body to ensure that no physical discomfort is adding to your tense mental state.
2. Dedramatize. Remind yourself that these are just physical sensations. Right now, nothing serious is actually happening. This only *feels* uncomfortable because of the way your brain is wired. Zoom out your focus to see yourself as one little person sitting in a room with certain chemicals flooding his system. Nothing more.
3. Destigmatize. Remind yourself that what you're experiencing is normal and everyone goes through it from time to time. Imagine countless people all over the world feeling the exact same thing.
4. Neutralize. Remind yourself that thoughts are not necessarily real. There have been many times when you've been certain that a client was disappointed, only to discover that the exact opposite was true.
5. Consider a few alternate realities. Michael considered:

Maybe the tension in John's voice had nothing to do with me. Maybe he felt harried because he's running late on that project he mentioned last week.

Maybe he fears that *I* might terminate our engagement. Maybe he's worried that he's not as important to me as my other clients. Maybe *he's* afraid of losing *me*.

6. Visualize a transfer of responsibility. Feel the weight of responsibility for the outcome of this situation lifting off your shoulders. Tell yourself it's all taken care of.

As Michael went through the checklist, putting each of the techniques to good use, he felt his tension gradually ease. Going through this sequence helped him put his initial pessimistic prediction into perspective as just one of many possible explanations for the tone of John's message. With a newfound calm, Michael picked up the phone ready to talk to his client with charismatic confidence.

## Getting Comfortable with Discomfort

You've come a long way already. Since the beginning of this chapter you've gained an arsenal of techniques to help you overcome the most common obstacles to charisma. But there's one more thing you need to learn. If you want to reach advanced charisma levels, where the masters operate, the next tool is what will take you there. This technique helps you get back into charisma no matter how difficult your internal state. It's a bit like having an ace up your sleeve. Just knowing it's there for you when and if you need it will give you a solid foundation of confidence.

This technique will give you the edge in negotiations, presentations, social situations—anytime your performance matters. It is, however, not an easy tool to acquire, as it requires going against your most primal instincts. So what's this secret weapon?

Being comfortable with discomfort.

Sounds simple? It is. Simple, but not easy.

Imagine that you're sitting in an airplane that's stuck on the ground, waiting in line for takeoff. You're trapped in a tiny, cramped seat. The air-conditioning has broken down, the temperature is rising, the air is growing stale, and you can feel sweat start to trickle down the back of your neck. Just when you think things can't get worse, an infant starts to howl in the row right behind you. You can feel the discomfort building, tension rising through your body, irritation taking hold of your mind. Your carry-on bag with all of your reading materials has been whisked away by the flight crew and stowed out of reach, so you have nothing with which to distract yourself. *And you have no idea how long this will last.* You do know that your mounting tension serves no useful purpose. But how can you stop it?

The answer, surprisingly, is to *delve into* those very sensations of discomfort. That's right. Though it sounds counterintuitive, rather than trying to suppress, ignore, or power through them, your goal is to give your full attention to the very sensations you'd instinctively want to push away.

Focusing on the minute sensations of your physical discomfort serves a dual purpose: it gives your mind something concrete to focus on other than its growing conviction that this situation is unbearable. It also has the advantage of bringing you instantly into full presence, a key component of charisma. In fact, this technique, called *delving into sensations*, can help you access charismatic presence even during highly uncomfortable situations.

•  •  •

## Putting It into Practice:
## Delving into Sensations

This exercise will create an uncomfortable situation and then help you practice getting comfortable there. You'll need to find a quiet, relaxing spot to sit, along with a trusted friend or colleague as your partner.

Once you start the exercise you cannot stop to check the instructions, so read over the script below once or twice before you begin. If you'd rather have my voice guiding you from start to finish, go to the Charisma Myth Web site: http://www.Charisma Myth.com/discomfort.

♦ Set a timer for thirty seconds and then look into your partner's eyes. Keep your gazes locked from now on.

♦ As soon as you become aware of any discomfort, pay very close attention to it. Notice where the feelings are located in your body. Mentally name the sensations—constriction, pressure, tingling?

♦ Delve into each sensation as much as you can; aim to feel its texture. Describe each one as if you were a chef describing a specialty dish.

♦ Let the awkwardness build. How does it manifest itself physically? Do you feel tightness in your jaw? Is it tension in your stomach?

♦ Imagine yourself as a scientist investigating this experience. Name the sensations you feel. Observe them as objectively as you can. See them purely as physical sensations, like hot and cold.

♦ When you feel the urge to laugh, talk, or relieve the discomfort in any way, resist it. This is your chance to practice delving into the sensations, not avoiding them.

If you and your partner last all thirty seconds, pat yourselves on the back. It takes a strong will to fight your instincts in this way.

Now try the same exercise again and see if you can increase your effectiveness by using two additions:

1. Give yourself continuous encouragement. Throughout the exercise, remind yourself that you're doing courageous, advanced work and that your efforts will yield rewards.

2. Remind yourself that this discomfort will pass, as did all other emotions you've ever had before it. Though it may feel unbearable in this moment, it *will* subside.

An hour or two after doing this exercise, check your level of discomfort. You might be astonished at how far away it seems, even though while you were in the middle of the experience it felt as if it would never end. If indeed your discomfort seems distant, make a strong mental note to remember this the next time your mind insists that an experience is endless and unbearable.

Robert, one of my favorite clients, is a brilliant, quick-witted, highly effective, and highly creative executive. He's incredibly fast on his feet. He also has very limited patience. For Robert, daylong company meetings were pure torture. He would feel the rising tide of impatience but felt powerless to stem it. He would desperately fight against the "I cannot bear this a minute longer" feeling, coming out of these experiences with his body tied up in knots.

As far as his charisma was concerned, the energy he was using to try to suppress his impatience was only making things worse. Waging this kind of internal war is not good for charisma. Nor is zoning out, which would only decrease his presence and make him appear at best uncharismatic and at worst uncaring. So I suggested he give the delving into sensations practice a try.

Robert took this practice to heart to such a degree that it became second nature to him. Nowadays, whenever he feels the first glimmers of impatience, he instinctively and immediately delves into his physical sensations. He says he describes them to himself "as a sommelier would describe a fine vintage." Doing this, he says, "is a very useful technique, simultaneously distracting me from the impatience while still keeping me fully present in the moment."

The ability to handle discomfort is a highly valuable skill. The less discomfort affects you, the fewer the situations that can impair your charisma potential. When you know how to handle discomfort, no situation can shake you; whether business or personal, there is no feeling that can make you run away.

One CEO told me that "the most effective thing you can do for your career is to get comfortable being uncomfortable." Think of the plethora of discomforts that come with leadership, from having to fire employees to taking the heat for a team failure, or simply enduring painful meetings. Think of how critical it can be to handle the discomfort of silence during negotiations. I've often heard professional negotiators tell me that they could accurately predict the outcome of negotiations fairly early on using one simple clue: whoever has less endurance for silence loses.

Try the exercise in the box below to increase your resilience. To make things easier, consider this a new skill you're practicing, rather than tests with which to evaluate your performance. Imagine that you're learning a new piece of music or a new way of tossing a ball. Just as you lift weights at the gym to increase your physical strength, here you're growing and strengthening your resilience muscles.

## Putting It into Practice: Stretching Your Comfort Zone

Here are more techniques to help you broaden your comfort zone and build comfort with discomfort. Since most of these involve some degree of awkwardness, it's best to use them in low-stakes encounters rather than with key clients or with your boss.

♦ Hold eye contact longer than is comfortable. One of my students started practicing this on passengers in passing cars while waiting at a bus stop. He said the reactions he'd get were amazing, from smiles and waves to honks and shouts.

♦ Experiment with personal space. Move closer to people than you usually would in an elevator, for instance. Notice how strong the urge is to revert to your standard behavior. Try not to give in.

♦ Hold the elevator door open for everyone entering, and then get in last. Stand with your back to the elevator door, facing everyone else.

♦ Strike up a conversation with a complete stranger. For instance, as you wait in line at a coffee shop, comment on the pastries and then ask your neighbor an open-ended question, such as: "I'm trying to decide which is the most sinful: the muffin, the brownie, or the cake. How would you rank them?"

These exercises may feel acutely uncomfortable and perhaps a bit embarrassing the first few times you do them. Remind yourself that you're not doing anything illegal! The only thing that's holding you back is social customs. You can also remind yourself that you're doing important personal work, increasing your skills and expanding the boundaries of your comfort zone. And remind yourself that, like every other experience, this one, too, will pass. However uncomfortable it feels, it will fade as completely as all the previous experiences you've ever had. You will also get better and more comfortable with practice. So if you can bring yourself to talk to strangers whenever you're waiting around in lines, or on buses or trains, do it. Grab every opportunity, and you'll improve fast.

You can practice this technique with any discomfort, physical or mental. Whether you're too hot, too cold, angry, impatient, annoyed, or fearful, you may be surprised to find that some feelings you usually don't welcome can even become mildly pleasant.

You now have all the tools you need to get into charismatic mental states, no matter what the obstacle. The three-step process of destigmatizing, detaching, and rewriting is one you can use anytime a difficult experience arises. Come back to this chapter whenever a situation in your life calls for these tools until they become second nature.

## KEY TAKEAWAYS

- To be charismatic, you must first learn to overcome the primary obstacle to charisma: internal discomfort.
- Skillfully handle internal discomfort with a three-step process: destigmatize your discomfort, neutralize your negative thoughts, and rewrite your perception of reality.
- Destigmatize and dedramatize uncomfortable feelings by remembering that they are survival instincts and a natural part of the human experience. Think of others who've gone through this before—especially people you admire—and see yourself as part of a community of human beings experiencing the same feeling at the same moment.
- Neutralize unhelpful negative thoughts by remembering that the mind often distorts reality and filters your environment to highlight the negative. Think of your negative thoughts as graffiti on a wall—you may find it an ugly sight, but just because you see an ugly sight doesn't mean you're an ugly person.
- Rewrite reality by considering a few helpful alternatives to your current perspective. For maximum effect, write down your new realities by hand and describe them in vivid detail.
- For advanced practice, delve into the physical sensations of discomfort. Focusing on the sensations gives your mind something concrete to focus on, drawing your attention away from your feeling that the experience is unbearable.

# 5

## Creating Charismatic Mental States

IN THE PREVIOUS chapter you learned how to skillfully handle the most common charisma-inhibiting obstacles. You're now ready to create the right mental states that will help you reach your full charisma potential. You'll learn how to increase confidence and how to emanate warmth and power—two of the three crucial components of charisma. You'll also discover ways to craft any mental state you want, from serenity to triumph.

### Visualization

Golfer Jack Nicklaus said that he never hit a shot, even during practice, without visualizing it first. For decades, professional athletes have considered visualization an essential tool, often spending hours visualizing their victory, telling their mind just what they want their body to achieve.

"There is good evidence that imagining oneself performing an activity activates parts of the brain that are used in actually performing the activity," Professor Stephen Kosslyn, director of Stanford's Center for Advanced Study in the Behavioral Sciences, wrote me. This is the reason why visualization works so well—in fact, some athletes report feeling physically exhausted after intense visualization sessions. Visualization can even physically alter the brain structure: repeated experiments have shown that simply imagining yourself playing the piano with sufficient repetition leads to a detectable and measurable change in the motor cortex of the brain.[1]

The brain is extraordinarily changeable: it's constantly rewiring itself. The previously held notion that past a certain age it becomes set in its ways has now been proven to be quite dramatically wrong.[2] Whenever we use our brain, we fire certain neuronal connections, and the more these connections get used, the stronger they become. We're essentially wearing grooves into our brain—whichever mental processes are used on a consistent basis will strengthen. You can build and then strengthen whichever mental tendencies you focus on.

Mental preparation techniques have also become standard practice in Hollywood, where a technique known as Method acting is used by many of the Hollywood's most respected stars. Sean Penn, Meryl Streep, Robert DeNiro, Marlon Brando, and Paul Newman all hail from this school of acting.

Method acting evolved to help actors with their most difficult task: getting their body language right. Consciously trying to control as much of their body language as possible was both exhausting and doomed to fail: even with years of training, it's impossible to control the flow completely. If their internal emotions were not what they wanted the outside world to see, sooner or later, something of these underlying thoughts and feelings would show.

Method acting took a different approach. Rather than having people try to control their body language, it went straight to the body language source—the mind—and had the actors strive to *become* the characters they were aiming to play so that they would really feel the emotions they wanted to convey. Then the thousands of body language signals would flow naturally and congruently.

Because of its powerful mental and physiological effects, visualization is one of the most effective charisma-boosting tools available. The right visualization can help you increase your internal feeling of confidence as well as your ability to project it. Just by using the right mental images, your subconscious mind will send a remarkable chain reaction of confidence signals cascading through your body. In fact, you can display nearly any body language just by picking the right visualization.

The box below is a step-by-step guide to visualization that you can use whenever you want to change your internal state. You'll practice visualizing confidence here, but later in the book you'll find other useful exercises for visualizing warmth and empathy, or calm and serenity.

## Putting It into Practice: Visualization

The following visualization is a great tool to increase the amount of power you want to convey. You can try this exercise at home on the couch, at work sitting at your desk, or even in an elevator—whenever you have an opportunity to close your eyes for a minute.

♦ Close your eyes and relax.

♦ Remember a past experience when you felt absolutely triumphant—for example, the day you won a contest or an award.

♦ *Hear* the sounds in the room: the murmurs of approval, the swell of applause.

♦ *See* people's smiles and expressions of warmth and admiration.

♦ *Feel* your feet on the ground and the congratulatory handshakes.

♦ Above all, *experience* your feelings, the warm glow of confidence rising within you.

(continued on next page)

*(continued from previous page)*

Do you feel more confident? Some people experience very strong results from their first visualization and others less. But, as with any other skill, your ability to create realistic visualizations will improve with practice.

The next time you do this exercise, aim to create images that are even more detailed. Guided imagery must be precise, vivid, and detailed to be effective, says Harvard-trained visualization specialist Stephen Krauss. When visualization is used with Olympic ski teams, skiers visualize themselves careening through the entire course, feeling their muscles tensing, experiencing each bump and turn in their minds.

Some people find it simple to think through a visualization scenario. However, others are more sensitive to auditory cues, so here's an alternative to visualization: select key phrases to mentally focus on. My clients have found a wide variety of phrases useful, so here are a few examples, which could help you access calm and serenity. They run the gamut of tastes and styles, so you may find that some raise your hackles while others strongly resonate:

- A week from now, or a year from now, will any of this matter?
- This, too, shall pass. Yes, it will.
- Look for little miracles unfolding right now.
- Love the confusion.
- What if you could trust the Universe, even with this?

Axioms like these can be a saving grace in moments of panic, when our brain goes blank and all we can remember are simple phrases. Beginning white-water rafters are taught an easy rhyme to remember—"toes to nose"—to remind them of the sequence of moves they should execute if the boat flips over. Even veteran firefighters sometimes fall back on a mantra like "Put the wet stuff on the red stuff" to snap them into action during a fire.

You can also add real sensory input to your visualizations. For instance, play music while you verbalize or subvocalize, choosing songs that you know make you feel especially energized and confident. Movie themes seem to be particularly useful. The executives I coach often mention the musical scores from *Rocky III* ("Eye of the Tiger"), *Chariots of Fire* (instrumental by Vangelis), or *Top Gun* ("Top Gun Anthem"). My personal soundtrack comes from the movie *Peter Pan:* "Flying," by James Newton Howard. Don your headphones and let the music of your choice set the mood for whatever mental state you want to achieve.

If you're ready to go all out, add movement to make your visualizations reach an entirely new level. Because physiology affects psychology (yes, your body affects your mind—more on this in the next chapter), creating certain movements or postures can bring up specific emotions in your mind.

Try to think of what gesture you tend to make when you achieve something, like a good golf shot, or when you get really good news. Is it the classic fist pump? Or maybe you raise both arms in the air and shout "YES!" By adding this particular gesture (and words, if any) to the end of your visualization, when your confidence is soaring, you'll engage your entire physiology and "lock in" the triumphant feeling, maximizing the effect of the exercise.

With all of these dimensions—visual, auditory, kinesthetic—keep refining as you go along. If you feel that a particular image, phrase, movement, or song works well, tweak it a little and observe how that affects the results. Notice what happens when you zoom in on visual details, sounds, or sensations. Whether you're hearing encouraging voices or feeling the warmth of the sun, keep making small changes. The combination of sights and sounds that works best for me has changed considerably over the years.

Visualization is truly a miracle method, helping you boost confidence, emanate more warmth, replace anxiety with calm serenity, or gain access to whichever emotion you'd like to feel and then broadcast it through your body language. In fact, it's worth taking the time to develop and practice a go-to visualization to effectively help you regain calm and confidence. That way, during times of stress, you won't need to come up with new imagery on the fly. You'll already know what works for you.

Here are three more visualizations to use when you want a charisma boost before giving a presentation, attending a key meeting, or anytime you're feeling anxious.

**Just before giving a presentation:** Some of this century's best-known speakers report using some version of visualization just before stepping into the spotlight. In fact, it would be unusual to find a great speaker who doesn't. When clients ask me if they should use visualization before an important speech, I answer, "Only if you want it to go really well!"

After fifteen years of speaking professionally, I find that doing even thirty seconds of visualization makes a substantial difference to my performance. It greatly affects how charismatic I am on stage. In fact, every time I *don't* run through a visualization just before stepping on stage, I regret it. Even when I know the speech so well I could say it backward, it's worth using visualization to ensure that I get into the right charismatic mental state.

To make the visualization most effective, I try to arrive at the venue early so that I can walk around the stage and get comfortable with the space. I take the right music along with me and start the visualizations right there on stage, aiming to link confident, triumphant feelings to being in that particular environment. While listening to an uplifting, energizing soundtrack, I create mental movies, vividly imagining how splendidly the speech is going, seeing and hearing the audience's enthusiastic response as I confidently move across the stage.

A few minutes before I'm due to walk out under the spotlights, I hide away in an unoccupied room (this is such a common practice for actors, politicians, speakers, and all other performers that a special room called the *green room* is often reserved for just this purpose) and run through my visualization, dancing around (yes, I'm serious) to my personal soundtrack.

**Before important meetings:** One of the most impressive young businesswomen I know seems to always float on a cloud of confidence, and things somehow always go well for her. When Silvia goes to pitch a deal, people who know her take for granted that she'll win the day.

Silvia recently confided that visualization is one of the secrets to her success. Before key meetings, she'll imagine "the smiles on their faces because they liked me and they are confident about the value I'm bringing them. I'll imagine as much detail as I can, even seeing the wrinkles around their eyes as they're smiling." She visualizes the whole interaction, all the way through to the firm handshakes that close the meeting, sealing the deal.

I've even found visualization helpful before writing important e-mails. Just as the right visualization helps you get into the right body language so that the right signals flow effortlessly, you can use visualization to get into specific emotional or mental states so that the right words flow as well.

If, for instance, your message needs to communicate warmth, caring, and empathy, you'll have a far easier time finding the right words if you can get yourself into a warm and empathetic state. Visualizing a scene that brings up these feelings—imagining a young child coming to tell you her troubles at school—will help prime your mind for the right language to flow.

**Anytime you're feeling anxious:** The surest way to feel better when you're feeling anxious is to flood your system with oxytocin. Often called the *neuropeptide of trust*, oxytocin instantly reverses the arousal of the fight-or-flight response.

One of my favorite neuroscience resources, the *Wise Brain Bulletin*, suggested that a twenty-second hug is enough to send oxytocin coursing through your veins, and that you can achieve the same effect just by *imagining* the hug. So the next time you're feeling anxious, you might want to imagine being wrapped up in a great big hug from someone you care about.

Time and time again, my clients are astounded by how effective these techniques are. "Visualization techniques have saved lives at MIT," one recent graduate told me. This famously high-achieving institution is also known for high rates of suicide, especially during final exams (MIT's suicide rate during the period was 38 percent higher than Harvard's, for instance[3]). The MIT Health Center now distributes visualization CDs to students during final exams.

One client called visualization techniques "real-life Jedi mind tricks." Another told me that while he'd always used visualization techniques in sports and music, he had never thought to apply the same techniques to business and daily life and was astounded at the results (and kicking himself for not having thought of it sooner).

Nineteenth-century author Napoleon Hill would regularly visualize nine famous men as his personal counselors, including Ralph Waldo Emerson, Thomas Edison, Charles Darwin, and Abraham Lincoln. He wrote: "Every night . . . I held an imaginary council meeting with this group whom I called my 'Invisible Counselors.' . . . I now go to my imaginary counselors with every difficult problem that confronts me and my clients. The results are often astonishing."

Choose your own counselors according to which emotions they embody for you. Hill's chosen self-confidence counselor was Napoleon Bonaparte. To boost your charisma, choose figures who represent complete self-confidence, or warmth and caring, or calm and serenity. Or you might even find some figures who embody all the elements at once. Visualize yourself going to these figures for a "pep talk" anytime you feel you need one. Thanks to the brain's wonderful placebo response, this will produce effects even if it doesn't feel real.

Visualization is indeed a powerful tool. Of all the charisma-boosting techniques, this is the one I recommend making a permanent part of your toolkit. If you gain nothing else from this book, this one technique will make a critical difference to your charisma.

## Gratitude, Goodwill, and Compassion

Warmth is one of the key components of charismatic behavior. It can make people like you, trust you, and want to help you. Unfortunately, for many people, warmth isn't an obvious, easy feeling to access; it just doesn't come naturally. Many of my clients confide in their first session that they aren't quite sure what warmth should feel like. In fact, I often hear new clients worry: "But what if deep down I'm actually heartless? What if I just *can't* access warmth?" The good news is I can absolutely guarantee that you're not heartless, and I know for sure that anyone can learn to better express warmth.

Warmth is difficult for a lot of us. This could stem from any number of reasons—upbringing, childhood, current environment, or just personality. Warmth certainly wasn't natural for me when I entered this field. To experience warmth, I had to use every tool in the book—every single tool you're about to discover. You're going to get a three-step gradual transition into warmth, from the least personal to the most personal.

The first step is to get in touch with warmth directed toward life in general, and your life in particular. This falls under the general category of gratitude. Gratitude has a special advantage for those of us who sometimes find it uncomfortable to connect with others. It can give us charismatic warmth without having to connect with anyone.

Then you'll experiment with warmth toward others—these are the realms of goodwill, altruism, compassion, and empathy.

Last, you'll explore what seems to be, for most of us, the least comfortable kind of warmth: warmth for yourself. This is the emerging discipline of self-compassion.

*Any* of these will bring you a measurable increase in charisma, so play around with all of them if you can, both those that feel natural and those that feel like a stretch.

### Step One: Gratitude and Appreciation

What's the opposite of gratitude? Resentment, neediness, and desperation—none of which is very charismatic. We all know that few things will ruin someone's chances more than giving off an impression of desperation, whether they're on a job interview or on a date. Gratitude is a great antidote to all of these negative feelings because it comes from thinking of things you *already have*—from material items or experiences to cherished relationships. Gratitude can be a great charisma conduit, bringing you back to the present and giving you immediate access to feelings of both confidence and warmth.

Everyone seems to be preaching gratitude these days. Oprah champions an "attitude of gratitude," and studies have come out showing that gratitude helps you live longer, healthier, and even happier.[4] The science is compelling, as are the ways in which gratitude can boost your charisma. If you can access gratitude, an instant change will sweep through your body language from head to toe: your face will soften, your whole body will relax. Your body language will emanate both warmth and a particular grounded confidence that people will find very appealing.

But few of us can simply decide to get into a state of gratitude. In fact, for most people, gratitude doesn't come easy. Human beings are instinctively wired for *hedonic adaptation*: the tendency to take our blessings for granted.[5] Telling yourself that you should be grateful is often counterproductive, as it only brings up guilt. Clients complain that when someone tells them "You should be grateful," it only makes them feel worse: either resentful or guilty for not being grateful.

One way to invoke a sense of gratitude is to focus on little things that are physically present. During a recent lunch meeting at a restaurant, for instance, I focused on little delights: the sun streaming through the window; blue skies; that the waiter got my order right; or the existence, availability, and wonders of ketchup.

Another good gratitude-enhancing tool is to view your life through a third-person lens, writing a narrative about yourself cast in a positive light.

For instance, Mary, whom we met earlier, wrote: "Mary has a pretty great life, really. She has a steady source of income. When so many others endure physical labor or can't find work, she gets to go to an office where she is treated decently and many colleagues respect her. She's well liked and appreciated by her friends and family. Many people truly care about her. She's often been a good friend. In several instances, she chose to be there for someone who needed her. And she's done decently well today: completed a full report, expressed appreciation for a colleague's help, even went to the gym." It doesn't have to be profound. Positive things like the ones Mary mentioned, which are small but significant in our lives, are great choices to be grateful for.

This is one of the many cases where the act of writing makes a critical difference to the exercise's effectiveness. It makes the positive perspective feel more real, more solid. If you simply imagine how someone else would see your life, it may not feel real at all, losing its substance and weight. Whereas if you write it out, even if it feels odd at first, by the end of the paragraph it'll feel oddly real.

Follow the exercises in the box below to try these approaches for yourself.

## Putting It into Practice: Gratitude

**Focus on the present:** The next time you find yourself annoyed at some minor thing, remember that letting your mind focus on the annoyance could impair your body language. To counter this, follow the suggestions below:

♦ Sweep through your body from head to toe and find three abilities you approve of. You could be grateful that you have feet and toes that allow you to walk. You might appreciate your ability to read. Try it right now:

1. _____

2. _____

3. _____

♦ Scan your environment. Look around and find three pleasant sights—even the smallest ones. Maybe you can see the sky and appreciate its shades of color. Perhaps you can notice the texture of the table you're sitting at or even the paper right in front of you. Try it right now:

1. _____

2. _____

3. _____

**Use a third-person lens:** For this technique, you'll need just a few minutes to sit down, a pen, and some paper.

♦ Start to describe your life as if you were an outside observer, and focus on all the positive aspects you can think of.

*(continued on next page)*

(continued from previous page)

♦ Write about your job—the work you do and the people you work with. Describe your personal relationships and the good things friends and family members would say about you. Mention a few positive things that have happened today and the tasks you have already accomplished.

♦ Take the time to write down this narrative. Just thinking about it won't be as effective.

**Imagine your own funeral:** The last gratitude-enhancing technique, used in many highly regarded leadership seminars despite its outlandishness, is the most intense—do not take it lightly.

Have you ever felt flooded with relief after finding an important item you thought had been lost or stolen? (It happens to me every time I lose my keys.) This instinctive sweeping sense of gratitude can be remarkably powerful, and it taps into wells of gratitude deeper than almost any other practice.

You can manufacture this gratitude-producing sense of relief by imagining your own funeral. Within seconds, this visualization can bring you into a state of emotional aliveness and, as you realize you *still* have your life, to a state of gratitude.

The main point of this exercise is to help you gain access to various shades of warmth and give you a chance to get comfortable with these feelings.

This is one of the few exercises that can fairly effectively help you feel gratitude for life. It can be very moving, bring you great insights, and give you clarity on deeply held values, but it can also make you feel quite stirred up. So for this one, please ensure that you're in an environment where you would feel comfortable being emotional. I often recommend doing this at home. Give yourself time to get into the exercise, time to experience it, and time to come out and process it. As with all visualizations, it's worth getting as detailed as you can—get all five senses involved. If you'd prefer to have my voice guiding you through the process, you'll find an audio recording online at http://www.Charisma Myth.com/funeral.

♦ Sit or lie down, close your eyes, and set the scene. Where is your funeral being held? What day of the week, what time of day? What is the weather like? See the building where the ceremony is being held. See people arriving. Who's coming? What are they wearing? Now move into the building and look around inside. Do you see flowers? If so, smell the flowers' scent heavy on the air. See people coming through the door. What are they thinking? What kind of chairs are they sitting in? What do these chairs feel like?

♦ Your funeral starts. Think of the people you care most about or whose opinions matter most to you. What are they thinking? See them stepping up one after another and delivering their eulogy. What are they saying? What regrets do they have for you? Now think: What would you like them to have said? What regrets do *you* have for yourself?

♦ See people following your coffin to the cemetery and gathering around your grave. What would you like to see written on your tombstone?

♦ Almost everyone, of all ages, genders, and seniority levels, gets a bit teary-eyed by the end. You might feel moved, touched, stirred. Stay with these emotions as much as you can and aim to get comfortable with them.

So this is how you can access gratitude for life. Gratitude is both a great first step toward warmth and a solid technique to get back into a good mental state even in the midst of a difficult situation. Simply considering the possibility of gratitude or looking for small things to appreciate will send a positive change sweeping through your body language. As an added bonus, it may also increase your sense of security and confidence, thus improving your mental performance.

## Step Two: Goodwill and Compassion

Have you ever been with someone who you felt truly had your best interests at heart? How did that feel? You likely experienced nice, warm feelings. Goodwill is a highly effective way both to project warmth and to create a feeling of warmth in others. When you truly focus on someone's well-being, you feel more connected to them, it shows across your face, and people perceive you as someone full of warmth. Your charisma quotient soars.

Goodwill is the second step on the road to accessing warmth and, ultimately, charisma. Using goodwill in your daily interactions can instantly infuse your body language with more warmth, kindness, care, and compassion—all very charismatic qualities.

I've often heard people say of meeting the highly charismatic Bill Clinton: "He makes you feel like you're the only person in the world for him." I know that every time I get myself into a state of goodwill, I feel an instant shift in the interaction; people immediately warm up and seem to like me more.

Goodwill improves how you feel as it floods your system with oxytocin and serotonin, both wonderful feel-good chemicals. In addition, in an interesting way, it lessens our need to make the interaction succeed. When our only aim is to broadcast goodwill, it takes the pressure off. We're no longer striving, struggling, pushing for things to go in a certain direction. And since we're less concerned about how the interaction goes, we can both feel and project more charismatic confidence.

Goodwill is the simple state of wishing others well. You can think of it as a mental muscle that can be strengthened through practice. Even if your goodwill muscles have atrophied, you can still build them back up. A recent study from the Wiseman Institute using functional MRI scans showed that these positive states could be learned, just like playing a musical instrument or being proficient at a sport. The scans revealed that the corresponding brain circuits were "dramatically changed" through training.

One simple but effective way to start is to try to find three things you like about the person you want to feel goodwill toward. No matter whom it is you're talking to, find three things to appreciate or approve of—even if these are as small as "their shoes are shined" or "they were on time." When you start searching for positive elements, your mental state changes accordingly and then sweeps through your body language.

Below are more intense goodwill exercises to experiment with. For some people, they work instantly. For others, they feel alien. Just try them out—if these don't work for you, we'll have others for you to experiment with.

First, a visualization. This one comes from neuroscientist Dr. Privahini Bradoo, a highly charismatic person whose radiating warmth and happiness I've long admired. I was grateful when she shared one of her secrets with me: in any interaction, imagine the person you're speaking to, and all those around you, as having invisible angel wings.

This can help shift your perspective. If even for a split second you can see someone as a fundamentally good being, this will soften and warm your emotional reaction toward them, changing your entire body language. So give it a try: as you're walking around, or driving around, see people with angel wings walking and driving. It's worth imagining yourself with wings, too. Imagine that you're all a team of angels working together, all doing your wholehearted best. Many of my coaching clients (even hardened senior executives) have told me how extraordinarily effective this visualization has been for them. They can instantly feel more internal presence and warmth, and I can see a great increase in the amount of both presence and warmth that their body language projects.

If you respond better to auditory guides, try a few different phrases. For instance, while looking at someone, think, *I like you. And I like you just for you.* Or try to remember this guideline: *Just love as much as you can from wherever you are.* Remind yourself of these maxims several times a day, and notice the shift this can make in your mind and body. Another saying people often find equally effective: *Of all the options open to me right now, which one would bring the most love into this world?*

For some people, these three techniques are all they need to feel goodwill and, thus, charisma-enhancing warmth. For them, simply focusing on wishing others well helps them to access warmth. For others, it may not be enough. Perhaps the person we'd like to show goodwill toward is being cantankerous. Perhaps we're feeling annoyed or resentful toward them. Or perhaps they just feel too remote.

In these cases, try going a step beyond goodwill to empathy and compassion.

- Goodwill means that you wish someone well without necessarily knowing how they're feeling.
- Empathy means that you understand what they feel; perhaps you've had a similar experience in the past.
- Compassion is empathy plus goodwill: you understand how they feel, and you wish them well.

Paul Gilbert, one of the main researchers in the field of compassion, describes the process of accessing compassion as follows: first comes *empathy*, the ability to understand what someone is feeling, to detect distress; second, *sympathy*, being emotionally moved by distress; and third, *compassion*, which arises with the desire to care for the well-being of the distressed person.

The good news is that we have a natural tendency for compassion; it's profoundly hardwired into our brains, even deeper and more strongly than cognitive abilities. Neuropsychologist Rick Hanson asserts that humans are by far the most empathetic species on the planet. You can think your way into compassion even if you don't naturally feel it, Hanson assures us.

Your *willingness* to focus on others' well-being is all you need to positively change your body language. This will be enough to give people the feeling that you really care about them, and is one of the core components of charisma.

You learn to swim by swimming. And you learn to be compassionate by practicing compassion, even if it feels awkward at first. Try the exercise on the following page to grow your capacity for compassion.

• • •

## Putting It into Practice: Compassion

Goodwill and compassion give you warmth to balance your power, and can save you from appearing overconfident or, worse, arrogant. They can also be a stealth tool, a silver bullet that turns around difficult conversations.

Take the three steps below to practice compassion for someone you know:

1. Imagine their past. What if you had been born in their circumstances, with their family and upbringing? What was it like growing up in their family situation with whatever they experienced as a child? It's often said that everyone you meet has stories to tell, and that everyone has a few that would break your heart. Consider also that if you had experienced everything they have experienced, perhaps you would have turned out just like they have.

2. Imagine their present. Really try to put yourself in their shoes right now. Imagine what it feels like to be them today. Put yourself in their place, be in their skin, see through their eyes. Imagine what they might be feeling right now—all the emotions they might be holding inside.

3. If you really need compassion dynamite, look at them and ask: What if this were their last day alive? You can even imagine their funeral. You're at their funeral, and you're asked to say a few words about them. You can also imagine what you'd say *to* them after they'd already died.

Though it may feel awkward, uncomfortable, or downright mushy, goodwill and compassion truly are valuable business skills—even in fields as dry as accounting. For Tom Schiro, one of the key executives at Deloitte, compassion is one of the top three qualities he seeks when evaluating potential leaders, and he sees it as a core tenet of charisma. Angel Martinez, chairman of the multinational conglomerate Deckers Outdoors, agrees. "Embedded in the notion of charisma is empathy," he told me. "I don't see how you can be an effective leader without this ability."

So that's how you can effectively access goodwill and compassion for others. Now let's look at the most personal, and often the most challenging, form of compassion: compassion for yourself.

### Step Three: Self-Compassion

Helen was clearly very bright. She could make forceful and persuasive arguments, and she came across as organized, trustworthy, and a good listener, intensely focused on what people were saying. But she wasn't charismatic, and she realized it. "I know I'm *interesting*," she told me. "I'm a good listener, and a good conversationalist. But I don't think I'm *likable*, and I'm definitely not charismatic."

Helen had plenty of self-confidence. So what was she lacking? Warmth. People were impressed by how much she knew, but they didn't feel cared for. Helen couldn't emanate warmth because she had a hard time feeling it—whether for others or for herself. Instead, she usually felt a little alienated, disconnected. In our first meeting together, she very sincerely wondered aloud, "Why would people like me? Even I don't find myself likable." As you can imagine, this cold internal message resonated in her head, played across her body language, and diminished how much warmth she could emanate.

For Helen, the path to charisma was through *self*-warmth. Warmth as we've described it so far is directed outward—toward other people, or toward life in general. But warmth can also be directed inward, toward ourselves. This self-directed warmth is called *self-compassion*, and though it can sound (and feel) uncomfortable, it can be a life-changing (and certainly charisma-enhancing) practice.

First, let's distinguish three key concepts:

**Self-confidence** is our belief in our ability to do or to learn how to do something.

**Self-esteem** is how much we approve of or value ourselves. It's often a comparison-based evaluation (whether measured against other people or against our own internal standards for approval).

**Self-compassion** is how much warmth we can have for ourselves, especially when we're going through a difficult experience.

It's quite possible for people to have high self-confidence but low self-esteem and very low self-compassion. Like Helen, these people may consider themselves fairly competent, but they don't necessarily like themselves any more for it, and they can be very hard on themselves when they don't succeed.

Recent behavioral science research indicates that it may be healthier to focus on self-compassion than on self-esteem.[6] The former is based on self-acceptance, the latter on self-evaluation and social comparison. Self-esteem is more of a roller coaster, contingent on how we believe we compare to others. It also tends to correlate with narcissism.

Individuals who score high on self-compassion scales demonstrate greater emotional resilience to daily difficulties and fewer negative reactions to difficult situations, such as receiving unflattering feedback.[7] Higher self-compassion predicts a greater sense of personal responsibility for the outcome of events: it helps predict levels of accountability. People who score high on self-compassion also have a lower tendency for denial. This makes sense: personal mistakes would generate less self-criticism, so people would be more willing to admit to them.

When they hear the term *self-compassion*, people often assume it is synonymous with self-indulgence or self-pity.[8] Surprisingly, the opposite is true. Solid behavioral science research shows that the higher one's level of self-compassion, the lower one's level of self-pity. You can think of the difference between the two this way: self-compassion is feeling that what happened to you is unfortunate, whereas self-pity is feeling that what happened to you is unfair. In this way, self-pity can lead to resentment or bitterness, and to feeling more isolated and alienated. In contrast, self-compassion often leads to increased feelings of connectedness.

Self-compassion is what helps us forgive ourselves when we've fallen short; it's what prevents internal criticism from taking over and playing across our face, ruining our charisma potential. In this way, self-compassion is critical to emanating warmth.

Interestingly, self-compassion can also help you emanate greater self-confidence. One of my clients was a high-performing, high-achieving bank executive who was always incredibly hard on himself.

In our very first session, Brian blurted out: "You know, that inner critic thing, man, it's a real problem for me." He told me he could feel his internal critic nitpicking every imperfection throughout his day.

Within minutes of trying the self-compassion technique I suggested, Brian already felt a difference. He told me: "I felt an immediate effect. I exhaled, felt relief, my chest expanded. I immediately had more presence, I felt myself being more of an 'alpha male' taking up more space!" Because self-compassion dispels the inner critical voice that affects body language, it can actually give you a more expansive, confident posture. For Brian, paradoxically, self-compassion was the route to being perceived as more of a confident alpha male.

Self-compassion delivers an impressive array of benefits: decreased anxiety, depression, and self-criticism; improved relationships and greater feelings of social connectedness and satisfaction with life; increased ability to handle negative events; and even improved immune system functioning.[9]

Sounds great, doesn't it? Unfortunately, self-compassion isn't taught in school. In fact, in today's culture it sounds indulgent and unjustified, and can feel very alien. Many of us don't have a very clear idea of what it is to begin with.

So first, let's get a solid definition. Kristin Neff, one of compassion's foremost researchers, defines self-compassion as a three-step process: First, realizing that we're experiencing difficulties. Second, responding with kindness and understanding toward ourselves when we are suffering or feel inadequate, rather than being harshly self-critical. Third, realizing that whatever we're going through is commonly experienced by all human beings, and remembering that everyone goes through difficult times.

When things go wrong in our lives, it's easy to feel that other people are having an easier time. Recognizing instead that everyone at some point has had or will have the very experience you're having now can help you feel like part of the larger human experience rather than feeling isolated and alienated.

When our inner critic starts pointing out our misdeeds and imperfections, it will often make us feel that everyone else is doing better, that we're the only ones who are this flawed. Self-criticism is much stronger when our suffering seems due to our own perceived failures and inadequacies than when it seems due to external circumstances. This is when self-compassion is the most precious.

How does one go about cultivating self-compassion? The good news is that intention is the most crucial component of treating yourself kindly. Christopher Germer, author of *The Mindful Path to Self-Compassion*, is adamant that "self-compassion is not a gift you're either born with or not. It's a skill, a trainable mental skill that each and every one of us, without exception, can develop and strengthen." Germer suggests starting where you are right now: discovering the ways in which you already care for yourself, and then reminding yourself to do these things when negativity hits.

## Putting It into Practice: Self-Compassion

You can do this simple exercise in minutes. Just list five ways that you already care for yourself when you're having a hard time.

1. _____

2. _____

3. _____

4. _____

5. _____

Star the ones you've found particularly effective, and that's it. You've started your self-compassion list.

You're now ready for the more intense self-compassion practices.

The highly charismatic Dalai Lama is known for being such a radiant presence of warmth and caring that even the most cold-hearted characters melt in his presence. He ascribes much of his effect on people to Buddhist compassion practices, one of which you're about to learn, called *Metta*.

Metta is a millennia-old Buddhist compassion and self-compassion practice that roughly translates as "loving kindness." Simply put, Metta is the conscious practice of developing kind intentions toward all beings. When the brains of dedicated Metta practitioners were examined and tested by neuroscientists, significant differences came to light. Not only did they emit deeper brain waves, they also bounced back from stress scenarios much faster, and they showed particular enhancement in the left frontal lobe of their cortexes, the "happy region" of the brain. [10]

Metta is the single most powerful tool you can use to counter your inner critic's attacks, and, with its many benefits, it is wonderful for boosting charisma. This is, however, a highly uncomfortable practice for many of us. Frankly, when I started this practice, it was more than uncomfortable—it was downright awkward. Even if it feels this way for you, too, do it anyway.

## Putting It into Practice: Metta

The visualization below will guide you through a custom-tailored form of Metta, step by step. It has been crafted to take advantage of two instinctive human tendencies: our absorption of images and our respect for authority. If you'd prefer to hear me guide you through this exercise, you'll find a recording online at http://CharismaMyth.com/metta. Throughout this exercise, you may notice a certain rhythm created by the repetitions. That is indeed their purpose; just be willing to give it a try.

♦ Sit comfortably, close your eyes, and take two or three deep breaths. As you inhale, imagine drawing in masses of clean air toward the top of your head; then let it whoosh through you from head to toe as you exhale, washing all concerns away.

♦ Think of any occasion in your life when you performed a good deed, however great or small. Just one good action— one moment of truth, generosity, or courage. Focus on that memory for a moment.

♦ Now think of one being, whether present or past, mythical or actual—Jesus, Buddha, Mother Teresa, the Dalai Lama—

who could have great affection for you. This could be a person, a pet, or even a stuffed animal.

♦ Picture this being in your mind. Imagine their warmth, their kindness and compassion. See it in their eyes and face. Feel their warmth radiating toward you, enveloping you.

♦ See yourself through their eyes with warmth, kindness, and compassion. Feel them giving you complete forgiveness for everything your inner critic says is wrong. You are completely and absolutely forgiven. You have a clean slate.

♦ Feel them giving you wholehearted acceptance. You are accepted as you are, right now, at this stage of growth, imperfections and all.

> You are perfect. At this stage of development, you are perfect.

> At this stage of growth, you are perfect.

> At this stage of perfection, you are perfect.

> With everything that's in your head and heart, you are perfect.

♦ With all your imperfections, you are perfect.

♦ For this phase of growth, you are perfect.

♦ You are fully approved just the way you are, at this stage of development, right now.

After going through the Metta exercise, my clients often report a physical sense of relief, their shoulders sagging during the forgiveness visualization, and then warmth rising during the self-approval process. Many people feel warmth in their solar plexus region. Some describe a kind of "exquisite ache," or feeling "very tender." No matter what you experience, if you are feeling anything, it means it's working.

Even when the experience itself doesn't "feel" like it's working, Metta is worth doing because of the spillover effect it produces. Often, though the exercise itself feels awkward, you will notice throughout the rest of the day that you are more present, connecting better with others and better able to absorb and enjoy the good moments in your life. As Germer puts it: "A moment of self-compassion can change your entire day. A string of such moments can change the course of your life."

You can use Metta visualization anytime you experience an attack of the internal critic. As Germer suggests, you can think of self-compassion as standing up to self-harm, the same way you'd stand up to something threatening a loved one.

Researchers who started experimenting with these kinds of visualizations with highly self-critical people reported "significant reductions in depression, anxiety, self-criticism, shame, and inferiority" while noting a "significant increase in feelings of warmth and reassurance for the self."[11]

If the Metta visualization didn't work for you, try putting up, throughout your home or office, photographs of people for whom you feel affection. These pictures could be of friends or family members, or even public figures who you feel *could* have affection for you, such as the Dalai Lama, Nelson Mandela, or whichever figures resonate with your personal beliefs or bring warmth to your heart (pets and stuffed animals included).

To nurture my internal warmth I set up a "Metta circle" of photographs in the area where I practice every morning. I also carry a small book of favorite wisdoms with me when I want to ensure that I'll be in the right charismatic mental state. The heart-softening and rising warmth I feel every time I glance through it is invaluable. It boosts my charisma within minutes, moving me from a state of worry or irritation to one of calm, confidence, and warmth.

One of my clients put together what she calls a "lovable book." Anytime anyone says something kind, complimentary, or affectionate to her, she jots it down in this book. She's even gone through her past journals and gleaned pearls of warmth. Every time she reads it, she says, it makes her feel warm, secure, and cherished. She feels that she has a "cheerleading squad" in the back of her mind, supporting her throughout the day.

## Using Your Body to Affect Your Mind

So far, we've focused mainly on the ways that our mind affects our body—the many ways in which our mental and emotional states affect our posture, body language, and facial expressions. But did you know the process also works in reverse? Emotions and body language are so linked that adopting a certain posture or facial expression will, in fact, create the corresponding feelings in your mind. Just as with visualization, where the right image will create corresponding emotions and body language, you can reverse-engineer many emotions by adopting the corresponding body language.

Harvard and Columbia psychology researchers found that subjects who assumed a strong, confident physical posture and then spoke with a strong voice and imposing hand gestures actually produced a biochemical reaction that made them feel and seem more confident and powerful. In contrast, those who adopted a hesitant, submissive demeanor experienced the exact opposite biochemical reaction.[12]

Displaying confident body language will actually make you *feel* more confident; these feelings will in turn affect your body language, which will adapt accordingly, displaying yet more confident signals. This will give you yet another feeling boost, and the cycle will build upon itself. All you have to do is get it going.

---

### Putting It into Practice:
### Using Your Body to Change Your Mind

Try out the following postures to see for yourself just how powerfully the arrangement of your body can affect your mind and your feelings.

♦ First, adopt the body language of someone who's utterly depressed. Let your shoulders slump, your head hang, your face sag. Now, *without moving a muscle*, try to feel really,

(continued on next page)

*(continued from previous page)*

truly excited. Go ahead, try to see if you can create any excitement without moving. It's nearly impossible.

♦ Now do the opposite. Physically spring into excitement. Jump up and down as if you've won the lottery, smile the biggest smile you can, wave your arms in the air, and while doing all this, try to feel depressed. Again, it's nearly impossible.

Here are a few more physiological changes to play with:

♦ For confidence, assertiveness, and to be able to emanate gravitas, imagine playing the role of a military general—take a wide stance, puff up your chest, broaden your shoulders, stand straight, and confidently put your arms behind your back. Feel the effect of this posture internally.

♦ For a boost in both energy and warmth, stand up, stretch your hands as high up as possible, inhale as much as you can—imagine your rib cage expanding, doubling in size—make the biggest smile you can and look upward, hold for a second, and then relax everything.

You can use these quick tools in pretty much any situation—anytime you'd like an internal-state change, whether just before an important business meeting or a social gathering.

When I explained this technique to one of my close friends, she exclaimed: "I know exactly what you mean! In Madrid, I had an experience that has influenced me ever since. I call it my Miss Piggy Moment." When *The Muppet Show*'s Miss Piggy is about to go on stage in front of an audience, she pauses for a second, looks in the mirror, preens, and then announces, "I feel beeyootiful!" And then, shoulders back, head held high, she swoops out to make her grand entrance. This is how my friend told me her own story:

> I was walking up the Gran Via in Madrid, feeling tired, hungry, lonely, unfashionably dressed, and the epitome of an ugly

American. The attitude was definitely not working for me, so what to do? I decided that I was a movie star incognito. I stood up straighter, shoulders back, head erect, with the posture that I imagine I would have if I were royalty. Suddenly the dress that had seemed so out of place a moment ago felt like an amazing fashion statement, something that everyone else should copy. I noticed as I walked down the street that heads were turning, all of them. When I asked a man for directions, he said he would be honored if I would allow him to show me the way. It was amazing. From one second to the next, I went from a dowdy, frumpy, ugly stranger to a head-turning movie star. It was memorable. And enlightening.

When I tell them they can be perceived as powerful simply by projecting a more confident body language, my clients are sometimes concerned that confidence is something you're either born with or acquire during early childhood experiences. They believe that just changing their body language would be faking it.

In fact, you really can gain actual self-confidence as well as the instant perception of greater self-confidence just by changing your body language. Yes, it might feel unfamiliar or awkward at first, a bit like riding a bike without training wheels. But if you use the techniques, it *will* work. And if you keep at it, you will get comfortable with it. Eventually, it will become second nature.

## Warming Up for Key Moments

Imagine that you've been training to run a marathon. You've completed several other races, you're in top form, you're ready. On the day of the marathon, what would you do as you arrived? Would you just stand around until the starting gun and then tear off at top speed? Of course not. You'd probably take care to warm up carefully.

You can do the exact same thing with charisma. Plan a warm-up period that allows you to gradually ramp up to the level you want. When you want to ensure peak charismatic performance, don't ex-

pect yourself to be on top of your game, going from zero to full
charisma instantly and at will. You can't rely on pure willpower to get
you there. In fact, it's important to understand just how limited our
daily reserves of willpower really are.[13]

Behavioral science researchers have come to the conclusion that
willpower is a bit like a muscle that fatigues depending on how much
we use it. If we draw on our willpower to resist a temptation or to put
up with a certain annoyance, it will be weaker when we need it for
another activity soon after. In fact, exerting willpower physically fatigues us.[14] It is a finite resource, so be strategic about where and
when you expend it.

Remember Robert, the quick-thinking, impatient executive? He
told me that he would often be annoyed at himself for his inability to
be patient with people. He noticed that when he spent time during a
meeting or a conversation fighting his internal rising impatience,
he'd perform less well for hours afterward. When several such interactions happened in the morning, his ability to be charismatic later
in the day clearly suffered.

I explained to Robert that every time he used his willpower, he
depleted his willpower reserves. He could stop berating himself and
instead realize that it was simply a matter of allocating his willpower
resources appropriately. I asked him to carefully consider which of
these daily interactions were worth spending his precious willpower
capital on. For the interactions that were not worth it, I recommended that Robert either delegate them to a junior employee or ask
a colleague to handle them in exchange for taking on a task that
would be less willpower-depleting for him.

Here's how this could all play out for you in practice. Let's say
you're attending a dinner that could significantly affect your career,
so you'd like to be particularly charismatic. To optimize your chances
of being most charismatic, you know you need to get into a mental
state of warmth and power. If, at dinner, you want to broadcast absolute self-confidence, make sure that the day of and especially the
hours leading up to the dinner do not include meetings or interactions that could make you feel bad about yourself. Rather than just
showing up at dinner, plan a warm-up that will boost your self-

esteem: have coffee with someone who makes you feel good about yourself, or plan an activity (play a sport or a musical instrument) that makes you feel competent or accomplished. If there is a cocktail reception before the dinner, interact with people who make you feel good about yourself, not those who criticize or tease you, even in jest. Yes, making fun of one another can be highly enjoyable—but save that for evenings when charisma is less critical.

Just like an athlete who is careful to stay centered on the morning of a big race, when you need to be at your most charismatic, be highly vigilant about what's entering your mind. Even the music you listen to can affect your emotional and mental state. You know how listening to sad songs can make you feel sad? Be aware that *everything* that enters your mind affects your internal state.

I curate my playlists considering both tempo and lyrics, and when preparing for a key moment, I'm careful to choose songs that correspond with the mood I'm trying to achieve. I have playlists for self-confidence, warmth, empathy, and patience. I've found that it really makes a difference. These playlists are also organized as "pre-speech," "morning wake-up," and even "pre–family gatherings" (yes, I'm serious).

One of my clients wrote me excitedly after first using the warming-up technique. He said: "I just tried it, and it worked! I'm usually uncomfortable in large groups and think about how unpleasant the experience will be. Before this gathering, I scheduled dinner with a longtime friend and went on a walk. I felt great when I entered and saw a friend I hadn't seen in a while so I pulled him aside for a quick catching up, which I knew would also make me feel great. From then on the occasion was a breeze. Several people even commented on how relaxed I looked, giving the impression that I was definitely enjoying myself. And I was!"

Another one of my clients who regularly hosts parties told me that he often plays his planned party-music playlist as he's getting his apartment ready. "This helps get my energy level up and gets me in the mood so I'm ready to play host. I sometimes do it before interviews, too."

The next time you have a key meeting, follow the exercise in the box below to plan the ramp-up. When you need to be particularly charismatic, the following tool can be a great reinforcer.

---

### Putting It into Practice: Warming Up

When warming up for an important event, follow this checklist to prepare your internal state and maximize your charisma.

♦ Go over your schedule for the hours leading up to the event. Think about how the activities and meetings you have planned will affect you.

♦ If you can, avoid any difficult encounters and aim for confidence- or warmth-boosting experiences instead.

♦ Create your own music playlist for the internal state you'd like to have. You could make one for energy and confidence, one that makes you feel warm and empathetic, and another that makes you feel calm and serene. This exercise is a lot of fun in itself, and you can add new songs as often as you'd like.

---

This is also a great substitute for the previous chapter's visualization exercises for anyone who doesn't yet feel comfortable with them. It can be used in place of visualizations, or you can plan a warm-up in addition to visualization if you really want to maximize your charisma power.

Let's say that you're about to discuss a difficult issue with someone who intimidates you. To warm up for the meeting, practice first in your mind, visualizing the scene as you would like it to unfold. Then ask someone with whom you feel comfortable to role-play the situation with you. Make sure you adopt a strong, confident posture. Imagine yourself as a four-star army general reviewing his troops. Take a wide stance, puff up your chest, broaden your shoulders, stand straight, and confidently put your arms behind your back. Practice making your arguments with a strong voice and imposing hand gestures.

When you have a series of meetings, calls, or interviews, whether in one day or over the period of a week, it's well worth scheduling them from least to most important, so that you can practice, learn, and gradually increase in skill and confidence as you go along. Think of yourself as an athlete going for test matches or trial races.

You can also try this with letters or e-mails if you have several to write on the same topic. Write the least important e-mails first and finish with the most important ones. By the time you've written four or five e-mails, your mind will be more practiced, your writing more fluid.

Now that you've learned how to access the right mental state for charisma, how can you ensure that these positive changes are here to stay? This is where charisma maintenance comes in. If you reached a new standard of physical fitness and wanted to maintain it, you'd keep up your fitness regime and adopt a healthy diet. You wouldn't expect to stay in shape without regularly going to the gym and eating right. Charisma operates on the same principle: stay charismatic by regularly using all the tools you've learned in the previous chapters.

## KEY TAKEAWAYS

- Creating an optimal mental state is crucial to unleashing your full charisma potential.
- Visualization can help you create the right mental state and thus the right charismatic body language. To make visualizations most effective, vividly engage all five senses in your imagination.
- You can increase both warmth and confidence by practicing gratitude, goodwill, and compassion for others as well as for yourself.
- Just as professional athletes and performers do, plan a gradual warm-up to reach your peak charismatic performance. Before important events, avoid experiences that would impair your mental state and plan warmth- and confidence-boosting activities instead.
- Your body affects your mind. Flip the visualization technique on its head and practice adopting the right posture and facial expressions to access more of almost any desired internal state.

# 6

## Different Charisma Styles

JUST AS THERE are different leadership and personality styles, there are also different charisma styles. Both Madonna and His Holiness the Dalai Lama draw crowds and are seen as charismatic, but for different reasons.

Throughout this chapter we'll look at four distinct kinds of charisma: focus, visionary, kindness, and authority. We'll see how each of these is perceived, how to develop it, and when to use it.

There are, of course, other kinds of charisma we could consider, but these four are the most practical for daily life, the easiest to access, and thus the most useful to study.

### Focus Charisma: Presence and Confidence

Elon Musk, cofounder of PayPal and current CEO of Tesla Motors, embodies focus charisma. As he'll tell you himself, Musk is very much an introvert. In Tesla's open office space, his nearly empty desk is in the far right corner, two huge monitors arranged to create a cocoon, shielding him from the rest of the office.

However, when he emerges from behind the screens, he is fully present and fully focused. You can feel the intensity of his attention, how keenly he listens to and absorbs everything you say. And he doesn't need to say a word to show you that he understands you: his nonverbal body language makes you feel completely listened to and understood. (You'll learn the secrets to this kind of listening in chapter 8.)

Focus charisma is primarily based on a perception of presence. It gives people the feeling that you are fully present with them, listening to them and absorbing what they say. Focus charisma makes people feel heard, listened to, and understood. Don't underestimate this kind of charisma; it can be surprisingly powerful.

Focus charisma can be highly effective in business. One executive who has worked closely with Bill Gates told me:

> Most people think of charisma as people who are larger than life, who command a room with an over-the-top personality. But despite his unassuming appearance, being slight in build and looking like the stereotypical geek, Bill *does* command the room; his presence is immediately felt. If your definition of charisma is that when you walk into a room all eyes are on you, then Bill has it. If it's that quality that draws people toward you and makes them want to listen to what you have to say, then Bill has that, too.

Jack Keeler, former president of IBM, was known as a very charismatic figure who embodied another key component of focus charisma: the ability to communicate respect. Remember that one of the foundations of charisma is making other people feel good about themselves. Keeler knew how to make others feel that their opinions mattered, and that they were important. He truly believed that even the most junior staff could have pearls of wisdom to impart. One executive who worked with him told me: "You'd see him go to plant manufacturers and engineers, and you could see that he held them in such high regard; he revered them. And in turn, they revered him—they'd light up when he'd walk into the room."

**What people notice:** We assess focus charisma entirely through demeanor. Presence is key: because we can perceive any distracted, inattentive body language, such signals would quickly undermine focus charisma.

### Developing Focus Charisma

Focus charisma requires, of course, the ability to focus and be truly present. Good listening skills are nonnegotiable, as is a certain degree of patience. To develop focus charisma, cultivate your ability to be present: make use of the techniques from the "Presence" section in chapter 2 (get into your toes!). You'll also need the skills to handle charisma-impairing internal discomfort, so tools such as the responsibility transfer and delving into sensations are worth acquiring.

**Once you have it:** Focus charisma is perhaps the easiest form of charisma to access, and can be surprisingly effective, but it comes with two main risks. The first is that if you display too little power you could come across as too eager, and consequently low-status or even subservient. You'll learn in chapter 9 how to increase the amount of confidence you broadcast. A less common risk is exhibiting too little warmth, which leads to attention that is too intense. If you become laser-focused, your interaction may start to feel like an interview, or, worse yet, an interrogation. This is where you need to balance focus with warmth and acceptance or genuine respect, and the following two chapters will show you just how to do that. Though it is primarily based on presence, focus charisma still requires a modicum of both confidence and warmth. You can't discard either dimension entirely.

**When to use it:** Focus charisma is appropriate for almost all business situations. It's particularly useful when you need people to open up and share information. In fact, this is a great charisma style for management consultants or those in other professional services, such as lawyers, accountants, and financial advisers. Focus charisma can also be very helpful in difficult situations, such as negotiations or to defuse hostile conversations. On the other hand, avoid focus charisma when you need to appear authoritative or during emergencies when you need immediate compliance.

## Visionary Charisma: Belief and Confidence

Visionary charisma makes others feel inspired; it makes us *believe*. It can be remarkably effective even though it won't necessarily make people like you. Steve Jobs was notoriously feared inside Apple and had many detractors both within and without, but even these detractors readily admitted to his being both visionary and charismatic. One recent attendee to a Steve Jobs presentation told me: "He spoke with such conviction, such passion, he had all of our neurons screaming, *Yes! I get it! I'm with you!!!*"

Why is visionary charisma so effective and powerful? Because of our natural discomfort with uncertainty. In a constantly changing world, we crave something solid to cling to. During George W. Bush's first presidential campaign, polls of his supporters revealed that a key to their attraction to him was "his conviction and certitude in his beliefs."

Conveying visionary charisma requires the ability to project complete conviction and confidence in a cause. In this way, visionary charisma is based on power. However, it is also based on warmth. Visionary charismatics aren't necessarily warm people, but they do feel strongly, even passionately, about their vision. And to be truly charismatic, their vision must include a certain amount of nobility and altruism.

One reporter described Steve Jobs as being "driven by a nearly messianic zeal. . . . Jobs doesn't sell computers. He sells the promise of a better world." Visionary charismatics often promise redemption—think Joan of Arc or Martin Luther King Jr. With visionary charisma, you're selling people on the vision more than on yourself.

**What people notice:** We assess visionary charisma primarily through demeanor, which includes body language and behavior. Due to the fact that people tend to accept whatever you project, if you seem inspired, they will assume you have something to be inspired about. For visionary charisma, appearance matters far less than it does for other charisma styles. You could be wearing rags and still successfully convey visionary charisma.

### Developing Visionary Charisma

The message matters for visionary charisma. This means knowing how to craft a bold vision and knowing how to deliver the message charismatically (see chapter 11).

One of the keys to communicating your visionary charisma is getting yourself into a state of complete conviction, shedding any doubt. You can use the tools you gained in chapters 3 and 4, such as rewriting reality, to strengthen your belief, or the responsibility transfer, to free yourself from the effect of uncertainty.

**Once you have it:** Visionary charisma can inspire fervent belief and lead monumental change. However, it can also inspire fanatical belief and lead people to disastrous decisions (cult leader Jim Jones persuaded nine hundred people to commit mass suicide).

**When to use it:** Visionary charisma is important at times when you need to inspire people. It's particularly helpful when you want to inspire creativity.

## Kindness Charisma: Warmth and Confidence

When you're a baby, no matter what you do your parents will think you're perfect just as you are. But after a few months, their acceptance becomes conditional. You now have to eat your carrots and smile at Grandma to earn approval. Seldom will you feel again such complete unconditional acceptance from anyone, with the exception, perhaps, of the first few stages of falling in love.

One of the reasons that the Dalai Lama has such a powerful effect on people is his ability to radiate both tremendous warmth and complete acceptance. People who may have never felt completely, wholeheartedly accepted suddenly feel truly seen and enveloped in acceptance. This is kindness charisma in action.

Kindness charisma is primarily based on warmth. It connects with people's hearts, and makes them feel welcomed, cherished, embraced, and, most of all, completely accepted.

**What people notice:** Like visionary and focus charisma, kindness charisma comes entirely from body language—specifically your face, and even more specifically your eyes.

### Developing Kindness Charisma

You, too, can learn how to emanate some of the Dalai Lama magic, though it does require willingness, patience, practice, and the right tools. Start with the mindset: practice accessing warmth with internal tools such as gratitude, goodwill, compassion, and self-compassion from chapter 5. You'll learn in chapter 9 how to emanate warmth from your face, body language, and demeanor and how to make the right kind of eye contact.

Because kindness charisma is heavily dependent on warmth, it is vital to avoid any body language of tension, criticism, or coldness. The internal tools for dealing with mental or physical discomfort from chapter 4 can be invaluable here.

**Once you have it:** Though kindness charisma is based primarily on warmth, without power you risk coming off as overeager to please. This is where the ability to convey a modicum of power becomes important.

The tools you gained in chapter 5—visualization, warming up, and using your body to change your mind—will help you get the right mindset. The following chapters will help you balance warmth and power in your body language.

Kindness charisma has its costs. One of my dear friends radiates such kindness charisma that people become enraptured wherever she goes. From colleagues at the office to cashiers at the supermarket, people feel accepted and cared for as soon as they're in her presence. This can be lovely, but it can also be a heavy burden for her to carry. She suffers pain and guilt when these people, having become enchanted, feel hurt or resentful when she can't make room for them in her life. This is one of the downsides of kindness charisma: it can lead to adulation and, potentially, overattachment. You will gain tools to prevent these side effects in chapter 13, on living a charismatic life.

**When to use it:** Kindness charisma is perfect anytime you want to create an emotional bond or make people feel safe and comfortable. It can be critical in some situations, such as when you have to deliver bad news (see chapter 12). It can also be a surprisingly effective tool when dealing with difficult people (and chapter 12 will cover that, too). However, just as with focus charisma, you may want to avoid it when you need to appear authoritative or when there's a risk that people might get *too* comfortable and share too much (thankfully, you have chapter 13 to help you avoid this).

## Authority Charisma: Status and Confidence

This form of charisma is possibly the most powerful one of all. Our instinctive deference to authority can take epic proportions, and, of course, can be equally turned toward good or evil. Colin Powell and the Dalai Lama embody authority charisma, but so did Stalin and Mussolini. The human reaction to authority runs deep; it's hardwired into our brains.[1]

Those who possess authority charisma are not necessarily *likable*. Michael Jordan, at the height of his career with the Chicago Bulls, told a journalist that he cared much more about being a leader than about being liked. The reporter wrote: "He rankles, sometimes infuriates, his teammates. But he uses his charisma to lift the whole team's level of play."

**What people notice:** Authority charisma is primarily based on a perception of power: the belief that this person has the power to affect our world. We evaluate someone's authority charisma through four indicators: body language, appearance, title, and the reactions of others.

We appraise body language first and foremost. Does it emanate confidence in the person's power to influence others, or to affect the world around them?

Second, we assess appearance. We are biologically programmed to care about status and to be impressed by it because this instinctive reaction favors our survival: high-status individuals have the power to help or hurt us. To survive, we need to know where in the pecking order we stand. As a consequence, we're exquisitely fine-tuned to any clues that can help us determine other people's status.

Clothing is one of our first and strongest clues in evaluating status, thus potential power, and thus authority charisma. We look for signs of expertise (doctors' white coats) or high authority (military or police uniforms). We pay particular attention to signs of high social status or success, such as expensive clothing. In one experiment conducted in New York City, people tended to follow a jaywalker dressed in an expensive suit sooner than one dressed in more casual clothing.[2]

In another experiment, a researcher conducted fake surveys in shopping malls wearing either a designer-logo sweater or a no-logo sweater. When faced with the designer label, 52 percent of people agreed to take the survey, compared with only 13 percent who saw no logo. Expensive logos also affected people's charitable impulses. Research assistants brought in nearly twice as many donations when their shirts bore a visible designer label than they did when they wore (otherwise identical) no-label shirts.[3]

Finally, a person's title and the way others react to them give us more clues about their authority charisma, though these last two factors carry less weight than the previous two. Instinctively, we understand that someone who has a high title but garners little respect has less real power than someone of lower title who is greatly respected.

Though all these assessments can happen in less than a second, the order is nonetheless important. If there is a conflict between signals, we'll trust the signals in the order you've just seen. As always, body language trumps all other signs of charisma. Even if all the other signals are present, a body language of insecurity will undermine any possibility of authority charisma. Conversely, you can gain a certain measure of authority charisma through body language alone if it's strong enough.

## Developing Authority Charisma

Your main aim if you want to gain authority charisma is to project power by displaying signs of status and confidence. Luckily, the two most important dimensions of status and confidence are also the ones over which you have the most influence: body language and appearance.

Because it is affected so strongly by body language, your authority charisma depends on how confident you *feel* in that moment. This is where the tools you gained in chapter 5 come in: you can use visualizations, warm-ups, or your body to change your mind to get into a confident mental state.

To project power and confidence in your body language, you'll need to learn how to "take up space" with your posture, reduce non-verbal reassurances (such as excessive nodding), and avoid fidgeting. You may need to speak less, to speak more slowly, to know how and when to pause your sentences, or how to modulate your intonation. We'll cover all the specifics of emanating power through your body language in chapter 9.

As far as appearance goes, choosing clothing that appears expensive or high-status is one of the easiest ways to look authoritative.

**Once you have it:** Authority charisma has the advantage that you get listened to and often obeyed. It does, however, have several disadvantages:

- It can inhibit critical thinking in others.
- It doesn't invite feedback, so you risk not receiving information you actually need.
- It can easily make you appear arrogant.

This is where learning to emanate warmth can be your saving grace. Not only will your warmth reduce the risk of your being perceived as arrogant or intimidating, it will also be more highly valued because you're now seen as high-status. If a low-status person is eager to please us, we may find this pleasant, but we don't necessarily value their eagerness very highly. After all, they can't do much for us; it's rather we who can do things for them. On the other hand, if a high-status alpha grants us attention and warmth, we're thrilled, because they can move mountains.

**When to use it:** Authority charisma works well in many business situations, and in any situation where you want people to listen and obey. It's particularly useful during a crisis (see chapter 12), and whenever you need immediate compliance from people. On the other hand, you might want to avoid it in social settings such as weddings or funerals or in sensitive business situations such as delivering bad news. Avoid it also when you want to encourage creativity or constructive feedback, as it can inhibit critical thinking in others. In these cases, use visionary, focus, or warmth charisma instead.

## Choosing the Right Charisma

There isn't just one way to be charismatic, nor does one charisma style work in every situation. When are certain styles more effective? Which style will suit you best? Determining your preferred charisma style and knowing when to use it is a crucial step toward fulfilling your charisma potential.

Different kinds of charisma will be appropriate in different circumstances. And different kinds of charisma will be a better or poorer fit for you. To decide which elements of charisma to bring out you'll need to assess three indicators: what's best suited to your personality, your goals, and the situation.

- **Your personality:** It's important to know what feels right for you, and to choose the styles, tools, and techniques that match your signature strengths.
- **Your goals:** You also need to be clear on what you want to achieve. Some modes of charisma will make people obey you, others will lead them to open up and share.
- **The situation:** What context are you stepping into? The situation sets the stage upon which your charisma will play out.

### The Right Charisma for You

The first consideration is your fundamental character.

One of John Kerry's mistakes during the 2004 presidential campaign was trying to "dumb down" his focused, intellectual charisma to become more "accessible." Not only was this ineffective, it also backfired by alienating those who had been drawn to his original personality. His discomfort made him appear awkward and inauthentic.

On the other hand, in the world of business, Steve Jobs cultivated and stayed true to his kind of visionary charisma and, despite what may be said of his personality or leadership style, always came across as authentic as well as powerful. Oprah Winfrey has spoken about her decision to be authentic as a critical turning point in her career. Once she gave up her attempts to be "the next Diane Sawyer," she flourished as "the best Oprah she could be."

You don't have to force yourself into one particular style to be charismatic, and I firmly advocate not doing something that goes against your values: it would only work against you. Trying to force yourself into a charisma style that really isn't right for you can be as unpleasant as it is counterproductive. For example, an introvert forcing himself to be extroverted might feel unnatural and awkward, and be perceived that way by others. Not only would he put himself through an unpleasant experience, he would also fail in his quest to appear naturally extroverted. Instead of fighting it, knowing how to work with your natural style can reap major rewards.

### Putting It into Practice:
### Working with Introversion

If you're naturally uncomfortable in large social gatherings, the next time you're at a party, don't force yourself to be sociable right away or to be "on" for the whole evening. Instead, try these easy tweaks. Give yourself five minutes after you arrive to hang back and observe. Then give yourself little "introversion breaks" during the party: five-minute pockets of solitude. I know one highly charismatic introvert who often does exactly that during both social and business events. When she reemerges to mingle, people frequently comment on how radiant she is.

Not only do you not have to force yourself into one particular charisma style, you don't have to limit yourself to just one style. These styles are just examples of how the different elements of charisma play out in the world around us. In reality, you can alternate between several modes of charisma, from one moment to the next. The more modes you master, the more versatile you can be.

The ability to adapt to a variety of social situations is characteristic of highly charismatic people. Hayes Barnard, the charismatic CEO of Paramount Equity, told me that he sees himself as a Swiss Army knife, adaptable to any situation. When he moves through a room, he intentionally varies his voice and body language according to the person or people he is speaking to. In selecting leaders, he looks for people who have a similar ability to adapt in multiple ways.

This is really just a matter of accessing different aspects of your personality and getting comfortable expressing them—we all have within us a measure of kindness or a modicum of authority. As you practice each style, it will gradually become more natural. Practice enough, and these behaviors become as easy and comfortable as brushing your teeth.

Not only can you flow from one mode of charisma into another, you can also mix and match, adding a dash of kindness to your authority charisma or infusing some confident authority into your focus charisma. Oprah can demonstrate focus, kindness, and in some cases even visionary charisma during a single interview.

Presidents Clinton and Obama both embody visionary charisma. Both have a touch of authority. However, Obama leads with focus. People who meet him say that his intelligence is palpable, and that he intensely focuses on whomever he is interacting with. Clinton, on the other hand, leads with warmth. He's known for being "off-the-charts empathetic."

When choosing a charisma style, remember to check in with your mental and emotional state. If you're feeling insecure, don't try to pull off authority charisma until you've regained your confidence. Instead, choose a charisma style that demands less confidence, such as focus or kindness, and then gradually move to authority if you so desire. Or take the time to ramp up your confidence so you will be ready to broadcast authority charisma.

The second consideration when choosing a charisma style is the goal you want to accomplish. How do you want to make others feel? How do you want them to react to you? For instance, if you want to be listened to and obeyed, authority charisma is ideal. The previous sections gave you an idea of which charisma style can best support which goal. As you practice each style you'll get a feel for which works best in different situations.

### The Right Charisma for Each Situation

The third consideration when choosing a charisma style is the situation you're in.

There are scores of situations in life where certain kinds of charisma, no matter how powerful, are not welcome. On the other hand, certain situations specifically call for certain kinds of charisma. For example, studies consistently show that in times of crisis, people turn to individuals who are bold, confident, and decisive.[4] This is the time to bring out authority or visionary charisma.

The context in which you operate sets the lens through which others will perceive you and your charisma.

First, let's look at the emotional context. People's emotional states influence their perception of you, and either enhance or inhibit the power of your charisma. Certain emotional states, such as a feeling of crisis or urgency, increase the chance that people will find you charismatic. However, there can be charisma without crisis: President George W. Bush was considered charismatic well before the turmoil of 9/11.

To get a sense for the emotional context around you, simply ask yourself: How are the people around you feeling? What do they need in this moment? If you're firing someone, authority charisma might not be most fitting—you may want to bring out focus or kindness charisma instead. And just like Oprah, you can alternate among several modes of charisma, playing on different parts of your personality as you respond to different aspects of the situation.

Social context matters, too: one behavior could be seen as charismatic in the United States but not in Japan. The same amount of eye contact that would be welcomed as an honest, straightforward gaze in most of North America could be seen as aggressive and obnoxious in parts of Asia. Though presence, warmth, and power are the fundamental elements of charisma, how they get expressed varies somewhat from culture to culture.

However, with all this said, if you get your mental state and behavior right, you're 80 percent of the way there. Facial expressions are universal,* so an expression of goodwill, empathy, or concern would be perceived in New York exactly as it would be in New Delhi or even Papua New Guinea.

More important, people give great credence to the intentions they perceive you to have. So if, for instance, you can get yourself into a mental state of goodwill, this would show in your facial expressions and body language and register with people on a deep emotional level. People perceiving this would *want* to like you, *want* to see your behaviors and actions in the most positive way. Think of goodwill as your charisma safety net: as long as you can get into a state of goodwill, you will have the absolute best chances of getting your charisma right (you can refer back to chapter 5 for goodwill-boosting techniques).

In addition, you can be strategic in choosing when to try out new charisma styles: choose low-stakes situations to expand the boundaries of your comfort zone. If, for instance, you're going to a networking event or a cocktail party that will have little impact on your career or your social life, use it as a testing ground. This is the time to experiment and try out new behaviors. Use these occasions to get progressively comfortable with new charisma styles. You could even

---

* Paul Ekman's fascinating research on this topic led him to travel around the world, going to the most remote locations and studying tribes of hunter-gatherers, cataloging and testing more than ten thousand facial expressions.

practice new techniques in short, casual interactions with cashiers or doormen.

On the other hand, when you're in a high-stakes situation—about to give a key presentation, or going for a job interview—don't take the risk of coming across as uncomfortable or inauthentic. In cases like these, it's best to stick with the behaviors and charisma styles that are most natural to you.

|  | AUTHORITY CHARISMA | VISIONARY CHARISMA | FOCUS CHARISMA | KINDNESS CHARISMA |
|---|---|---|---|---|
| *Foundation* | Confidence | Belief | Presence | Caring |
| *Examples* | Colin Powell<br>Winston Churchill<br>Margaret Thatcher | Steve Jobs<br>Joan of Arc<br>Martin Luther King Jr. | Gandhi<br>Chairman Mao<br>Bill Gates | Dalai Lama<br>Mother Theresa<br>Princess Diana |
| *Makes people feel* | Impressed<br>Intimidated<br>Cowed | Inspired<br>Certain | Heard<br>Listened to<br>Understood | Accepted<br>Embraced<br>Cherished |
| *How to get it* | Project high status and high confidence in your ability to impact or influence others | Project absolute conviction in a noble cause, faith, or vision | Project attention, focus, and presence | Project warmth, caring, and acceptance |

*(continued on next page)*

*(continued from previous page)*

| | AUTHORITY CHARISMA | VISIONARY CHARISMA | FOCUS CHARISMA | KINDNESS CHARISMA |
|---|---|---|---|---|
| *What people notice* | Demeanor: facial expressions, body language, behavior<br><br>Appearance: status symbols, clothing<br><br>Other people's reactions, titles | Demeanor: facial expressions, body language, particularly voice | Demeanor: facial expressions, body language, particularly eyes | Demeanor: body language through eyes and voice |
| *Pros* | You will be listened to and obeyed<br><br>Helpful in a crisis | Inspires fervent belief<br><br>Inspires creativity and teamwork | Easy to access<br><br>Surprisingly powerful | Creates an emotional bond and safe space<br><br>Makes you likeable |
| *Cons* | Inhibits critical thinking<br><br>Discourages feedback<br><br>Can seem arrogant | Can inspire fanatical belief<br><br>Can seem overzealous<br><br>Very context-dependent | Can seem eager or subservient<br><br>Can seem intense or interrogating | Can lead to over-attachment, oversharing<br><br>Can be inappropriate in business situations |
| *How to balance* | Increase warmth | Show vulnerability | Increase confidence<br><br>Increase warmth | Increase confidence |

## KEY TAKEAWAYS

- Choosing the right charisma style depends on your personality, goals, and the situation.
- You can alternate among different charisma styles or even blend

them together. Don't force yourself into a charisma style that is just too awkward for you. Doing so would negatively affect how you feel and how others perceive you.

- The more charisma styles you can access, the more versatile and confident you will be.
- Stretch out of your comfort zone in low-stakes situations.
- Stick with styles you already know well in high-stakes situations.
- Let goodwill be your safety net. Coming from a place of genuine goodwill gives you the best chance of getting your charisma right.

# 7

# Charismatic First Impressions

YOU NEVER GET a second chance to make a great first impression. Within a few seconds, with just a glance, people have judged your social and economic level, your level of education, and even your level of success. Within minutes, they've also decided your levels of intelligence, trustworthiness, competence, friendliness, and confidence. Although these evaluations happen in an instant, they can last for years: first impressions are often indelible.

Is it possible to overcome a bad first impression? Yes, it is. Over the course of several meetings, you can sometimes change a person's initial perception of you. But you'll have to work much harder than if you'd come across as charismatic from the start.

Why do split-second impressions last for so long? One reason is that, according to economist John Kenneth Galbraith, when "faced with the choice between changing one's mind and proving there is no need to do so, almost everyone gets busy on the proof."[1] Behavioral research has since proven him right. Once we've made a judgment about someone, we spend the rest of our acquaintanceship seeking to prove ourselves correct. Everything we see and hear gets filtered through this initial impression.[2]

If you make a favorable impression when first meeting someone, the rest of your relationship will be colored by it, thereby tipping the scales in your favor. On the other hand, an unfavorable first impression can prove impossible to overcome, often deciding the outcome of a meeting even if the rest of the interaction is impeccable. Litigators know just how much a client's first impression on a jury can affect the outcome of the trial, and often spend hours preparing them for this first moment. This is why, even if you're really late to a meeting, it's worth taking just thirty seconds to get back into the right mental state and body language. Otherwise you risk giving a very uncharismatic first impression.

The other reason first impressions have such an impact is that often they actually *are* right. In one study conducted at the University of Texas at Austin, people were able to accurately judge nine out of ten personality traits by looking at a single photograph. The traits in question were extroversion, openness, agreeableness, conscientiousness, emotional stability, likability, self-esteem, loneliness, religiosity, and even political orientation.

"We have long known that people jump to conclusions about others on the basis of very little information," said one of the researchers, "but what's striking about these findings is how many of the impressions have a kernel of truth to them, even on the basis of a single photograph."[3]

Further studies confirmed that we're often quite accurate in our perceptions of personality, even after meeting someone for only a few seconds.[4] One Harvard research team showed students a two-second silent clip of a teacher they had never seen before, and asked them to evaluate the teacher's effectiveness. The researchers then compared these evaluations with those of students who'd experienced this same teacher for a full semester. Both sets of evaluations were impressively similar.[5] This means that without hearing a word from the teacher or attending one class, complete strangers could predict with fair accuracy the ratings this teacher would receive.

CEOs as well as human resource professionals will often admit that they decide whether they'll hire a job applicant within the first few seconds of the interview. As one senior executive once told me, "The rest of the interview is just window dressing."

The Harvard team realized that first impressions are generated by the fastest part of the brain, which is also the most primitive. This reptilian brain generates our instinctive, primal reflexes and may have been a key to our ancestors' survival. In hunter-gatherer times, we often had only a split second to determine whether shapes entering our field of vision were animate or inanimate, human or nonhuman, friend or foe—in other words "fight, flight, or relax?" Those able to accurately make these split-second decisions survived, thrived, and multiplied. Those who couldn't ended up as somebody else's protein snack.

Today, even in sophisticated business settings, we still operate on hunter-gatherer survival instincts. When we first meet someone, our instinctive question is: friend or foe? How friendly are their intentions likely to be? To find an answer we still look to the clues that were so useful in tribal times: appearance and demeanor.

If there's any chance the person could be a foe, our next question is: fight or flight? If they did have ill intentions, would they have the power to enact them? To find the answer, our brain tries to determine which of us would win in a fight. We take into consideration factors such as height and size, age, and gender.

It's only after both of these evaluations have taken place that the content of what we say and how we say it comes into play.

## The Golden Rule

So how can you make a fantastic first impression? Our default setting here is actually quite simple: people like people who are like them. During the vast majority of our history, from which our current instincts are drawn, people lived in tribes. In such an environment, the ability to accurately recognize whether or not someone was of your tribe could have life-and-death implications. If you know how to get these instinctive responses working in your favor, you've won half the battle.

When people are similar in terms of attire, appearance, demeanor, and speech, they automatically assume they share similar social backgrounds, education, and even values. They feel like part of the same tribe—or, as Rudyard Kipling wrote in *The Jungle Book,* "We are of one blood, you and I."

Overall appearance is evaluated before demeanor and body language. This may be because clothing can be seen from farther away, and would help us determine more quickly the likelihood of the other person being friend or foe, fellow tribesman or not. Clothing, essentially, is modern-day tribal wear.

## Tribal Wear

Can you imagine a U.S. president delivering the State of the Union address in a bathrobe? Of course not. No matter how hard we try to be objective, clothing matters. The exact same speech will be perceived very differently when delivered in a suit versus a bathrobe.

One Danish manager told me: "I've found that the more formal my clothing is, the more respect my opinions get!" For him, the difference is striking. Presenting the very same opinion in casual clothing one day and in a suit the next produced dramatically different results. In the first case, he says, "people barely listened." In the second, "everyone listened and I got my way."

In the 1970s, when young adults' dress styles tended to fall into either the "hippie" or the "straight" category, researchers experimented with the effects of clothing choice. They approached college students on a campus, sometimes wearing hippie clothes and other times wearing straight clothes, and asked for change to make a phone call. When they were dressed in the same style as the student, the student said yes two-thirds of the time. When they were dressed in the opposite style, the student said yes less than half the time.[6]

One company that understood this principle and used it to its advantage was American Express. They made their first good move when they started sending their salespeople to college campuses dressed like college students. They then went one step further. They didn't just *dress* them like students, they *hired* students. And that's when they saw their sales rates soar.

---

### Putting It into Practice: Tribal Wear

Blend in or stand out? The answer depends on your goals. If you want to make others feel comfortable, adapt to their tribal wear. IBM managers, when sending their salespeople to call on traditional corporate clients, were known to tell them, "You can wear anything you want, as long as it's a navy blue suit."

You wouldn't wear a Hawaiian shirt in an investment bank, nor would you wear a three-piece suit in a start-up. Dress codes can vary even within the same industry—a tax lawyer might not wear the same suit as an entertainment lawyer.

If you want to impress others, look at the range of choices within that environment and choose the upper end. There's a reason the phrase "Dress to impress" exists.

---

It's worth doing your research. If you're going to a party, call the host; if you're going on a job interview, go by the office a few days before to see what people coming in and out of it are wearing.

On my first visit to Oracle, I made the mistake of showing up in a New York–style black business suit. Oracle was not only a West Coast firm (read: casual) but a high-tech one to boot; they quickly advised me to lose the suit. These days, when I'm leading consulting projects at the Google headquarters, I blend in with jeans, while the brilliant engineers I coach slouch around in shorts, T-shirts, and flip-flops.

## The Power of a Good Handshake

A Fortune 500 CEO once said that when he had to choose between two candidates with similar qualifications, he gave the position to the candidate with the better handshake. Extreme? Perhaps, but management experts at the University of Iowa analyzing interactions in job interviews declared handshakes "more important than agree-ableness, conscientiousness, or emotional stability."[7] Other studies determined that a handshake improves the quality of the interaction, producing a higher degree of intimacy and trust within a matter of seconds.

I often tell my clients that no matter how expensive their suit, watch, or briefcase, if their handshake is bad, their first impression will take a hit. The right handshake costs far less and will do far more for you than a designer suit can. Having a great handshake is critical to authority charisma—can you imagine a powerful figure with a limp, weak handshake?

Though it may seem inconsequential, a handshake is indeed a serious step in intimacy. The physical contact involved requires that the personal space barrier be suspended, if only for a moment. It therefore requires trust. If the trust is validated (the handshake goes well), the first step in a relationship is made.

The first commonly known depiction of a handshake was found in Egyptian frescoes dating back to around 2800 B.C. To this day, across cultures and hemispheres, the handshake remains surprisingly common—and always features the right hand. Since that was the one traditionally used for wielding weapons, shaking the right hand was symbolic of a suspension of danger, showing that the greeter's weapon hand was unarmed.

In Roman times, the handshake was in fact an arm clasp. Each man would clasp just below the elbow of the other. This gesture afforded a better opportunity to feel for daggers hidden in sleeves. Medieval knights took precautions a step further by adding a shake to the clasp to dislodge any hidden weapons, and thus the handshake was born.

Of the many handshake blunders people can make, let's discuss the worst offenders.

**The Dead Fish:** This is perhaps the worst. Here, a limp, lifeless hand is extended and just barely shaken. This handshake can ruin a meeting before it even begins. And, unfortunately, I have met scores of women with this particular affliction.

**The Knuckle Cruncher:** This grip may be a demonstration of machismo, but it could also be the result of a person genuinely unaware of his (or her) strength. Alternatively, it might be the result of misguided teachings—some women have been taught that the stronger their grip, the more seriously they will be taken. Hence, they conclude that they should clamp down as if their life depended on it.

**The Dominant:** In this case, the hand is extended palm down, perhaps conveying the intention of having the upper hand in the interaction. A variation of this shake would be **The Twisting Dominant,** where the hand is extended innocently straight outward, but twists once the shake is initiated to gain the upper hand.

**The Two-Handed:** We'll close this woeful list with the classic two-handed handshake. In this case, you'll feel your partner's left hand at work, closing in on your right hand, wrist, arm, shoulder, or neck. It's also known as **The Politician's Handshake,** which gives you an idea of how little regard people have for those who proffer it. The only exception is when the person you're meeting is already a good friend, and even then I'd reserve it for those times when you want to convey special warmth (to be used sparingly).

Many of my clients were shocked to learn that they'd been guilty of one of the above without realizing it, and in doing so lost charisma points before they had even said a word. So what, then, are the ingredients for a perfect handshake? Check out the box below for the ten components of a gold-star handshake.

## Putting It into Practice: The Perfect Handshake

Follow these ten steps to get it right every time, or go online to http://www.CharismaMyth.com/handshake to see a step-by-step live demonstration of good, bad, and absolutely great handshakes.

1. First things first: make sure your right hand is free. Shift anything it may be holding to your left hand well in advance. You don't want to have to fumble at the last moment.

(continued on next page)

*(continued from previous page)*

2. Avoid holding a drink in your right hand, especially if it's a cold drink, as the condensation will make your hand feel cold and clammy.

3. Before shaking someone's hand, whether you are a man or a woman, rise if you're seated. And keep your hands out of your pockets: visible hands make you look more open and honest.

4. Make sure to use plenty of eye contact, and smile warmly but briefly: too much smiling could make you appear over-eager.

5. Keep your head straight, without tilting it in any way, and face the person fully.

6. Keep your hand perfectly perpendicular, neither dominant (palm down) nor submissive (palm up). If you're in doubt, angle your thumb straight to the ceiling.

7. Open wide the space between your thumb and index finger to make sure you get optimal thumb-web contact.

8. Ensure contact between the palms of your hands by keeping your palm flat—not cupped—and by draping your hand across your partner's diagonally.

9. Try to wrap your fingers around your partner's hand, scaling them one by one, as if you were giving a hug with your hand. You will almost have your index finger on their pulse—*almost,* but not quite.

10. Once full contact is made, lock your thumb down and squeeze firmly, about as much as your partner does. Shake from the elbow (not the wrist), linger for a moment if you want to convey particular warmth, and step back.

Several of my clients have come back to me amazed by what a difference a good handshake makes. Practice with friends or family—people who will give you truly candid feedback. Have them read this section. (And remember, everything here is North American specific.)

So you've made a fantastic first impression. You've given a great handshake. You walk up to them and what happens next? You speak. Charismatic conversationalists know how to start conversations easily, make people feel special, and end conversations gracefully. Let's see how you can create positive associations from start to finish, from the way you open a conversation to the way you exit it.

## Break the Ice

An easy way to start interactions in a way that both communicates warmth and sends the conversation down the right path is to offer a compliment about something the person is wearing. This would be a great opener when you're aiming to broadcast either kindness charisma or focus charisma. It can also be a good way to balance out the power in your authority charisma if you think a more subdued version of your power is needed.

Continue with an open-ended question, such as "What's the story behind it?" The word *story* has a very strong emotional effect on most people—it sends them straight into storytelling mode, which instantly changes the rapport between the two of you. In addition, because they chose to wear this item, they most likely have a positive feeling about it.

Another good question to break the ice with is "Where are you from?" No matter what the answer, it will encourage further dialogue. Whether they answer "New York" or "New Delhi," if you're not from that area, you can follow up with "What was it like growing up there?" The smaller the town of origin, the more delighted they will be that you have expressed interest.

To keep people talking, simply ask open-ended questions, such as "What brought you here tonight?" or "How are you connected to this event?" Closed questions, by contrast, can be answered by yes or no, and once answered, they land you right back where you started, trying to think of something else to keep the conversation going.

Aim to keep your questions focused on positive subjects because people will associate you with whatever feelings your conversation generates. Instinctively, you would probably know to avoid asking "So how's the divorce going?" Instead, focus on questions that will likely elicit positive emotions. With your questions, you have the power to lead the conversation in the direction you want.

If they start asking about you and you want to refocus the conversation on them, use the *bounce back* technique. Answer the question with a fact, add a personal note, and redirect the question to them, as follows:

Other Person: "So where are you moving to?"

You: "To Chelsea [fact]. We fell in love with the parks and the bakeries [personal note]. What do you think of the neighborhood [redirect]?"

Remember, it's all about keeping the spotlight on them for as long as possible. "Talk to a man about himself, and he will listen for hours," said Benjamin Disraeli. In fact, even when you're speaking, the one word that should pop up most often in your conversation is not *I* but *you*. Instead of saying "I read a great article on that subject in the *New York Times*," try "You might enjoy the recent *New York Times* article on the subject." Or simply insert "You know . . ." before any sentence to make them instantly perk up and pay attention.

To make yourself even more relatable, adjust your choice of words, your breadth and depth of vocabulary, and your expressions to suit your audience: focus on their fields of interest and choose metaphors from those domains. If they're into golf and you want to talk about success, speak of hitting a hole in one. If they sail, a catastrophe becomes a shipwreck.

One of my clients, a Deutsche Bank analyst, told me she couldn't seem to establish a good relationship with her boss. She described him as rather brusque, almost militaristic in his demeanor, "and, in fact, he often uses battle language in our daily interactions." That, to me, was just the clue we needed. I suggested adopting military analogies in which she would liken herself to a "loyal soldier" or a "good lieutenant," and gradually increasing the use of military vocabulary in their conversations. Within a week, she told me that their interactions had significantly improved—he now seemed to regard her as "one of his people," and someone he could count on.

This was a high return on investment for just adding a few words to her vocabulary!

## Graceful Exits

Just as a first impression can color the rest of the interaction, so can the last few moments. Becoming a charismatic conversationalist means that people will really enjoy being around you, and may be increasingly reluctant to let you go. In fact, the more charismatic you become, the harder it will be to escape your newfound fans. Many charismatic people mention this as one of their biggest challenges. So how can you gracefully exit a conversation?

First, don't wait too long to end it. Otherwise, you and your partner will feel the strain and become uncomfortable. The easiest way to exit is, of course, to have an official reason for doing so. That's one of the many reasons to be a volunteer or acquire some official duty at parties. When you're "on duty," people will actually expect you to spend no more than a few minutes with them.

Another way to exit a conversation with grace is to offer something of value:

- Information: an article, book, or Web site you think might be of use to them
- A connection: someone they ought to meet whom you know and can introduce them to
- Visibility: an organization you belong to, where you could invite them to speak
- Recognition: an award you think they should be nominated for

Offering value will often create in others a feeling of warmth and goodwill toward you, and your departure from the conversation will be haloed by the impression of generosity you've created.

Wait until your conversation partner has finished a sentence, and say something to the effect of, "You know, based on what you've just said, you really should check out this Web site. If you have a card, I'll send you the link." As soon as your counterpart gives you a business card, you have the perfect opportunity to say, "Great! I'll e-mail you soon. It was a pleasure meeting you."

Alternatively, if the person has agreed to meet someone in the room, simply say, "Let me introduce you," and bring them together. Because you've just generously given them something, your conversation partner can't help but have positive feelings for you. You can also draw others into the conversation as they pass by—a group of three or four is always easier to take leave of.

What if you're the one breaking up a group? Perhaps you're rescuing someone from a conversation they've indicated they wanted to leave, or you need to introduce them to someone else, or one of the group is needed for another duty.

In this case, focus all your attention, with particularly warm eye contact (see chapter 9 for this), not on the person you're taking with you but on the person who is being left behind. This minimizes the chances of their feeling excluded and is particularly important for conveying either kindness charisma or focus charisma.

A good way to phrase things is: "I'm *so* sorry, but Christopher is needed to [fill in the blank]. Would you allow me to bring him over there?" This also gives them at least a nominal feeling of having a choice in the matter.

Once a conversation is over, don't waste time worrying about what you said, what you wish you hadn't said, or what you'll say next time. As the MIT Media Lab studies showed, what impacts people isn't the words or content used. Rather, they remember how it *felt* to be speaking with you.

You might not remember the exact content of conversations you had a week ago, but you probably do remember how they felt. It's not the words but the conversation's emotional imprint that remains. And if you use all the tools we've just covered, the emotional imprint will be simply splendid.

## KEY TAKEAWAYS

- First impressions happen within seconds and can affect not only the rest of the interaction but also the rest of your relationship with that person.
- People feel most comfortable with those who are similar to them in some way, including appearance and behavior. Do your homework and decide how much you want to adapt your dress and word choice to your environment.
- A good handshake can go a long way. Likewise, a bad one can leave an unfavorable and lasting first impression. It's worth spending some time perfecting the right way to greet someone.
- Great conversationalists keep the spotlight on the other person and make them feel good about themselves.
- Know how to gracefully exit a conversation, leaving others with positive feelings.

# 8

## Speaking—and Listening—
## with Charisma

AS WE'VE SEEN, body language and other nonverbal signals can emit a variety of messages and can be used to project charisma even before a single word is spoken. Managing a charismatic mental state is the first step, but this chapter will reveal specific verbal and vocal techniques to successfully broadcast your charismatic mental state. You'll learn how to communicate presence when listening, and power and warmth when speaking.

### Charismatic Listening

When I ask my clients to name the first skill they would improve upon in their people if they could wave a magic wand, most of the CEOs say, "Better listening skills." They may not sound complex or glamorous, but listening skills are an absolute requirement for charisma, and most charisma masters possess them in abundance. By being a great listener you can make people feel completely heard and understood without saying a word. In fact, it's remarkably easy to impress people just by listening attentively.

We're about to cover three keys to communicating presence: attentive listening, refraining from interrupting, and deliberate pausing. Listening comes first and foremost, because listening lays the groundwork for the presence that is fundamental to charisma.

John F. Kennedy was known as a "superb listener" who made others feel like he was "with them completely." Great listening skills helped him pay extremely close attention to the feelings of whomever he was interacting with, enabling him to establish rapport on a very deep, emotional level.[1]

I'm sure you know that listening is important. But did you know that just a few tweaks can bring your listening skills from good to truly extraordinary? Great listening skills start with the right mindset: both the willingness and the mental ability to be present, pay attention, and focus on what the other person is saying. As you can imagine, this is absolutely key for conveying focus charisma, though it can boost any of the other charisma styles, too.

One of the most common mistakes my clients make is equating listening with "letting people talk until it's my turn." Sorry, but that's not sufficient. Even if the other person is doing all the talking, you can't let your mind wander while waiting for your turn to speak. Even if what you're thinking about is what you want to say next, your lack of presence will be written all over your face. The other person will see that you're not fully present and are just waiting for them to finish so you can jump in.

Presence is a cornerstone of effective listening. You already have all the tools you need to avoid mind-wandering while someone else is talking:

- If zoning out is the issue, bring yourself back to the moment by focusing on physical sensations, like the feeling in your toes or your breath flowing in and out of your body.
- If impatience is the issue, handle it by *delving into* the minute physical sensations you're feeling. Then get back to the person.

Once you have the right mindset, how do you ensure the right behaviors? Effective listening means behaving in a way that makes whomever you're speaking with feel truly understood.

*Good* listeners know never, ever to interrupt—not even if the impulse to do so comes from excitement about something the other person just said. No matter how congratulatory and warm your input, it will always result in their feeling at least a twinge of resentment or frustration at not having been allowed to complete their sentence. One of my clients told me: "This one practice alone is worth its weight gold. To stop interrupting others could be the single most important skill I've learned from working with you."

*Great* listeners know to let others interrupt them. When someone interrupts you, let them! Were they right to interrupt you? Of course not. But even if they were wrong, it's not worth making them feel wrong; your job instead is to make them feel right. In fact, if you notice the other person repeatedly agitating to speak, keep your sentences short and leave frequent pauses for them to jump in.

People really do love to hear themselves talk. The more you let them speak, the more they will like you. One young executive told me: "In job interviews, I've gotten offers simply by going in for an interview and letting the interviewer talk for ninety percent of the time. I walk out and they absolutely love me since we talked about what mattered most to them."

*Master* listeners know one extra trick, one simple but extraordinarily effective habit that will make people feel truly listened to and understood: they pause before they answer. The pianist Artur Schnabel once said, "The notes I handle no better than many pianists. But the pauses between the notes—ah, that is where the art resides."[2]

Knowing how and when to pause is also an art in business conversations, and something that most charismatic conversationalists do naturally. Considered a key tool in negotiation, pausing can also play a wonderful role in making people feel good about themselves when they're around you—it's an easy way to make people feel intelligent, interesting, and even impressive.

When someone has spoken, see if you can let your facial expression react first, showing that you're absorbing what they've just said and giving their brilliant statement the consideration it deserves. Only then, after about two seconds, do you answer. The sequence goes like this:

- They finish their sentence
- Your face absorbs
- Your face reacts
- Then, and only then, you answer

Now, I'm not saying this is easy. It takes confidence to bear silence, both because of the awkwardness you may feel and because of the uncertainty of not knowing what they're thinking during those two seconds. But it's worth it. Several of my clients told me that this one simple technique had a major impact for them. The people they interacted with seemed to feel more relaxed and better understood, and they were willing to share more and open up—a high return for just two seconds of patience.

Great listening skills will give you presence—the foundation of charisma—and boost any charisma style. Now that you've laid a solid foundation for communicating presence, let's move on to communicating charismatic warmth and power.

## Charismatic Speaking

Imagine yourself one morning in a hurry to get to work. You scramble through your routine, rush out the door, and at the very first street corner, while waiting for the red light to turn green, you witness a deadly traffic collision. From now on, what are you going to think of whenever you pass that corner? The accident, of course. It would be nearly impossible to pass that specific street corner without thinking of it. You might remember the feelings of horror and dread or the way your blood seemed to turn to ice in your veins.

Our minds link the sensations we're experiencing to the places, people, and physical sensations we notice while we're experiencing them. This is why car manufacturers often include highly attractive female models in the ads promoting their cars. (It works: in a study, men asked to evaluate cars whose ads featured attractive female models rated *the cars* as faster, cooler, and more desirable.)[3]

The same association happens with negative feelings, which is why TV weather forecasters often receive hate mail from viewers who so strongly associate the meteorologists with the weather they report that they believe these folks actually cause the weather. It's not unusual during nasty seasons for a forecaster to receive at least one death threat.[4]

Now imagine a big corporation in which one employee (say, the human resources director) is responsible for all employee termination. Whenever people think of her, they immediately think of the negative associations tied to her job duties. In fact, the long-term negative effects of such associations are so well-known that an entire industry developed around being the bearers of bad news—firing people, closing plants, etc. These specialized firms will come in to deliver the blow, serve as the focal point for people's resentment, and then leave, presumably taking the worst of the negative associations along with them.

Have you ever heard the phrase "Don't shoot the messenger"? Back in ancient Persia, a messenger would be dispatched after a battle to bring the king news of either victory or defeat. If the messenger reported victory, he was treated to a feast. But if he came bearing news of failure, he was immediately executed. Though we no longer execute people on a whim, the underlying basis for this custom remains: people will associate you with whatever feelings you produce in them on a consistent basis.

In 1904, Ivan Pavlov (who would later go on to win the Nobel Prize) was studying the process of digestion in animals; in this case, the dogs kept at his laboratory. To call the dogs' attention once their food had been put out, he would ring a bell. As he was idly playing with the bell one day, he noticed a curious phenomenon: just by hearing the sound of the bell, the dogs not only rushed up to the usual feeding place but also started drooling.

Many cat owners will tell you that they barely have to start opening a can of cat food for their feline to appear at its bowl. As it turns out, we humans work exactly the same way. Are there certain songs that make you feel energized? How about one that makes you feel nostalgic and misty-eyed? Have you ever been brought back to a specific moment from your childhood just by experiencing a certain taste or smell?

We associate feelings with sights, sounds, tastes, smells, places, and, of course, people, which is why others will associate you with the way you make them feel. For most charisma, but especially kindness charisma, it's critical to make others feel good about themselves. Benjamin Disraeli's genius was his ability to make whomever he was speaking with feel intelligent and fascinating. People would associate the wonderful way they felt around him with the man himself.

Because we're constantly creating associations in people's minds, it's crucial in both business and social situations to be aware of how you're making people feel. To be charismatic, you need to create strong positive associations and avoid creating negative ones.

When one of the world's largest accounting firms asked me to coach their "rising stars," I was struck by how earnest, hardworking, and well-intentioned these bright young managers were. Chosen for their high level of knowledge and competence, they served a two-year term in the firm's headquarters before returning to their local offices. And yet they were intensely disliked by the rest of the firm.

During these two years, the young managers served as experts for all local offices, who would turn to them in difficult situations, e.g., when questions were tricky or when things had gone wrong. Because they spent their time finding mistakes and providing the right answers (or explaining what the answer should have been), these back-office experts had become associated with difficult situations and unpleasant feelings.

You can imagine how hard it was afterward for the rest of the firm to be warm and welcoming to these same experts when they "repatriated" to the very offices whose failings they'd had to point out. Talk about bad associations! Because of this setup, making others feel supported and being positively associated was a challenge for these rising stars.

To reverse this negative connotation and broadcast as much warmth as possible, we worked to ensure that they communicated a better ratio of neutral or good news to bad news. They learned to highlight what people had done *right;* they started sending out e-mail updates with useful tips, and would even include a "kudos" section to congratulate any local office that had done a good job. These techniques helped them use their high-status position as experts to give their warmth and praise even more weight.

## Take a Compliment

We often impair our warmth with negative associations without even realizing it. Negative associations can happen anytime someone feels bad when they're around us, and they are a particular risk if we make people feel bad about themselves—wrong, inadequate, or stupid.

How do you feel when someone pays you a compliment? For instance, when someone says you look good or you have accomplished something impressive, do you instinctively downplay it? For many people, compliments feel both pleasant and a little awkward, and they don't quite know how to handle them. Many of us either turn bashful or modestly deflect the compliment by saying something like "Oh, it's nothing . . ."

Unfortunately, doing this sends a message to your admirer that they were wrong to compliment you. They will probably feel rather foolish, and there's even a chance that they will associate this experience of feeling foolish with you. If you do this enough, pretty soon they'll stop trying. If, on the other hand, you make them feel good for complimenting you, they'll enjoy feeling good about themselves, and so will want to do it again.

The next time you're given a compliment, the following steps will help you skillfully handle the moment:

1. *Stop.*
2. Absorb the compliment. Enjoy it if you can.
3. Let that second of absorption show on your face. Show the person that they've had an impact.
4. Thank them. Saying "Thank you very much" is enough, but you can take it a step further by thanking them for their thoughtfulness or telling them that they've made your day.

Imagine giving a compliment to Bill Clinton. How do you think he would take it? I'd been making this suggestion to clients for some time when one of my friends told me he'd had that exact experience in person, when the former president was touring Google's headquarters:

> Seeing him come down the hall, I wanted to approach him but had only a second to come up with something to say other than just "Hi!" I found myself saying, "Uh, thank you for your service to this country." He paused and looked thoughtful for a second, as if the idea had never occurred to him. Then he appeared to let it sink in as if it were the kindest thing anyone had ever said to him. His shoulders dropped, he got this big "aw, shucks" smile, and he responded as though *he* were a starstruck Cub Scout and *I* were the president: "Oh, it was an honor." What a way to take a compliment! He really nailed it perfectly.

Creating positive associations to highlight the warmth dimension means that you make a person feel good when they're around you. Clinton is known to make everyone he's speaking to feel as if *they* were the most important person in the room. How can you make people feel this way?

First, think about how you would behave if you were indeed speaking to the most important person in the room. You would probably want to hear everything they had to say. You'd be truly interested, maybe even impressed, and that attitude is exactly what will make people feel great about themselves and associate all those feelings with you.

As Dale Carnegie said, "You can make more friends in two months by becoming truly interested in other people than you can in two years by trying to get other people interested in you."[5] One great trick is to imagine that the person you're speaking with is the main star in a movie you're watching right now. This will help you find them more interesting, and there's even a chance that you'll make them feel like a movie star, too. Charismatic people are masters at using positive associations, whether consciously or subconsciously, and you'll often hear people rave about how "special" and "wonderful" these charismatics made them feel.

I tell all my clients: Don't try to impress people. Let *them* impress *you*, and they will love you for it. Believe it or not, you don't need to sound smart. You just need to make them feel smart.

### Get Graphic

If you were told the number of deaths caused by smoking every year, would you remember that exact figure three months from now? Probably not. But what if you were told that this figure was equal to three fully loaded Boeing 747 planes crashing into the earth every day for a year, with no survivors? *That* image you'd remember for a while.*

A picture is worth a thousand words, indeed—and for good reason. Image generation has a powerful impact on emotions and physiological states and a high impact on brain function.[6] Our brain's language-processing abilities are much newer and less deeply wired than are our visual-processing abilities. When you speak in words, the brain has to relate the words to concepts, then translate the concepts into images, which is what actually gets understood. Why not speak directly in the brain's own language? Whenever you can, choose to speak in pictures. You'll have a much greater impact, and your message will be far more memorable.

Visionary charismatics make full use of the power of images. Presidents rated as charismatic, such as Franklin Delano Roosevelt and Abraham Lincoln, used twice as many visual metaphors in their inaugural addresses as did those rated as noncharismatic.[7]

When Steve Jobs launched the iPod Nano, he needed a dramatic way to illustrate its small size and light weight. First, he pulled it out of the smallest pocket of his jeans, giving tangible proof of just how small and slim it was. Second, he compared the Nano's weight to eight quarters: his presentation slide shows the iPod on one side and eight quarters on the other.

---

* This image isn't just powerful, it's also frighteningly accurate. In the United States alone, 530,000 people die each year from diseases caused by smoking. This is equivalent to 1,325 crashes of a Boeing 747 (more than 3 crashes per day).

During Chrysler's remarkable turnaround, Lee Iacocca initiated a series of factory closings, which of course meant that thousands of workers would be fired. To mitigate the emotional backlash that could have ensued, he used a battle metaphor, comparing himself to an army surgeon, a job he called "the toughest assignment in the world." In the midst of battle, with wounded men everywhere, doctors must prioritize which ones to attend to. This is called *triage:* helping those with the best chances of survival and ignoring the rest.

With this one metaphor, Iacocca made people feel that the plant closings were painful for everyone but done in the general good interest, and that he himself was in the trenches with his men, a lifesaver treating an organization at war.

When you craft your images and metaphors, try to make them sensory-rich: involve as many of the five senses as possible. Believe it or not, you can do this in almost any situation, even with the driest of subjects.

One of the aforementioned accounting firm's rising stars asked me to help him communicate the importance of a complex new regulation in such a way that everyone would realize just how critical it was to ensure clients' abidance. Here's the metaphor we came up with: "If you don't bring your clients into compliance, it's as if they're innocently paddling along a river, and you know there's a waterfall coming, yet you do nothing to stop them from going over the waterfall, watching as they crash down to the rocks below, their bodies mangled, blood spilling through the water." Harsh? Yes. Effective? You bet.

Of course, you'll want to take great care in choosing the right metaphor for your particular goal. In the previous example, we wanted to shock people and frighten them into remembering something important. I was quite comfortable in suggesting a rather unpleasant metaphor. Be aware of the emotional tenor of your metaphor and choose accordingly.

### Avoid White Elephants

This tendency of the brain to think in pictures can sometimes be problematic. Once an image is imagined, it's nearly impossible to unimagine it. Remember the white elephants exercise? When entreated to *not* think of a white elephant, your brain sooner or later (usually sooner) will focus exactly on what you want to avoid.

One young CEO told me: "We've had some revenue trouble. When I talked about it with my team, I would occasionally use the phrase 'It's nothing that will sink the company.' One of my employees told me that every time I said that, it made him imagine the company sinking. I stopped using the phrase."

It's not just metaphors that can paint the wrong picture. Some common phrases can have the same effect. When you tell someone, "No problem," "Don't worry," or "Don't hesitate to call," for example, there's a chance their brain will remember "problem," "worry," or "hesitate" instead of your desire to support them. To counter this negative effect, use phrases like "We'll take care of it" or "Please feel free to call anytime."

### Deliver High Value

Attention is a precious resource, just like time and money. Anytime you ask people to listen to what you say or read what you've written, you're asking them to *spend* both their time and their attention on you. You're asking them to give you some of their resources.

What are you giving them in return? Whenever people are asked to expend any of their scarce resources, you can bet that they are (at least subconsciously) measuring the return on their investment. You can deliver value to others in multiple ways:

- **Entertainment:** Make your e-mail or meeting enjoyable.
- **Information:** Give interesting or informative content that they can use.
- **Good feelings:** Find ways to make them feel important or good about themselves.

The longer you speak, the higher the price you're making them pay, so the higher the value ought to be. Professional speakers, when rehearsing a new presentation, will often have their first attempt taped and transcribed, and then go over each sentence, aiming to tighten their speech as much as possible.

In fact, aiming to deliver high value for low effort brings together all the points we've covered in this section. When you speak or write, use few words and lots of pictures, and strive to make your communications useful, enjoyable, and even entertaining.

## Tuning Your Voice

Voice fluctuation is the foundation for both vocal warmth and power. In 1995, Cornell professor Stephen Ceci taught a developmental psychology course in the fall and spring semesters to about three hundred students each time. During the winter break that separated the two semesters, he worked to improve his presentation style. He received training to increase the fluctuation of his tone of voice, to use more gestures while speaking, and to communicate an overall body language of enthusiasm.

When spring came, he delivered a course that was identical in content to the one he'd delivered in the fall. Ceci and his colleagues even compared recordings of both sets of lectures to verify that they were word-for-word copies. The only differences were the variations in his tone of voice and the addition of gestures. Grading policy, assigned textbook, office hours, tests, and even the basic demographic profile of the class remained the same.

And yet students rated all aspects of the spring semester class and instructor far higher. Even the textbook was rated better, gaining nearly 20 percent higher approval ratings. Spring semester students also believed they had learned far more, even though their actual performance on tests remained identical to the performance of the fall semester students. Ceci himself was rated as more knowledgeable, more open to others' ideas, and better organized even though (as he told me himself) none of these factors had changed from the previous semester.

Studies have consistently shown that audience ratings of a lecture are more strongly influenced by delivery style than by content.[8] Your voice is key to communicating both warmth and power, but there isn't just one charismatic voice. You can choose to play up different aspects of your voice depending on what you want to convey and with whom you're communicating.

When the MIT Media Lab concluded that they could predict the success of sales calls without listening to a single word, these are the only two measurements they needed:

- Ratio of speaking to listening
- Amount of voice fluctuation

Earlier in this chapter, we explored how to balance speaking with listening. The second important vocal feature is fluctuation. The degree to which your voice fluctuates affects your persuasiveness and your charisma. Increasing voice fluctuation means making your voice vary in any of the following ways: pitch (high or low), volume (loud or quiet), tone (resonant or hollow), tempo (fast or slow), or rhythm (fluid or staccato).

## Putting It into Practice: Voice Fluctuation

You can gain great insights into your own voice fluctuation by practicing sentences with a tape recorder. Repeat a sentence several times with as wide a variation in emotions as you can. Try to say it with authority, with anger, with sorrow, with empathetic care and concern, with warmth, and with enthusiasm.

### Vocal Power

If your goal is to communicate power, set the pitch, tone, volume, and tempo of your voice in the following ways:

**Pitch and tone:** The lower, more resonant, and more baritone your voice, the more impact it will have.

**Volume:** One of the first things an actor learns to do on stage is to project his voice, which means gaining the ability to modulate its volume and aim it in such a targeted way that specific portions of the audience can hear it, even from afar. One classic exercise to hone your projection skills is to imagine that your words are arrows. As you speak, aim them at different groups of listeners.

**Tempo:** A slow, measured tempo with frequent pauses conveys confidence.

## Putting It into Practice: Vocal Power

The guidelines below will help you broadcast power through your voice.

1. Speak slowly. Visualize the contrast between a nervous, squeaky teenager speaking at high speed and the slow, emphatic tone of a judge delivering a verdict.

2. Pause. People who broadcast confidence often pause while speaking. They will pause for a second or two between sentences or even in the middle of a sentence. This conveys the feeling that they're so confident in their power, they trust that people won't interrupt.

3. Drop intonation. You know how a voice rises at the end of a question? Just reread the last sentence and hear your voice go up at the end. Now imagine an assertion: a judge saying "This case is closed." Feel how the intonation of the word *closed* drops. Lowering the intonation of your voice at the end of a sentence broadcasts power. When you want to sound superconfident, you can even lower your intonation midsentence.

4. Check your breathing. Make sure you're breathing deeply into your belly and inhale and exhale through your nose rather than your mouth. Breathing through your mouth can make you sound breathless and anxious.

## Vocal Warmth

There's only one thing you need to do in order to project more warmth in your voice: smile. Smiling affects how we speak to such an extent that listeners in one study could identify sixteen different kinds of smiles based on sound alone.[9] This is why it's worth smiling even when on the phone.

What about cases in which you don't necessarily want to smile? The good news is that you don't need to actually smile: often, just thinking about smiling is enough to give your voice more warmth. Although there isn't one single way to achieve a charismatic delivery, here's an effective visual to simultaneously convey power and warmth. Imagine that you're a preacher exhorting your congregation. Think of the rich, rolling, resonant voice of a preacher; he *cares* about his people (warmth), and, in addition, he feels he has the might of God behind him (power, authority, confidence).

Now that you have the tools you need to communicate presence, warmth, and power through speaking and listening, let's take a look at body language.

## KEY TAKEAWAYS

- Power, presence, and warmth are important for both charismatic speaking and charismatic listening.
- Great listening skills are key to communicating charismatic presence.
- Never interrupt people, and occasionally pause a second or two before you answer.
- People associate you with the feelings you produce in them. Avoid creating negative associations: don't make them feel bad or wrong.
- Make people feel good, especially about themselves. Don't try to impress them—let them impress you, and they will love you for it.
- Get graphic: use pictures, metaphors, and sensory-rich language to convey a compelling, charismatic message.
- Use as few words as possible, and deliver as much value as possible: entertainment, information, or good feelings.
- To emanate vocal power, use a slow, measured tempo; insert pauses between your sentences; and drop your intonation at the end.
- To emanate vocal warmth, you need to do only one thing: smile, or even just imagine smiling.

# 9

## Charismatic Body Language

It was the last day of my vacation, and I intended to enjoy every minute of it. I was strolling through a small park in the center of town, drinking in the sun, when suddenly, something caught my attention.

Perched atop a white bandstand, a short, middle-aged man was making an impassioned speech. A crowd was quickly gathering, and somehow, I felt myself being drawn in, too. There was something in the manner of his speaking—his expansive and flowing gestures, the tempo of his speech—that was captivating.

For more than forty minutes, his growing audience and I were held spellbound. To this day, I have no idea what this man was speaking about. You see, this scene took place in a small town in Mexico—and my Spanish was nearly nonexistent.

FOR NEARLY AN hour, Ronald Riggio, one of charisma's main researchers, had been fascinated, without understanding a word of content. *What* the speaker was saying was clearly not important to his spellbinding power. *How* he was saying it was enough.

Words are grasped first by people's cognitive minds, their logical side, which gets to work on understanding their meaning. Body language, in contrast, affects us on a visceral, emotional level. It's this emotional level that you need to access in order to inspire others to follow, care for, or obey you. Business guru Alan Weiss likes to say, "Logic makes people think. Emotion makes them act." Which would you rather have? If you speak only to people's logical mind, you're missing half the playing field.

Charisma, which makes us feel impressed, inspired, or thrillingly special, speaks to our emotional side. It bypasses our logical thinking. Just as the feeling of awe goes beyond our understanding and touches us at an emotional level, so does charisma.

Nonverbal modes of communication are hardwired into our brains much deeper than the more recent language-processing abilities and they affect us far more strongly. When our verbal and nonverbal signals are in congruence (when they "agree" with each other), the nonverbal amplifies the verbal. When they conflict, we tend to trust the nonverbal over the verbal. If your body language is anticharismatic, it doesn't matter how great your message is. On the other hand, with the right body language you can succeed even with an imperfect message.

In some situations, the delivery of a message has a much greater impact than the message itself. For instance, the *Harvard Business Review* detailed research showing that when negative performance reviews were accompanied by positive body language, employees received them far better than they received positive reviews delivered with negative body language. [1]

Our tendency to react to *how* something is said more than to *what* is said is particularly strong in high-stakes situations—whether it's trying to win a new client, impress a new boss, or make a new friend.

In high-stakes situations we react more strongly to body language than to words because our fight-or-flight response activates and a more primal part of the brain takes over. This part of the brain does not directly comprehend words or ideas. Instead, it's immediately impacted by body language.

## Emotional Contagion

Your body language is particularly important if you're in a position of leadership because of the process known as *emotional contagion*. Behavioral scientists define this as "the process by which the emotions expressed by one individual are 'caught' by another." Charismatic people are known to be more "contagious"; they have a strong ability to transmit their emotions to others. As a leader, the emotions conveyed by your body language, even during brief, casual encounters, can have a ripple effect through your team or even your entire company.

This ripple effect is due to the mirror neurons in our brain, whose job it is to replicate or mirror in our own mind the emotions we observe in someone else. When we detect someone else's emotions through their behaviors or facial expressions, our mirror neurons reproduce these emotions. This is what makes empathy possible.

I'm often called in by leaders with strong personalities who already have powerful charisma and need to learn how to manage their emotional contagion. We analyze what impact they're having on whom, and then give them the skills to control it at will.

Let's imagine that you interact with someone while in an anxious emotional state. As they read your body language, their mirror neurons fire up, mirroring that state. They go on to meet someone else, replicating the process—and your emotional state spreads. Emotional contagion "triggers arousal in others, in a sort of chain reaction."[2] Within organizations, leaders' emotions always propagate fastest because people are strongly affected by those in a position of power (we can thank our survival instincts for this, too). Through emotional contagion, your emotions can strongly affect your followers' effectiveness.

When positive, emotional contagion can be a wonderful thing. In controlled experimental settings, leaders' positive emotional contagion was shown to improve not only their followers' moods, performance, and effectiveness but also the followers' perception of the leaders' effectiveness.[3]

Emotional contagion can of course have a corresponding negative effect, and it's worth increasing your awareness of your own internal states, as well as your skill in handling your emotions, in order to manage the consequences of this propagation. Chapter 12 will help you do this.

The potency of your emotional contagion is one good measure of your level of charisma. When researching *Social Intelligence,* author Daniel Goleman analyzed a video of Herb Kelleher, the charismatic cofounder of Southwest Airlines, strolling through the corridors of the airline's hub. Goleman said, "We could practically see him activate the oscillators in each person he encountered."

## Conscious Mirroring

Have you ever noticed that people who have been married for many years often end up looking like each other? It's actually a well-documented fact that as we spend time together, we tend to adapt to each other's body language.[4] This naturally includes our facial expressions, which end up shaping our faces in similar ways by repeatedly using the same facial muscles.

This tendency to mimic the body language of others is technically called *limbic resonance,* and it's hardwired into the human brain. Limbic resonance is made possible thanks to a certain class of neurons called *oscillators*, which coordinate people physically by regulating how and when their bodies move together. Daniel Goleman details in the *Harvard Business Review* what happens when two accomplished cellists play together. Not only do they hit their notes in unison, but, thanks to oscillators, their right brain hemispheres are more closely coordinated to each other's than they are to the left hemispheres of their own brains![5]

Imitating someone's body language is an easy way to establish trust and rapport. This technique, which is often called *mirroring* or *mimicking,* is the conscious application of something that many charismatic people do instinctively.

When you consciously mirror someone's body language, you activate deep instincts of trust and liking. For this reason, it can be a

great aid when you need people to open up. A former political journalist mentioned how effective mirroring was during interviews.
"People get share-oriented," he told me. They just instinctively start
sharing more.

Several studies across the world have found that mirroring someone's body language can get them to pick up your dropped items, buy
your products, or give you a better deal. Mirroring even makes you
more attractive to others.[6]

During your next few conversations, try to mirror the other person's overall posture: the way they hold their head, how they place
their feet, the shifts in their weight. If they move their left hand,
move your right hand. Aim also to adapt your voice to theirs in
speed, pitch, and intonation.

Because people focus primarily on themselves while interacting,
they usually won't notice that you're mirroring unless you are exceed-
ingly obvious about it. However, here are some ways to increase
subtlety:

- Be selective: do only what feels natural to you. For instance,
  some gestures are gender-specific.
- Use variations in amplitude: if they make a big gesture, you
  could make a smaller one.
- Use lag time: let a few seconds elapse before you move into a
  mirrored position.

Over the years, I've had the privilege to coach a few extraordinary
individuals who dedicate their lives to improving those of others.
One of my all-time favorites is Darius, the young cofounder of New
Scholars, a nonprofit dedicated to creating "a Peace Corps for entrepreneurs."

Early one morning in Nairobi, Kenya, Darius was on his way to
meet the director of Africa's largest entrepreneurial network. This
was a critical moment for him, his one chance of cementing a partnership between his young organization and an industry behemoth.
Darius decided that this would be the perfect place to put the mirroring technique to the test:

When we arrived, we were greeted by George, one of the organization's executives. He invited us to the boardroom, where we made small talk over tea. I paid close attention to George while we were talking. He was sitting away from the table, legs crossed, and leaning forward. Gradually, I moved into a similar position. This had a noticeable effect: George started getting more excited, speaking faster, and getting really engaged in the conversation. So I matched his excitement and pace. This felt natural and easy.

The organization's director, Nathan, arrived shortly thereafter. The minute he walked in, I felt the energy in the room change. It became less relaxed, more tense. Nathan sat farther away from the table, leaned far back in his chair, and crossed his legs in a different way from George. So I gradually matched his posture, moving farther from the table, leaning farther back, and recrossing my legs.

Noticing that Nathan's tone was slow and deliberate, I matched my tone according to his. As he waved his hands occasionally to emphasize a point, I responded in kind. At one point, he turned sideways and leaned an arm on the table.

When it was my turn to speak, I inched close enough to place my arm on the table and turned sideways, too. Though I knew I was copying his moves, it still felt natural, and Nathan was obviously completely unaware of what I was doing. As I did this, I could feel the atmosphere getting more comfortable and more relaxed.

Finally, as our conversation came to a head, I asked Nathan how he saw this partnership coming together. He sat up, turned to face the table, and firmly tapped it with each point he made. My heart sank—what he had just announced was very different from what we had been hoping for. But I let him finish without interruption; and when it was my turn to speak, I sat up, faced the table, and said, "Here's how we see it." With each point, I firmly tapped the table just as he had.

I was shocked by what happened next. Nathan sat up, looked around the room, and agreed to every single one of our requests, even those we didn't think we had any hope of obtaining! I couldn't believe it. I still can't believe it. I don't know if it was entirely due to the mirroring, but I can tell you that I've never had a meeting start the way this one did and yet end the way this one did. We got everything we wanted, without giving up anything. This is the most important deal we've had to date.

As Darius's story shows, mirroring someone's body language is often enough to achieve rapport and sometimes enough to bring them around to your point of view. Mirroring is also one of the few techniques that can help overcome a bad first impression. It's extraordinarily effective. In fact, I can tell you that although I teach this material, the techniques still work on me even when I realize people are using them!

But what about cases in which the other person is exhibiting negative body language? Do you still mirror then? Well, it depends. In some situations, you want to first mirror their body language, then gradually lead it in a more positive direction.

Let's say that one of your colleagues comes in to see you, clearly upset about something. She timidly taps on your open door to ask permission to enter. As she walks in, her steps are hesitant. As you invite her to tell you what's going on, she seems anxious and drawn into herself, having trouble even finding words to express her concerns.

This is where mirroring could be useful in establishing rapport. What you could do in this situation is carefully observe her posture—the way she's sitting, how she's holding her head, what her shoulders are like—and gradually move into the same position. Look for rhythms. Is she nodding her head periodically? Tapping her knee? Fidgeting with a button? You can find a way to loosely mirror that, too. And, of course, match your voice to hers: adopt a similar cadence, tempo, and volume.

Once you're in a mirrored position, spend your entire listening time in that mode: as long as you're listening, match your body language to hers. Only when it's your turn to speak should you start infusing the interaction with warmth, caring, and compassion through your voice, face, and eyes. As you speak, gradually shift into a more relaxed, calm, and, eventually, confident posture. There's a good chance that she'll follow.

Mirror-then-lead is a smart strategy when the person you're interacting with needs reassurance—when they're feeling nervous or timid, anxious or awkward, stiff or withdrawn. With any of these emotional states, mirror them to establish comfort and rapport, and then gradually draw them out. In these situations, it's not a good idea to try to influence their body language too forcefully.

On the other hand, there are instances where you do not want to mirror a person's body language. If their demeanor is angry or defensive, mirroring would only escalate the tension. Say you're meeting with a manager who has denied a request you made, and who is sitting in a defensive position—leaning back with his arms and legs crossed and his hands balled into fists. Rather than mirroring, try breaking him out of his posture by handing him something: a piece of paper or a pen—whatever works. And then, as soon as he's in a new position, distract him by giving him new information or changing the subject while you mirror his posture to reestablish rapport.

Remember, our physiology affects our psychology. This link between physiology and psychology is also the reason it's so important to get someone who is in an angry, stubborn, or defensive posture to change their body language before you attempt to change their mind. As long as their *body* is in a certain emotional mode, it will be nearly impossible to get their mind to feel something different.

## Personal Space

Behavioral scientists can predict which stall people will choose in a communal bathroom with startling accuracy. People consistently follow a specific pattern, depending on which stalls are already occupied. Our adherence to personal space rules is so strong, it's even been found that people who play virtual-reality games obey real-life personal space rules within the game.

The concept of personal space evolved from mid-twentieth-century studies of zoo animals' behavior.[7] In the same manner that animals define and defend their territories, we humans feel "ownership" of the space around us. This territory, even if it's just a few inches, is felt as an extension of our bodies, and we act to preserve this space and react strongly if it is invaded.

Being charismatic means making others feel comfortable, at ease, and good about themselves when they are around us. In nonverbal communication, one crucial element for making people feel at ease and establishing rapport is respecting the amount of personal space people need to be comfortable. Conversely, not respecting people's personal-space preferences can create high levels of discomfort, and those emotions could become associated with you. It's worth paying attention.

Let's say you're in a conversation, and you notice your conversation partner leaning away with her upper body, pulling her head backward, or even physically stepping away from you. This may be a sign that she needs more personal space. The worst thing to do would be to move in closer. That would heighten her discomfort, and there's a good chance that those feelings would get associated with you. Instead, give her space: lean away or move back a few inches.

The size of personal space varies by culture, by population density, and by situation. A single individual's comfort zone is in fact highly variable. We will accept personal space restrictions in certain situations, such as when we're in a crowded elevator, bus, or subway.

I realized just how ingrained our sense of personal space is by trying to overrule my own instincts while standing in a crowded subway car. When the doors opened and people poured out, creating pockets of empty space, I resisted the urge to move away from my nearest neighbor. Instead, I made myself stay in the same spot and the same position, as close as we'd been when the crowd pushed us together. I had been wondering whether my knowledge of our instinctive tendencies would free me from their hold. Clearly, this was not the case: I realized, to my amusement, that I was feeling physically uncomfortable, almost unbearably so! And despite my best efforts to stay in place, I discovered too late that my body had gotten away from me:

though I hadn't moved my feet, the rest of my body was leaning away as much as balance and gravity allowed.

Personal space affects our interactions with others and how we perceive situations. For example, that's why negotiators choose their seats around a table so carefully; they know their seating choice can influence the outcome of the entire negotiation. When people are sitting across from each other with a table dividing them, they tend to speak in shorter sentences, are more likely to argue, and can recall less of what was said.[8]

### Putting It into Practice: Charismatic Seating Choices

The next time you want to establish warm rapport with someone, avoid a confrontational seating arrangement and instead sit either next to or at a 90-degree angle from them. These are the positions in which we feel most comfortable. In fact, this is an exercise you can try out with a partner.

♦ Start a conversation sitting next to each other.

♦ After five minutes, change positions so that you're sitting across from each other. You'll likely feel a clear difference in comfort level.

♦ After another five minutes, move to a 90-degree angle and feel the difference.

♦ Finally, come back to your original position sitting next to each other.

Pay close attention to the rise and fall of feelings of trust and comfort throughout the exercise.

If you want someone to feel comfortable, avoid seating them with their back to an open space, particularly if others are moving behind them. This kind of seating position causes the breathing rate, heart rate, and blood pressure to increase rapidly, especially if the person's back is toward an open door or a window at ground level.[9] And by association, their discomfort would likely affect their perception of you.

## Your Eyes, the Windows to Your Soul

Have you ever been in a conversation with someone who kept looking over your shoulder to see if someone more important and interesting than you might be arriving? Those roaming eyes are definitely not charismatic.

Good eye contact is incredibly important. Profound eye contact can have a powerful impact on people; it can communicate empathy and give an impression of thoughtfulness, wisdom, and intelligence. You simply cannot be charismatic without it. In fact, eye contact is one of the main ways charismatic masters make you feel that you are the most important person in the room.

Anthropologist Helen Fisher explains that when you stare with intensity at someone, it can speed up their heart rate and send a hormone called *phenylethylamine*, or PEA, coursing through their bloodstream. PEA is the same hormone that produces the phenomenon we call love at first sight.

In one study, complete strangers were asked to count the number of times the person across from them blinked. This was just a ploy to get people to look deeply into each other's eyes without feeling the awkwardness that usually arises. Within just a few minutes, people reported increased affection, and some even passionate feelings, for each other.[10] So obviously, you don't want to overdo it, but it can be very effective.

Our eyes are a key part of our nonverbal communication, perhaps the single most important one. Why are eyes called the "windows to the soul"? Because they are the most mobile part of the entire face—and so, the most expressive.

Imagine that you're in a conversation with someone who's wearing sunglasses. Wouldn't you find it harder to read them? This is why poker players wear sunglasses, as did shipping magnate Aristotle

Onassis during tough negotiations so that his adversaries wouldn't know what he was thinking.

Eye contact is so meaningful to us that our brains are hardwired to experience *separation distress* whenever someone with whom we have significant eye contact turns away. One good way to avoid creating this anxiety is to keep eye contact for three full seconds at the end of your interaction with someone. This may sound short, but it'll actually feel endless! If you can get into the habit of doing this, you'll find it well worth the effort. With just a few seconds' investment, people will feel you have truly paid attention to them.

Two of the most common eye-contact issues people have are lack of eye contact due to shyness and lack of eye contact due to distraction. Either, unfortunately, can ruin your charisma potential. One technique works equally well for both of these: delving into sensations. As you look into someone's eyes, pay attention to the physical sensations you are feeling in that very moment. If shyness is the issue, this helps to dedramatize the discomfort. If distraction is the issue, this technique will help you keep your mind focused in the present moment. You can also look at the different colors you see in their eyes, the different shades playing around their pupils.

Let's say you're at a party. Your boss's spouse grabs your arm and proceeds to talk your ear off about an impossibly boring subject. You might be tempted to let your mind wander or your eyes roam. But you know that doing either of these would be visible and would diminish your charisma. This is where the presence techniques can help keep you focused.

These insights and tools will help you get the right amount of eye contact. But that's not enough—to be charismatic, you also need to know how to use the right *kind* of eye contact. The degree and the precise kind of tension that shows around our eyes dramatically impact how we are perceived.

Les Fehmi, a neuroscientist specializing in this field, found that it all comes down to the way we pay attention. If we're in narrow, focused, evaluative attention—imagine viewing the world through the eyes of a police officer—our stress system will be on constant, low-grade alert. This brings our eyes into sharp focus, increases our stress responses, and results in both our face and our eyes tensing.[11] It greatly inhibits the amount of warmth we can project.

Charismatic eye contact means switching to a softer focus. This immediately relaxes our eyes and face, and quiets down our stress system. Here are three simple steps to help you switch to a soft, open focus: First, close your eyes. Focus on the space around you, the empty space in the room. Now focus on the space filling the entire universe. That's it—you've moved into "soft focus."

## Putting It into Practice: Charismatic Eyes

To truly understand how different your face appears when your eyes are relaxed and open, go see the transformation for yourself.

- Find a room with a mirror where you won't be disturbed for a few minutes.

- Close your eyes and think of a recent annoyance—some minor issue that's been bugging you lately, or an unpleasant task such as doing your taxes.

- When you feel the irritation take hold, open your eyes and look closely in the mirror. Note the tension around your eyes, their narrowness.

- Now close your eyes and think of something that would induce warm feelings—a recent pleasant experience, like time spent with a good friend.

- When the warmth has arisen, open your eyes and look at that precise kind of relaxation. That's what warmth looks like.

- Close your eyes once more and think of an exciting time when you felt full of confidence and on top of the world—receiving a triumph, an award, some brilliant news.

- When you've accessed the feeling of confidence, open your eyes again and note closely what they look like now. That's what confidence looks like.

One of my clients mentioned that as he tried this exercise, he saw "how little effort it takes to make drastic changes in our eyes . . . literally, one-millimeter changes have a huge impact!"

You knew that eye contact mattered, and you were right. Few things impair charisma more than bad eye contact and few things gain you charisma points more than improving your eye contact. The next time you're in a conversation, try to regularly check whether your eyes are feeling tense. If you feel the slightest bit of tension around your eyes, aim to relax them. You can use any favorite quick visualization (just one heartwarming image can do the trick) or aim to move into soft focus.

Getting your eyes right is critical to emanating warmth. Now let's look at one element critical for power: posture.

## The Right Posture for Nonverbal Power

Because we can't peer into people's hearts and minds, we assume attributes from the clues we observe. When someone displays high confidence through their body language, we tend to assume they have something to be confident about: people simply accept what you project. Any increase in the amount of confidence your body language projects will bring you major charisma rewards.

Projecting power and confidence is what allows you to emanate warmth, enthusiasm, and excitement without coming across as overeager or subservient. Because body language is wired so deeply within us, signs of confidence (or lack thereof) in someone's body language have veto power over all other signs of power. No matter how many signs of power and high status we may project through our appearance, title, or even through others' deference, a body language of insecurity will kill charisma on the spot. On the other hand, a body language of confidence can endow its bearer with charisma even when no other power signs are present.

In the following sections, you'll learn how to broadcast power in your posture and poise in a way that's properly balanced with warmth.

### Be the Big Gorilla

It's a sweet spring day in California, and students are milling about the sunny campus of Stanford University. With its pastel Spanish-style buildings, palm trees, and profusion of wildflowers, the university feels like a cross between a posh country club and a Spanish hacienda.

Nervously making her way across campus, peering through thick glasses, Ella is a fragile-looking history major, her arms full of books, on her way to her very first class of Kickboxing 101.

As she enters the locker room, Ella has no idea what to expect. She changes into shorts and a T-shirt, suddenly feeling very breakable. *Maybe we'll start with push-ups,* she tells herself. *Or maybe punching sandbags? Oh, I hope we're not asked to fight right away in front of everyone. I've never thrown a punch in my life.*

To her relief, the class begins with neither punches nor push-ups. Instead, the coach announces a far more surprising assignment: "Go back out and find a busy, crowded space on campus right now. For the next hour, as you walk around, try to get other people to move aside for you." The only rule is that Ella isn't allowed to step aside to make way for others. If it means a mild collision, so be it.

So here's Ella, bracing herself to move through the crowded main quad. All she knows is that she somehow must make others move out of the way for her. What would you have done? Imagine being there with that mission—how would you get others to move aside for you?

When we think of boxing matches and what helps an opponent win or lose in the ring, most of us think of strength, speed, and agility. And these are all true. But as many professional boxers will tell you, a lot happens before the opponents even set foot in the arena, well before the first punch is thrown. The way the fighters carry themselves—how impressive and intimidating they seem—can play a decisive role in the fight.

Though you may not realize it, your subconscious mind is constantly scanning your surroundings as you move through your environment to glean the information you need to keep moving forward. Your eyes scan and assess potential obstacles, including other people in your way. To determine whether you need to modify your route to avoid them, you read their body language without even realizing it.

If they're broadcasting a body language that says, "You better move aside, baby," you will most likely pick up on it and make way for them. Conversely, if you feel that you're the bigger gorilla, you'll stay your course and expect them to deviate.

Right now, close your eyes and imagine a very large gorilla. A rival has just breached his territory, and the gorilla is furious. He goes charging through the jungle, reaches the top branch of the top tree, and from there wants to broadcast his presence all around and intimidate the rival off his territory. What would he do? He'd likely inflate his chest and pound it with his fists—both of these actions have the effect of making him look bigger. The pounding also makes him loud and scary. That's how a gorilla charging through the jungle wants to look: big, loud, and scary. In human terms, we read confidence the same way: how much space people are willing to take up.

Deborah Gruenfeld, organizational behavior professor at Stanford's business school, says that "Powerful people sit sideways on chairs, drape their arms over the back, or appropriate two chairs by placing an arm across the back of an adjacent chair. They put their feet on the desk. They sit on the desk." All of these behaviors, she says, are ways of claiming space.

The next time you're out in a crowded environment, practice getting people to move aside for you. You could even do this on your way to work. First, visualize what a big gorilla would look like charging down the street. Then adopt the corresponding body language: imagine you're a big gorilla about to go charging down the street and let your body express that. Take up as much space as you can. Inflate your chest and charge through the crowd. You might even swing your arms as you go, taking up yet more space.

When you first start trying out this confident body language, it can feel a little scary. But it's well worth it. What's the worst that can happen? You bump into someone. Use that as an opportunity to practice switching into kindness charisma with a quick visualization to increase your warmth. Imagine the person you've just bumped into is a good friend or see them with angel wings.

Your job is to learn how to take up space and get comfortable doing so. Keep in mind that you'll need the freedom of motion to inflate your chest, so avoid constrictive clothing that doesn't allow you to breathe. You can't be imposing without oxygen.

One of the first things I question my clients about when we work on projecting charismatic body language is: "What's your breathing like right now?" Anytime your breathing is shallow, you activate the stress response. It's hard to feel calm, relaxed, and confident when you're not getting enough oxygen and your body thinks it's in fight-or-flight mode.

## Putting It into Practice: Being the Big Gorilla

This is a great exercise to use before any meeting or interaction where you want to both feel and broadcast confidence—for instance, before a job interview, or before meeting someone who's a bit intimidating.

Follow these seven steps to convey confident body language:

1. Make sure you can breathe. Loosen any clothing if need be.

2. Stand up and shake up your body.

3. Take a wide stance and plant your feet firmly on the ground. A wide, stable stance helps you both feel and project more confidence.

4. Stretch your arms to the ceiling, trying to touch it with your fingertips.

5. Now stretch your arms to the walls on either side of you, trying to touch them.

6. Bring your arms loosely to your sides, and roll your shoulders up and then back.

7. INFLATE. Try to take up as much space as possible. Imagine puffing up like a gorilla, doubling in size.

*(continued on next page)*

*(continued from previous page)*

As Stanford's Gruenfeld found, people who assume expansive poses (taking up more space) experience a measurable physiological shift. In one experiment, assertiveness- and energy-promoting hormones rose by 19 percent, while anxiety hormones fell by 25 percent. Assuming a strong, confident physical posture will make you feel more confident and more powerful. As you feel more powerful, your body language adapts accordingly. This in turn gives you yet another biochemical boost, and the cycle builds upon itself. All you have to do is get the cycle going, and if you keep practicing, confident body language will become second nature.

## Regal Posture

Can you imagine James Bond fidgeting? How about tugging at his clothing, bobbing his head, or twitching his shoulders? How about hemming and hawing before he speaks? Of course not. Bond is the quintessential cool, calm, and collected character. He epitomizes confidence.

This kind of high-status, high-confidence body language is characterized by how *few* movements are made. Composed people exhibit a level of stillness, which is sometimes described as *poise*. They avoid extraneous, superfluous gestures such as fidgeting with their clothes, their hair, or their faces, incessantly nodding their heads, or saying "um" before sentences.

These gestures, which behavior experts identify as low-status, are often signs used by someone wanting to convey reassurance to the person they're interacting with. The desire to convey reassurance can stem from two different sources:

- Empathy: wanting to ensure that the other person feels heard and understood and knows you're paying attention
- Insecurity: wanting to please or appease the person you're interacting with

In contrast, people who come across as powerful, confident, or high-status are usually more contained; they don't feel the urge to give so much reassurance because they're not as worried about what their counterpart is thinking.

Imagine yourself in a royal court. Picture a nervous servant anxiously bobbing and curtseying. Now imagine the opposite: the king or queen. Poised and powerful, they don't need to make a move.

When you want to increase your poise, there are three major issues to look out for. The first is excessive or rapid nodding. Nodding once for emphasis or to express agreement is fine and can be an effective communication method, but nodding three or four times in rapid succession is not. This is what one of my clients has come to call "the bobble head."

The second hindrance is excessive verbal reassurance: making a sound, such as "uh-huh," or a half-sentence, such as "Oh, I agree." Done once, and consciously, this is fine; multiple times per sentence is not.

The third issue is restlessness or fidgeting (tapping your pencil or foot, or rearranging items on the table). Fidgeting decreases presence, thus charisma. Even when you have warmth, confidence, and are mentally present, if you are physically restless, you can't be charismatic. Your body language is sending distracting signals. I know one particular young entrepreneur who is both confident and warm, yet his restless tics and incessant fidgeting make him seem odd and eccentric. He comes across as a child who can't keep still and has a hard time being taken seriously.

How to break these habits? The first step is awareness—you need to see how you appear to others. One of the most valuable things you can do is to videotape yourself during a meeting or even a casual conversation. When you sit down to watch it, fast-forward ten minutes; you'll probably have forgotten about the camera enough to display uninhibited body language. Turn the sound off at first and just compare your body language (nodding, gesturing, etc.) to whomever is the most senior person in the room. Then watch again with the sound on and compare your verbal reassurance level with others'. Though the experience can be painful, it's often invaluable: realize that everything you see on that tape is what others are seeing. You might as well be aware of it, too.

With this newfound awareness, you may catch yourself throughout the day displaying high amounts of verbal and nonverbal reassurance and feel dismayed by how often it occurs. This is normal. Many of my clients tell me they feel incredibly frustrated for the first few days, noticing how often and how eagerly they bob their head.

Give yourself a break. Everyone goes through this period of frustration, and it really is possible to break these habits. The client who called her nodding bobble-heading proudly reported: "I still nod my head occasionally, but I now do it deliberately, in well-chosen moments."

Catch yourself when you find yourself nodding or verbally reassuring, and try to replace it with stillness and silence. Aim to get comfortable with silence, inserting pauses between your sentences or even midsentence. If you want to speed up the process, ask a friend or colleague to tell you whenever they catch you nodding or reassuring. One very effective trick is to carry around a stack of one-dollar bills and commit to ripping one up every time you trip. For maximum effectiveness, ask a friend, spouse, or colleague to help catch whichever habit you want to break.

Be aware, however, that broadcasting too much power can come across as either arrogant or intimidating for some people. The warmth-enhancing techniques you gained earlier in this chapter, such as keeping your eyes in soft focus, will counter this. You can also aim to bring your chin down a few degrees—imagine a king bowing his head to a noble emissary. This has a double benefit. It avoids giving the impression that you're contemptuously looking down your nose at someone (the impression given when your head is tilted back) and simultaneously makes you appear more thoughtful, attentive, and deliberate as your eyes automatically open wider.

## Knowing What to Do When

The same amount of nonverbal communication or reassurance can be appropriate and helpful in one context but hold you back in another. For instance, if you're seeking to make a shy colleague or subordinate feel comfortable and open up, you would be smart to punctuate your interaction with both nonverbal (nodding) and verbal (uh-huh) reassurance.

If they're looking insecure and you think they need to be reassured, ramp up the amount of warmth you're projecting. Use any of the warmth-enhancing visualizations you gained in chapter 5 or the verbal warmth techniques from chapter 8, and adapt your body language to theirs.

On the other hand, when you'd like to be seen as a confident peer or a respected boss, focus on poise and containment and limit your reassurance. Rather than synchronizing your body language with theirs (unless theirs is the very essence of confidence you want to display), keep to your own rhythms and maintain your confident, contained posture.

You now have the basics of projecting presence, power, and warmth through both verbal and nonverbal communication.

You first learned how to build a solid internal foundation for charisma, then how to bring your charisma into the world. Now you're ready to learn how to apply these tools in difficult situations. The next chapter will help you stay charismatic when it counts the most.

## KEY TAKEAWAYS

- While our words speak to a person's logical mind, our nonverbal communication speaks to a person's emotional mind.
- Nonverbal communication amplifies verbal communication when the two are congruent.
- When verbal and nonverbal messages contradict, we tend to trust what we see in the other person's body language more than what we hear them say.

- Through emotional contagion, your emotions can spread to other people. As a leader, the emotions conveyed by your body language, even during brief, casual encounters, can have a ripple effect on your team or even your entire company.

- To communicate warmth, aim to make people feel comfortable: respect their personal space, mirror their body language, and keep your eyes relaxed.

- When people come to you in need of reassurance, first mirror their body language, then lead them to more calm, open, and confident positions.

- When people are defensive, break their body language lock by handing them something to look at or something they will have to lean forward to take.

- To project power, take up space (be the big gorilla) and be still (adopt a regal posture).

- Cut out verbal and nonverbal reassurances like head bobbing and excessive uh-huh-ing.

# 10

# Difficult Situations

FOR THE MOST part, my clients report major success incorporating the charisma-boosting techniques you've just learned into their everyday social and business interactions. But, as you may well imagine, certain challenging circumstances may require a more nuanced approach. In this chapter you'll learn how to handle situations such as dealing with difficult people, delivering bad news or criticism, and giving apologies in the most charismatic way you can. It is actually possible to come out of each of these experiences with relationships intact, and possibly even strengthened.

## Dealing with Difficult People

Some people are just difficult. Some have egos that need to be stroked, some are always critical, others are deliberately confrontational. In many cases, these people make a point of being resistant to being won over. This section gives you techniques for disarming difficult people and getting them on your side.

Peter was the worldwide chairman of a global professional services firm. When he came to see me, he already had a level of charisma most executives would envy. But Peter had a different challenge: he wanted to take the entire global firm in a new direction.

"It's like herding cats," he grumbled as we sat down that morning. For his initiative to succeed, all eight members of the firm's international board would have to agree to it, and each of them, he told me, was "one big ego with a couple of arms and legs sticking out." He had only one chance to succeed: an imminent international board meeting. Failure was not an option, so Peter cleared his schedule and flew to New York to meet with me.

What magical charisma tricks might I have, he asked, to win over that entire board?

### Divide and Conquer

My first recommendation to Peter was simple: don't try to win them all over all at once.

Every time someone sees you, their perception of you is filtered through the context in which you both operate: their internal state and their personal and cultural filters. It's far more difficult to have charisma when you're dealing with a group because you must handle all the individual contexts on top of the group dynamic. The one exception is when you're on stage: the effect of being in the spotlight makes up for the multiple-context handicap. But in general, when you have a group of difficult people to convince, you'll have much greater chances of success if you work on each of them individually.

This is why Peter and I crafted an individual persuasion strategy for the CEO of each country, and he had a separate meeting with each of them. This allowed him to choose the right charisma style for each person and situation. As we saw in chapter 6, the "right" charisma style depends on your personality, the situation, your goals, and the person you're dealing with.

One situation might call for focus charisma. Perhaps you're dealing with a person who needs to feel heard and listened to. In Peter's case, the head of the firm's Spanish branch was feeling ill-treated. He thought that his opinions hadn't been given due consideration by the rest of the board. He also disapproved of Peter's recent "Message from the Chairman" firm-wide e-mail and wanted to make this known. "He really just wanted to get this all off his chest," Peter told me. "Focus charisma was perfect. It made him feel completely heard, listened to, and understood. After that, he was far more willing to consider anything I suggested."

Other situations might call for either authority or visionary charisma; for instance, when people are dealing with uncertainty and looking for a clear, compelling vision. In Peter's case, the head of Argentina was dealing with massive uncertainty. His country was facing a severe economic and social crisis. Peter told me that "they had run out of answers." Here, he drew mainly on visionary charisma, presenting a strategic plan that would give the senior executive team a solid framework to rely on as well as clear guidelines to follow.

Once you know whom it is you need to persuade and which styles might work best for each person, consider the following recommendations to help win them over.

### Make Them Rationalize in Your Favor

Benjamin Franklin's favorite way to win over his political opponents was not to do them favors but rather to *ask* them for favors. Franklin once wrote a note to one of his adversaries expressing his hope of reading a certain rare book he'd heard that this gentleman possessed, and asking the favor of borrowing it for just a few days. The gentleman complied. Franklin returned it as promised, with a second note warmly expressing his appreciation and gratitude for the favor.

In his autobiography, Franklin describes what happened as a result: "When we next met in the House, he spoke to me (which he had never done before), and with great civility; and he ever after manifested a readiness to serve me on all occasions, so that we became great friends, and our friendship continued to his death."[1]

This technique has become known as the *Ben Franklin Effect*.

Having lent Franklin the book, the opponent had to either consider himself as inconsistent (having done a favor for someone he disliked) or rationalize his action by deciding that he actually rather liked Franklin. "I did something nice for this person, so I must like him. I wouldn't have agreed to do a favor for someone I dislike. That wouldn't make sense." Using this technique encouraged the opponent to rationalize his actions in Franklin's favor.

How can you use this technique to your advantage? You could indeed ask your opponents for their help or ask them for a favor. Better still, ask them for something they can give without incurring any cost: their *opinion*. Asking for someone's opinion is a better strategy than asking for their advice, because giving advice feels like more effort, as they have to tailor a recommendation to your situation, whereas with an opinion, they can just spout whatever is on their mind.

Best of all is to call upon the benefits of rationalization through something they've already done for you. Find ways to remind them of any help they've given you in the past. Express your appreciation and gratitude, highlight the choice they made, the effort they put in; and if they put their reputation on the line for you in any way, play it up. Remember, it'll make them rationalize their actions in your favor. "Wow, I really did go all-out for this person. I must really like them."

### Expressing Appreciation

Way back in 1936, Dale Carnegie wrote the now-classic book *How to Win Friends and Influence People*. Though his original guidelines have since become clichés, some fundamental principles still hold; and in the case of praise, Carnegie's writings are just as applicable today. He writes: "We all crave honest appreciation. It's a gnawing and unfaltering human hunger; and the rare individual who satisfies it will hold people in the palm of his hand."

This simple recommendation is supported by recent science. People are indeed incredibly susceptible to praise. In fact, Keise Izuma's research showed that hearing a *computer* tell people "Good job!" lit up the same reward regions of their brains as a financial windfall.[2]

The most effective and credible compliments are those that are both personal and specific. For instance, instead of "Great job," you could say, "*You* did a great job," or, better yet, "The way you kept your calm when that client became obnoxious was impressive." The more appreciation you express and the more you show them the impact they've had on you, the more they will like you and feel invested in your success. They'll rationalize in your favor. When you show people how they've impacted you, they feel that they've in a sense *made* you. This sense of ownership gives them a vested interest, and they identify with you; you become part of their identity. Therefore, they feel more responsibility for ensuring your success.

Making people rationalize in your favor is a classic marketing technique often employed by commercial airlines. As they welcome us to our arrival city, the pilot or flight attendants now often say: "We know you have many airlines to choose from, and we thank you for choosing to fly with us." Hearing their appreciation reminds us that we had a choice, and that *we* chose *them*. What's the result? We will tend to view the airline with greater favor because, after all, we chose it, and we hate to be wrong. Remember John Kenneth Galbraith's quote about our strong preference to prove ourselves correct rather than change our minds. Most of us would much rather decide we're happy with our choice of airline than find fault with our decision.

Reminding people that they had a choice and that *they* chose you, your company, your service, or your suggestion is one of the most useful tools to maintain their support for you or your idea, particularly when the going gets rough and people start complaining.

And remember, this process also works in reverse, so avoid making other people feel wrong. If someone feels like they've done you harm, they will seek to rationalize their actions and will convince themselves that what they did was justified. They don't want to feel like a bad person, therefore you must have done something wrong in order for them to act this way toward you. Few people will blame themselves no matter how wrong they may be—even notorious gangster Al Capone saw himself as a public benefactor.

You can use rationalization not just for yourself but for the idea you're supporting. By showing someone the impact they've had on a project or an idea, they will feel a degree of ownership of it, and then instinctively will feel driven to support it. Show them how it changed as a result of their involvement, their actions, or their recommendations. Change is the sign of impact. As soon as we create change, we have created impact.

Better yet, show the person how this idea or project was, at its very core, in its very source, inspired by what they did in the past—a similar idea, project, or initiative they supported.

This is what Peter did with the chairman of the firm's French branch. He highlighted all the ways in which the endeavor was not just similar to but in fact inspired by past initiatives that the French contingent had launched.

## Don't Go in Unprotected

As with all toxic substances, toxic people should indeed be "handled with care." Not for their sake, but for yours. Dealing with a difficult person, like any hostile situation, can activate your stress system, sending adrenaline flooding through your body. And that can be a killer.

Dr. Redford Williams, professor of psychiatry at Duke University Medical Center, spent more than twenty years studying the impact of the mind and emotions on health. "Getting angry is like taking a small dose of slow-acting poison," he concluded. It leads to higher blood pressure and arterial damage, and it spurs cholesterol-filled fat cells to empty into the bloodstream. In brief, hostile feelings are apt to harm your health unless you know how to handle them.

To counteract the stress hormones that could flood your system, impair your mental functioning, and generate negative body language, flood your system with oxytocin instead. To do this when dealing with a difficult person, get into empathy and stay there. You can use any of the compassion-accessing tools you learned in chapter 5. It might also help to consider that this person may well be in a state of utter self-loathing. The internal world of difficult people can be pretty nasty— that's the very reason they're difficult. If their mental climate were one of peace and love, they'd be exuding warmth instead. Hostility is often nothing but the external manifestation of internal turmoil.

If you need a compassion boost, consider an alternate reality. Imagine that just a few hours ago they saw a beloved parent die. Remember, it's not for their sake that you're doing this but for yours. It will reduce the level of toxicity in your body and make the experience less frustrating for you. You can go back to this technique anytime you feel your frustration level rising.

Getting into empathy will protect your mental and emotional state, and give you the right body language throughout. If you're in an adversarial mindset, this will be written across your face. Empathy will help you get into a collaborative mindset instead, giving you a great body language in addition to making the interaction far easier to handle. This is why kindness charisma can be a surprisingly effective tool in dealing with difficult people.

Maria, a young MIT graduate who'd recently joined a new company in Boston, told me she combined several of the tools to alleviate the resentment she felt toward two of her colleagues. "They're good people, but their behavior really got me angry. And because they didn't apologize, the resentment just kept building." She didn't feel quite confident enough to demand an apology, but couldn't let this resentment simmer either, because she needed to work well with both of her teammates.

So Maria wrote a venting letter to get everything off her chest, describing in detail how she felt about the situation. Then she wrote out their imagined return apologies. "Writing the letter and receiving the apologies felt so liberating! I had a surprising feeling of satisfaction and could really feel the resentment dissipate."

The next day, in the hour before her team meeting, she reread the apologies and used the zooming-out technique to see the whole situation from afar, to see how small the whole thing really was. Finally, she visualized a warm moment of triumph. She also told me that during the meeting, imagining both of her colleagues with angel wings really helped. "This was a test for me. And it worked! I cannot tell you how different the experience and the outcome were. I cannot tell you how good it felt. I know I both felt and showed warm self-confidence. Wow."

Let's go back to Peter. By early September, he had met with every one of his board members. He'd used a slightly different mode of charisma with each, and he told me: "Well, they all *sound* like they're on board. But of course, I might be wrong—and one never knows what could happen during the meeting." Peter left nothing to chance. In the hours leading up to the big board meeting, he made sure his calendar was as charisma-inducing as possible, using the tools from the "warming up for key moments" section (see page 93). Just before the meeting began, he spent fifteen minutes getting into the right mental state.

He told me later: "When I walked into that room, I could *feel* the confidence, warmth, and calm radiating from me. It was amazing." As it turned out, the CEOs now felt so invested in the new direction he wanted to take the firm, all he had to do was sit back and let *them* push for it.

## Delivering Bad News

It was one of those rare cases where I got to hear both sides of the story.

One summer afternoon, Xavier started our coaching session with a request. "There's a voicemail I got a few hours ago that's been really bugging me. Would you mind listening to it and helping me get into a better mental state before I return the call? It's from Susan."

This is the message that Susan had left: "Xavier, I want to talk to you about your memo. I have bad news—well, I shouldn't say that, but it's something you may find insulting, and I guarantee I do not intend it that way. Anyway, call me back."

Ouch. Can you spot Susan's mistakes? First, she was creating highly negative associations: her message was unpleasant from beginning to end. Second, she had fallen into the white-elephant trap by telling Xavier he "shouldn't" feel insulted. Because our brain can't unprocess information it has received, it's likely that the word *insulted* is what Xavier's mind recalled most.

Third, by being vague in her message, Susan was letting Xavier's mind imagine the worst. With a brain wired to look out for the negative, when we hear "It's bad news," our brain automatically starts thinking of the worst possible scenarios.

Susan was also part of the team I was coaching, so when I saw her next I explained: "Put yourself in Xavier's place. Imagine getting a voicemail announcing bad news and being insulted, without any explanation. Yes, you've certainly grabbed his attention. But what kind of emotions do you think he'll associate with you from now on? Every time he thinks about that message he'll think about bad news and being insulted. Is that really what you want to be associated with in Xavier's mind?"

You won't always be able to choose the time and place for your difficult conversations. But when you can, by all means, consider both timing and location. Before you pick up the phone or sit the person down to talk, take a moment to imagine what mental state they might be in.

If you know they've just had a very rough, stressful, or tiring twenty-four hours and you can wait a day, do so. I've experienced the difference between receiving tough news on a day when I was operating well and on a day when I was sick or tired. In the latter case, the news was much harder to bear—molehills felt like mountains.

Before delivering bad news, think about the setting, remembering that people will transfer their feelings for the environment to the experience itself. As much as you can, choose a comfortable location. Don't try to hold a difficult conversation in a noisy place such as a train station or an airport.

Do whatever you can to increase their comfort. You can even use props for this. Have you ever noticed the way that people fidget with items in their hands or with their clothing—for instance, toying with their shirt buttons when they're in the middle of a difficult conversation or when they're having trouble expressing themselves? What they're subconsciously doing is finding objects on which to focus their mind to distract themselves from the discomfort of their immediate experience. Make it easy for them by having objects close by with which they can play, and thus more quickly feel at ease, while conversing with you. They won't even realize what's happening, and yet they'll sense the interaction become easier and more comfortable.

I always have Play-Doh on hand for people to play with when they come see me. It's particularly helpful with people who are naturally shy or when the conversation is difficult. It's fascinating to see throughout the interaction the way they'll bring their focus back to the Play-Doh in their hands whenever they're feeling a bit awkward and need to relieve the intensity of their discomfort.

Candles and firelight have the same positive distracting effect. This is why they're so prized in romantic situations, when comfort and ease are key. These constantly moving elements give people the feeling that there's something happening in the background that they can turn their attention to when they need a distraction. Background music, of course, serves partly the same purpose.

When you're delivering unpleasant news of any kind, your body language is everything. Remember the way negative performance reviews delivered with positive body language were far better received than positive reviews delivered with negative body language? In stressful situations, your body language carries far greater impact than your words. When the stress system is activated, a more primal part of the brain takes over, which does not directly comprehend words or ideas. Instead, it's immediately impacted by body language.

The right body language for delivering bad news is one of warmth: care, concern, understanding, and empathy. Essentially, demonstrate as much kindness charisma as you can. The worse the news, the more important it is for the recipient to feel that you truly understand them, and that you are there with them. This is where the internal tools of goodwill, compassion, and empathy come in.

- First, get yourself into the right internal state. Access compassion so that it plays out across your body language.
- Put yourself in their shoes; imagine in vivid detail what it's like inside their head, inside their life.
- Imagine both of you with angel wings working toward a common mission.
- Focus on a compassionate phrase, such as "Just love as much as you can from wherever you are."
- Try to convey empathy in your facial expressions, your tone of voice, and your words.

The right verbal language for delivering bad news depends on what kind of difficult message you have to deliver. In most cases, you can follow the suggestions covered in chapter 8: make the message relevant to them; use their words, analogies, and metaphors. If you're delivering this message to a larger audience, go to page 187 for the section on presentations.

Make sure that throughout your interaction you express your care and concern both nonverbally and verbally; tell them, if appropriate, what you would like to do to ease their discomfort. Show that you fully understand not just how unwelcome the news is but also the ramifications it could have for them.

Throughout the experience, turn your kindness charisma not just toward them but also toward yourself. Use all the internal tools you've gained to handle this difficult experience as best as you can and keep giving yourself praise and encouragement. You're doing your best.

## Delivering Criticism

"Honest criticism is hard to take, particularly from a relative, a friend, an acquaintance, or a stranger," said humorist Franklin Jones. Have you ever winced at the mere memory of a comment heard years ago? Few things sting as badly or last as long as a nasty comment.

For many of my clients, having to occasionally deliver negative feedback is the worst part of their jobs. Many tell me that when they know they have criticism to deliver, they walk around with a knot in their stomach all day, dreading the upcoming conversation.

Unfortunately, criticism—like dental exams, airport security, and, depending on whom you ask, taxes—is a necessary evil. You may not like it, but sometimes you just have to do it. At some point in your life, *someone*—whether it's a parent, spouse, friend, colleague, or boss—will do something wrong and you'll have to tell them about it. The question, of course, is how to do it right.

There are four crucial steps to charismatically delivering criticism.

First, **think about your timing and the location**. Try to be as empathetic as possible in your choice of both. Consider the individual's levels of stress and fatigue. With criticism (or with "constructive feedback"), try to provide it as soon as possible after witnessing the behavior you want to change. Just be sure the person is in a physically and emotionally receptive state when you do so.

Second, **get into the right mindset, one of compassion and empathy**. Yes, even when delivering criticism, your compassion will play out across your body language and affect the entire interaction in a positive way. Warmth is also important here. Accessing kindness or focus charisma will ease the situation, whereas authority charisma would worsen it.

When people feel that you have their best interests at heart, it can change the dynamic entirely. Chris, an executive from Los Angeles, told me about a former boss who he felt was truly invested in his success. This boss, when pointing out areas of improvement, would remind Chris that he wanted him to be promoted as soon as possible and that's why he was pointing out the things that needed to be better.

To access the right mental state, you can also try thinking of a person whom you highly respect just before you deliver criticism. You might think of a favorite grandparent, mentor, spiritual figure, or anyone who is important to you. If you were to make this comment to them, or in front of them, how would you word your criticism? In what ways do you see your comments changing now? Try to remind yourself of this regularly throughout the difficult conversation and imagine the respected mentor watching you.

Third, **decide exactly what points you want to make: be specific**. Focusing on a few key points rather than making an exhaustive list will prevent the other person from feeling overwhelmed. In addition, if your criticism is too general, their danger-wary brain might imagine the worst possible interpretations of your message.

Fourth, **depersonalize.** As much as possible, communicate that **what you're critiquing is the behavior, not the person.** It's harder to find common ground when someone feels that their intentions or character traits have been criticized. Be very wary of assuming you've accurately guessed a person's motives. Instead, focus on observed behaviors and verified facts.

Even when focusing on the behavior, aim to make the criticism as impersonal as possible. The wrong way to do this would be to say: "Why do you always procrastinate on presentations until the very last minute?" This is both personal and generalized. Instead, zero in on one observed behavior: "When you wait until the very last minute to prepare the presentation, I feel anxious." After all, *we* create the feelings of anxiety in our bodies—it's our decision to become upset. If possible, don't mention their actions at all. Just explain what's going on for you: "When I don't see a finished presentation until the last minute, I feel anxious."

### Critical Delivery

Now that you've thought about timing and location and chosen the specific, empathetically phrased points you want to make, you're ready to start charismatically delivering the difficult feedback. It's important to start off on the right foot. The way you begin will greatly affect people's perception of the conversation.

Human beings remember "firsts"—the first time something happens, or the beginning of an experience—and we tend to remember "lasts" as well. In a study done on patients who had received a colonoscopy exam, some were given a full exam for three minutes, while others received a longer exam but the device was held immobile during the final two minutes, thereby finishing the procedure on a far less painful note. This second group of patients remembered the entire exam as less painful, and they were more willing to undergo the procedure a second time. [3]

If you start your criticism with a positive beginning, it will affect the rest of the experience. In the first moments, when people are most apprehensive, what they need is reassurance. You can give them solid ground to stand on by expressing the fact that you value them—that you recognize their worth as human beings, and that they matter to you as colleagues, as clients.

Once they are reassured of their own worth, people will accept your comments far more easily, and they'll get less defensive. Indeed, this step may be the most important one to mitigate a defensive reaction. Defensiveness, after all, is often just the outward face of fear and insecurity.

Let's say a colleague has been falling behind on his commitments. Instead of pointing to this fact directly, first acknowledge his many positive contributions. This way, he will feel that his entire history is fairly recognized. It also recognizes the behavior as momentary, a lapse in otherwise good behavior.

Once you've started on a positive note, you can bring up the actual issue you want to address. Tell people exactly what you want to see from them, as opposed to what you don't want to see. Teachers are taught "Don't have *don't* rules," warning them that if they tell their class, for instance, to "not put the beans in their ears," they might find half the students promptly doing so.

When you tell the person you are criticizing the corrective action you'd like to see, depersonalize the behavior change just as you had the criticism. Rather than asking, "Could you get the presentation done earlier?" say, "In the future, I'd greatly appreciate it if the presentation could be ready a few days in advance." That takes who was right or wrong off the table and focuses instead on something you can both agree on without anyone having to win or lose.

Just as when dealing with a difficult person, try to avoid making people feel wrong when you're delivering criticism. When someone is told they're wrong, even when they do realize they're at fault, they will often strive to justify themselves; it can both wound their ego and arouse their resentment, leading them to discredit *you* in an attempt to lessen their own guilt.

Legendary diplomat Benjamin Franklin admitted in his memoirs to learning this lesson the hard way. As a young man, having found one of his adversaries in error, he felt quite right in pointing out the error, proving beyond the shadow of a doubt that the man had erred. He made his point—and he made an enemy for life. Franklin came to realize that the short-lived pleasure of being right was not worth the long-term negative consequences. From then on, he adopted the practice of "denying [himself] the pleasure of contradicting others." He would instead begin by observing that "in certain cases or circumstances his opinion would be right, but in the present case there appeared to be some difference."

You can take a similar path by saying: "You know, I might not be explaining this the right way. Let me try again." Choose the high road. Being a charismatic communicator means that others feel good about themselves when they are with you. It means that others look forward to being with you because they like themselves better as a result of being around you.

As always, body language matters here. You can tell someone that you think they're wrong with a look, intonation, or gesture just as eloquently as you can in words. So use all the tools in your arsenal to stay in an internal state of calm and goodwill. Your body language will follow.

It's absolutely critical throughout difficult conversations to stay attentive to any signals that the other person might be getting defensive. When you sense defensiveness, whether through their facial expressions, body language, or tone of voice, dial up your warmth to move them back into a more positive frame of mind. You can do this in two ways:

- **Verbally:** Encourage positive mental associations. For example, mention something they've done well in the past or something in this situation that you approve of.
- **Nonverbally:** Use your body language to influence theirs. Get back into a state of goodwill so that it plays out across your face. The mirror neurons in their brain will replicate the emotions they're seeing in you, putting them in a more positive state of mind as well.

When closing the conversation, if you can, aim to end on a positive note. Remember how important beginnings and endings are—they can color the whole interaction. This is when you can put the emphasis on three important points:

- **Next steps:** Review the steps that will be taken to improve the situation, particularly if you're going to do any of it together. Give the sense of constructive, forward motion.
- **Appreciation:** Tell them how much you appreciate how well they took your feedback. Praise even the slightest good effort

here; you're providing positive reinforcement so they'll improve over time.

- **A positive future:** Bring up anything that both of you can look forward to in the future, such as exciting events or upcoming projects—whatever conveys the fact that you're looking forward to future interactions.

## Apologies: What to Do When Things Go Wrong

So you screwed up. You hit REPLY ALL by mistake, you didn't check the numbers, the dog ate your homework. Call it what you will, something bad happened, and, whether they're right or wrong, someone thinks it's your fault. Fear not. If you play your cards well, even embarrassing blunders can be turned around.

Having a disagreement or a conflict can actually improve a relationship and be a great thing in the end. When a relationship has gone well from the start, there might be in the back of our mind a slight hesitancy. Everything has gone well so far, but what if that changes? How would they react then? Once you get through a difficult situation and it was well handled, you know that the relationship can withstand difficulty. The apprehension is resolved.

One of my very first clients told me that he actually welcomed making minor mistakes, especially early on in a business relationship. "Most people do such a piss-poor job of apologizing that just by being halfway decent at it, you'll be head and shoulders above the rest." Another entrepreneur told me: "I have a pretty good track record of turning screw-ups into up-sells." So let's see how you can approach, conduct, and conclude apologies charismatically.

First, as always, get into the right mental state. This means, first and foremost, forgiving yourself. Yes, I'm serious. Though it may sound counterintuitive, having warmth toward yourself—even though you may be at fault—is necessary to prevent making the situation worse through negative body language. It will greatly help avoid any sign of defensiveness in either your voice, your posture, or any part of your facial expression. So use all the tools we've covered to access and stay in a state of self-compassion.

Forgiving yourself and getting into a good mental state also helps you avoid appearing overly apologetic, subservient, or insecure. With the confidence that accompanies a positive internal state you can embody both warmth and contrition, yet still be seen as coming from a place of strength.

Now that you're in the right mental state, let's turn to the other person. The graver the offense, the more you should strive for a personal touch. To be satisfied, the person receiving the apology may need to see remorse in your face or, at the very least, hear it in your voice.

Because so much of our communication is nonverbal, when you apologize in person you have the greatest number of tools at your disposal: body language, facial expressions, and vocal tone, in addition to your choice of words. On the phone, you have only your voice and words to work with, and you have even fewer instruments at your disposal in an e-mail.

On the other hand, some people find it easier to handle such difficult situations with the distance that a written medium provides. Written communication has the advantage that you can put hours of thinking into a few lines of communication, and really get them right. Putting something in writing can also be a powerful statement. You are in a sense making it permanent; you are willing to be held to account.

In this case, as with so many of the charisma-enhancing techniques, it will be a question of what is the best fit considering *your* preferences, your best guess of *their* preferences, and what the logistics, timing, and context allow.

### Hear Them Out

Whether you're apologizing in person or on the phone, your first concern is to let the other person have their say. The simplest and most effective way to do so is just to listen: give them the complete presence of focus charisma. Now, I'm not saying that putting this into practice is easy. For each grievance your counterpart utters, you might have a dozen retorts bubbling up in your mind. But at this point, interrupting is the worst move you could possibly make. No matter how brilliant you are, no matter how right your rejoinder, they will feel belittled rather than accepted and understood.

While you listen, be fully present, and try to avoid preparing your response. Instead, focus your entire attention on determining precisely what the complaint is. Ask questions to make sure you understand. If someone says, "I just don't feel good about the way this meeting went," ask, "Could you tell me more? I really want to understand. What is it about the meeting that made you uncomfortable? Was it the people, the timing, or something else altogether?" You can also try to restate your counterpart's complaints in your own words. You'll know you've listened enough when they say, "Am I talking too much?"

### Goodwill Matters Here, Too

Just coming into a conversation with the mindset of "Help me understand how you see things" can change the outcome completely. The simple fact of being in an open mental stance affects your voice, your facial expressions, the words you use, and your body posture, and it dramatically changes the emotional tenor of the interaction. Your goodwill is written across your face and shows up in your every microexpression.

Use any of the internal tools we've covered to inject warmth into the interaction, and call on your kindness charisma. Think of keeping your chin down, your eyes wide open, and your voice warm and slow, leaving frequent pauses to make room for the other person to jump in should they feel the urge to do so.

Once you're sure that you fully understand the complaint, and if you agree that the fault was yours, a true-blue apology is in order. Surprisingly, your wording can be very simple (again, body language is what really matters). A simple "I'm very sorry" delivered with full presence and full warmth can work wonders.

What matters is the thoughtfulness, concern, and sense of personal involvement that you convey. There is, for instance, a significant difference between saying "I'm sorry" rather than just "Sorry." The first shows that you, personally, identify with and feel touched by the situation they're in. Sincerity is key: you need to sound as if you really mean it, rather than just apologizing to calm them down.

Show that you understand not only the direct consequences of your actions (or inaction) but also their ramifications. In a business context, you might show that you understand how this mistake impacts their goals or the success of their business. Then show what you will do to make things right or to make sure it never happens again. What steps will you take? Be as concrete as possible.

Mistakes happen, even to the best of us. But if you put these principles into practice, even your missteps can become opportunities. When well handled, these difficult interactions can become bonding experiences, and your relationships can gain a new depth.

## Phone and E-mail

As far as charisma is concerned, phone and e-mail communication come with specific challenges. Clearly, much of nonverbal communication is lost. On the phone, you lose all visual communication, and through e-mail you lose everything but words. In addition, e-mail doesn't allow you to make midcourse corrections based on how the other person is responding.

However, the main principles remain valid: think of the timing, the setting, and the situation the person may be in. Plan the order in which you write e-mails and phone calls from least to most important, to improve with practice. You can also use visualizations before important calls and e-mails to get into the right mental state so that the right words and tone flow effortlessly.

On the phone, always ask, "Is this a good time for you?" before launching into conversation. No matter how important your information or how pleasant your call, bad timing means bad results for you. The person may be under a deadline or in the midst of a crisis.

Once you're in a conversation, pay attention. You need to be as focused as if you were face-to-face—perhaps even more so, as you have fewer visual clues (such as body language) to read and must rely only on auditory signals. Focus and be quiet. Do you think you can get away with eating, drinking, or working on your computer while talking on the phone? Not so fast. Eating and drinking are out. Even if you think you're being quiet, the person will hear you chewing and swallowing because receivers are specifically made to amplify sound. People will just as surely hear you typing and wonder what it is you're really paying attention to.

Reading your e-mail or surfing the Web are also inadvisable—too often, this will cause a slight lag in your response time, which will make you sound like your mind is wandering.

Delayed vocal response can have the same effect as delayed facial expressions. If your mind is wandering, your distraction might show. Being present on the phone is at least as important as it is in person. In fact, it's easier to project presence in person because of the many different ways you can communicate. By phone, you need to work that much harder at it for it to be received.

To communicate presence, Michael Feuer, the founder of Office-Max, says that he often closes his eyes when listening. I was struck by how good a listener he was: even on the phone, I could *feel* the intensity of his listening, how well he absorbed everything I was saying.

For best results, get up from your desk and away from all distractions. Stay standing and walk around (your voice will sound more energetic) while focusing entirely on the phone call. Just as actors do when they lend their voices to puppets, use the same body language techniques as you would in person. As actors know, this will greatly enhance your voice. Remember the smile studies that showed that listeners could identify sixteen different types of smiles based on sound alone.

Listen to what the other person is saying and what's going on in the background. If you hear the other phone line ring, ask if he needs to answer it, and assure him that it's all right with you. He'll appreciate it, and you don't want his brain split between vaguely listening to you and trying to figure out whom the other caller may be.

Here's one specific—and surprisingly effective—recommendation for phone charisma, courtesy of author Leil Lowndes: Do *not* answer the phone in a warm or friendly manner. Instead, answer crisply and professionally. Then, only after you hear who is calling, let warmth or even enthusiasm pour forth in your voice. This simple technique is an easy and effective way to make people feel special. I recommend it to all my business clients whose companies have a strong customer service component. The gains in customer satisfaction are impressive.

When writing e-mails, you can apply all the tools and principles you've learned in the past sections. Review a few of your past e-mail messages. How often does the word *I* appear, as opposed to the word *you*? Does the e-mail speak about you and your interests first? Don't try to fight your natural tendency (we're hardwired to primarily care about ourselves, after all). Instead, write out the e-mail as you normally would, but before you send it, simply cut and paste so that whatever pertains to the other person appears first *and* most prominently.

You can also do this with your marketing materials, whether it be your Web site, brochures, or anything that represents you or your company to the world. When consulting to large firms I often recommend that they go through their marketing materials (you can do the same with your e-mails) using two different-colored highlighters, one for things relating to them and the other for sentences that speak to their potential clients. If the second color doesn't predominate, they have a problem.

Just as in speaking, watch the return on investment of your sentences: measure the length of your e-mail against the value it was delivering. I give many of my clients the assignment to read over their e-mails before they send them. They must trim as many extra words as possible until there is nothing left that could be deleted. To paraphrase Antoine de Saint-Exupéry, author of *The Little Prince*: perfection is not when there is no more to add, but when there is no more to subtract.

## KEY TAKEAWAYS

- Approach difficult people individually and choose the right charisma style for each person and each situation.
- Express appreciation for their help or positive impact: it'll make them rationalize their actions in your favor.
- When delivering bad news, get into a state of compassion, and show warmth and care in your timing, body language, and verbal language.
- When delivering criticism, get into a state of goodwill, and focus the request for change on specific behaviors rather than on personal traits.
- When delivering apologies, show presence in hearing them out completely, show warmth in your apology, and show power in how you'll correct the mistake or prevent its reoccurrence.
- With phone and e-mail communication, use all the tools you've learned for in-person communication.

# 11

## Presenting with Charisma

IT WAS THE make-or-break moment of David's career. He had joined the company six months before, and although he'd worked day and night to prove his value, his coworkers hadn't yet accepted him. The CEO, who had pushed for David's hiring and really believed in his potential, decided to give him one big chance to shine. He gave David the leadership role in a project that would define the company's future. David would be presenting his proposed strategy before the entire management committee. He knew that he would be given only one shot. "Which charisma style should I use?" he asked me. "I've got to get this perfect."

Charismatic public speaking engages several charisma styles. In this section, you'll learn how to:

- Construct an inspiring and motivational presentation using visionary charisma
- Command your audience's attention and respect using authority charisma
- Connect to your audience using kindness charisma

The following recommendations are valid whether you're presenting to a very small group or a very large one. In fact, these guidelines can even be highly relevant when you're aiming to inspire, influence, or persuade an audience of one. So whether you're delivering a keynote at a conference or pitching a new idea to your boss, the following techniques will guide you through crafting your message, choosing your words, and perfecting your delivery until your presentations are simply irresistible.

## Constructing a Charismatic Message

For most of us, presentations are about convincing people of something—an idea, an initiative, a course of action. Though we'll cover a complete set of techniques for charismatic messaging, it all starts with knowing whom exactly we're aiming to persuade.

The *New York Times*—one of the best and most respected newspapers in the United States—is purportedly written so simply that a tenth grader can understand it.[1] The paper's readership includes highly educated business executives, successful entrepreneurs, and CEOs. But the editors know that their readers are often thinking about six things at once, juggling far too many balls in the air.

You, too, will often be communicating with attention-starved audiences who will devote only part of their attention to what you are saying. If you can keep this one fact firmly in mind while you craft your presentation, and design your speech accordingly, you'll be more effective than 80 percent of the speakers out there.

Let's say you're giving a presentation at four P.M. on a Wednesday afternoon. Your audience has been thinking, acting, interacting, and dealing with issues since they woke up that morning. Whatever has been occupying their minds since then doesn't magically vanish when they enter the room to attend your presentation. It all stays in their heads, and you may have to compete with it for their attention.

Select the single most important idea you want to convey and make it as crystal clear and easy to understand as you possibly can. Ideally, you should be able to articulate your message in one sentence.

Within this one main message, have three to five key supporting points. The human brain thinks in triads (from Olympic medals to fairy tales, it's three medals, three princes, three bears), and it cannot immediately comprehend numbers greater than four.* Each one of your supporting points should open with entertaining anecdotes, fascinating facts, compelling statistics, great metaphors, examples, and analogies.

**Stories** have a particularly strong impact on people. In fact, audiences will often remember first the story, and only second the point the story was making. Since the dawn of time, people have been telling stories as a way to transmit information to one another.

For your stories to be most effective, choose characters that are similar to the people in your audience to make them more relatable and make them as entertaining (and short!) as a Hollywood sneak preview. When you're delivering a presentation, you're in the entertainment business, whether you know it or not. So make the story dramatic. You're calling on visionary charisma here; and as with all forms of charisma, you're tapping into people's emotional side.

Using **metaphors** and **analogies** can be a highly effective way of capturing your audience's imagination. For maximum impact, choose images and analogies that would appeal to a young audience. The speeches that give us a feeling of awe and wonder are those that appeal to our childhood roots. If you're mentioning the fact that there is untapped potential in your customer base, liken yourselves to "bounty hunters" or "treasure hunters" searching for "hidden gold."

Make even **numbers and statistics** personal, meaningful, and relatable for your audience. Steve Jobs did this masterfully when he gave his audience two ways of measuring iPhone sales: "Apple sold four million iPhones so far," he said. "That amounts to selling *twenty thousand iPhones every single day.*" He did even better with memory

---

* Above four, we must engage different, slower brain processes. It takes us more time to remember the items, and we do not remember them as accurately. Assessments of one to four items are rapid, accurate, and confident through a process called *subitizing*. As the number of items increases beyond this amount, judgments are made with decreasing accuracy and confidence. In addition, response times rise in a dramatic fashion.

cards: "This memory card has twelve gigabytes of memory. That means it holds enough music for you to travel to the moon and back."

Whether you use a story, example, number, or statistic, make sure that you close with either a clear point or a transition to the action step you want your audience to take. Remember to make this so simple that even a multitasking, partially listening audience member would get it.

When you craft the closing of your presentation, keep in mind that we remember primarily beginnings and endings. Just as you want to start on a high note, you also want to end on a high note, so avoid ending with Q&A. It's hard to have a question-and-answer period as compelling and energetic as your main speech. Almost inevitably, the Q&A period lowers the energy.

Personally, I avoid formal Q&A entirely. Instead, my introducer warns the audience that there will be no Q&A session at the end, so their one and only chance to ask questions is during the speech. This has the added advantage of increasing the audience's involvement, participation, and general energy level.

Once you've created your structure, you can start crafting your sentences. The pointers given in chapter 8 will also help you choose your words here:

- It's all about them. Use the word *you* as often as possible. Use their words, their stories, their metaphors: *hole in one* for golfers, *shipwreck* for sailors. Try also to match your verbs to your audience: *lead* or *initiate* for businessmen, *build* for engineers, *craft* for artists.
- Get graphic. The brain thinks in pictures, so choose language that is vivid and sensory-rich.
- Beware of negotiations: avoid the "no problem" trap.
- Keep it short. With each sentence, ask yourself: What value is this sentence delivering? Even when crafting stories, give only details that convey comprehension or enjoyment. Think sneak preview, not full-length movie.

## Creating a Charismatic Appearance

You're going to be in the spotlight, so think carefully about the message you want to convey through your clothing. Is it authority? Power? Warmth? Keep in mind what social psychologists' research reveals about chromatic effects:[2]

- Red conveys energy, passion. Wear red to wake up an audience.
- Black shows you're serious and that you won't take no for an answer.
- White exudes honesty and innocence, which is why defendants often choose it in the courtroom.
- Blue emits trust. The darker the shade, the deeper the level of trust it elicits.
- Gray is a good neutral, the quintessential color of business.
- Orange and yellow are not recommended. Because they are the first to attract the human eye, they are also the first to tire it.

Based on these guidelines, one of my clients adopted a go-to combination whenever she had a difficult message to convey: navy suit, white shirt, white pearl stud earrings (perhaps because pearls seem conservative, they have been shown to further enhance credibility).

In order to project confidence and move with ease on stage, you also need to *feel* physically confident. Make sure nothing is hindering your movements, impairing your balance, or in any other way diminishing your comfort. It's hard enough to feel fully comfortable on stage while facing an audience alone, without having to deal with physical discomfort on top of it all! This means wearing clothing you can breathe in and shoes that are stable. Your brain's first job is to monitor your safety, whether it's your ability to escape predators or your ability to stay upright. If it has to spend any of its attention worrying about your breathing or your balance, that means that at least one part of your attention can't be devoted to your speaking success. Why waste any of your focus?

## Rehearsing for Charisma

When celebrity comedian Jerry Seinfeld finally got his first chance at the big time—a six-minute spot on *The Tonight Show*—he practiced those six minutes for six *months*. As he recalls, "By the end of those six months, you could have slapped me, shaken me, or held me under water, I would have still given you those six minutes with pitch-perfect timing."

Charisma takes practice. Steve Jobs, who appeared so masterful on stage, was known to rehearse important presentations relentlessly. Just as a duck appears to be sailing smoothly on the surface of a lake while powerfully paddling below the waterline, it takes a whole lot of effort for a presentation to appear effortless. When a speech is important I practice until every breath is perfect, because knowing I've got the speech so well mastered allows me to be spontaneous. I know that I have muscle memory to fall back on.

When you know that a particular presentation will have a significant impact on your career, it's worth rehearsing until you feel that it's part of your very bones. One interesting technique used by magicians is to run through the entire presentation once with their eyes closed.

Another good practice is to have your speech audiotaped or, better yet, videotaped, and to count what professional speakers call *irritants*. These are any sounds or movements that do not add to your message. Because the audience is watching your every move, every sound and facial expression you make is a form of communication that demands a portion of their attention. Be strategic: make sure you're getting value out of each nonverbal gesture you make, and limit superfluous gestures to avoid wasting any bit of your audience's attention.

If you've been videotaped, ask three people to point out any unnecessary gestures—any tics or distractions. If you've been audiotaped, have the speech transcribed and ask them to note every "um" and "ah." Don't do it yourself—it's much harder to hear our own irritants, and transcription services are inexpensive.

If you can, perform the entire speech at least once in front of a live audience as a trial run. No matter how well you've practiced your presentation on your own, the dynamics change dramatically when you present the same information to living, breathing people.

Professional stand-up comedians organize trial runs for themselves, performing at smaller clubs where they can test out new material in a lower-stakes environment. Jerry Seinfeld still does this, occasionally making unscheduled appearances in New York City comedy clubs to work on his act.

Like comedians who perform at small clubs to perfect their acts, you, too, need a place where you can break in your sales pitch, your script, or your interview lines in front of real live people. Ideally, you would find an audience somewhat similar to the one you're going to address (whether in age or profession or level of experience), but in a pinch, friends and family will do.

## Projecting Power

Charismatic speakers know how to give the impression that they're as comfortable walking across the stage as they would be walking across their living room. This is called *owning the stage,* and there are three tricks to making it happen.

First, when you stand, be sure to have a wide stance, well balanced on both feet. Not only will you feel more confident, you'll also look more confident, more stable, than if you were standing on one foot. Wide, stable stances also help you to project confidence. Be the gorilla!

Second, practice without a podium or a lectern. Speaking behind one can give the impression that you're fearful to venture out, and prefer staying behind the safety of a shield. It also makes the presentation much more static. Think of the stereotype of a boring presentation: a lecturer who stands immobile at his lectern, reading from his notes in a monotone voice. Moving comfortably around the stage will make you appear much more confident, powerful, and charismatic.

Third, find the right volume to project confidence. This is tricky, as so much can depend on the microphone you're given that day or how the sound system is set up. Your best bet is, just before the speech, to ask a few people sitting in the back of the room to be your sound experts and give you a prearranged signal to raise or lower your volume if need be.

## Projecting Warmth

Franklin Delano Roosevelt changed everything. At least, as far as presidential speeches go.

Up until then, presidential addresses were formal affairs given in solemn tones. And then came FDR and his "fireside chats." Suddenly the experience of listening to the president of the United States became a warm, intimate conversation. Today, great public speakers emulate the fireside chat atmosphere: no matter how many people are in the audience, you feel as if they're speaking directly to you.

A fireside chat is a comfortable conversation that creates a sense of intimacy. Imagine sitting by a fire telling stories to your favorite friends or having a comfortable conversation with just one person. To make your audience feel particularly special, speak as if you were sharing a secret.

Another way to make people feel special as you roam about the stage is to give one to two seconds of eye contact per person. Though this may sound like a short amount of time, I promise that in the midst of a speech it feels like an eternity. But it's worth it. This is how charismatic speakers give you the feeling that they are speaking directly to you—giving each person in the audience the feeling that they shared a real connection. You can make this easier by making eye contact first with the people who seem the most animated—those who are smiling, showing interest, or nodding.

To create this sense of comfort and intimacy, David (the new executive who was preparing his crucial presentation) focused on projecting warmth. He made good use of the internal tools detailed in chapter 5, especially the angel wings visualization. He told himself that the people he was presenting to were *his* angels, gathered here to work together. He told me that he felt a kind of warm pride, a surge of affection for his audience that he knew was palpable.

David also focused on increasing his voice fluctuation to enhance persuasiveness, on smiling when he wanted a warm voice, and on dropping the intonation of his voice when he wanted to convey confidence and authority.

David called me within hours of delivering his presentation with the wonderful news that it had been a major triumph: he'd been so inspirational that people came up to him for days afterward to express their admiration.

## Pause, Breathe, and Slow Down

When I woke up on the morning of my very first speech, I was feeling quite confident. It was a short, easy piece, encouraging my fellow students to donate blood for the local children's hospital. I'd been granted the first five minutes of a plenary lecture, so I knew that I would be facing a full auditorium, but saying a few words for a good cause seemed easy. I was eighteen years old, and though I had never faced an audience of twelve hundred before, I thought, "Really, how hard could this be?" In fact, I was quite eager to bask in the spotlight and climbed the stairs leading to the stage with assurance and aplomb.

But with each step, more butterflies started fluttering in my stomach. By the time I reached the top, I was feeling ever so slightly out of breath. When I turned to face the audience, reality hit me like a ton of bricks: a sea of faces, twelve hundred pairs of eyes looking expectantly at me. My mind froze in panic, and I went through the entire speech nearly without breathing. In case you were wondering, this is officially *not a good idea*. By the time I finished I could barely see, the lights blurring in front of my eyes. To this day, I'm not quite sure just how I made it off the platform.

For the next five years, every speech outline I prepared was emblazoned with one bold word scrawled across the top of every page: *BREATHE!* Today, when learning a new speech, I'll often still include notes to myself every few pages: *Pause. Breathe. Slow Down.*

Though this may feel unnecessary in the comfort of home or office, things are very different on stage. In the heat of the moment, with adrenaline flowing through your veins, your brain speeds up.

This is why everything around you can seem to be happening in slow motion. With your brain going on hyperdrive, you'll also tend to speak faster. But your audience is still operating at normal speed.

In addition to practicing, it can be helpful to ask a member of the audience to give you a prearranged signal reminding you to slow down. It's really worth paying attention to your tempo because the slower you speak, the more thoughtful and deliberate you will sound, and the more attention people will give to what you say.

During that first speech, I felt certain that if I were to pause even for an instant, I'd lose my audience's attention forever. It takes courage to pause. But, just as in conversations, pausing regularly during your presentations is an important skill to acquire. It's one of the hallmarks of effective speakers and really is one of the key tools for great speaking. Throughout your speech, pause frequently, deliberately. Have the confidence to make your listeners wait for your words. It's called a *dramatic pause* for a reason: it adds drama.

After delivering a key point or an impactful story, pause for a few seconds to let your audience take it in. If you've just used humor, have the courage to wait for the laughter to swell and subside before you move on. Pausing is important both to begin and to end your speeches. When you walk on stage, come to the center, face the audience, and stop. Remain completely silent as you count three full seconds while slowly sweeping your eyes across the crowd and making eye contact. This may feel endless, but it will be well worth it. Nothing rivets an audience's attention like this kind of silence.

Pausing is equally critical to end your presentations. Don't run off stage. *Sicilienne* is a slow, somber piece of music by composer Gabriel Fauré. A young musician told me: "The pause at the very end, right after the last note, is so critical that without it, the entire performance is ruined. On the other hand, when done right, the audience is so spellbound that often not a single person stirs for a full minute." After your last words, pause, then say "Thank you" and stay there while you endure the applause for a few seconds.

If you're having trouble pausing, try color-coding your speeches. I used this technique for years when I first started out. I would use one blue bar for a one-beat pause, two red bars for a two-beat pause (having the difference both in color and in markings helps in the heat of the moment, when your mind is racing and you can't think clearly).

I would also underline any part that needed warmth, to indicate that I should smile. Yes, it really worked—people actually told me I seemed wonderfully at ease, fluid, spontaneous, and natural.

You can try out a lot of these tips in low-stakes situations, for instance, during a parent-teacher association, service club, or homeowners' meeting. Let's say you're at your next PTA meeting. You've always thought it would be nice if the school's fading hallway could be repainted. You're going to get a few minutes to present your case, and you need to keep everyone focused on what you're going to say. Since this issue is really not a big deal for you one way or the other, this would be a good time to try out the techniques you've just learned: voice fluctuation, strategic pauses, and intonation drops to make your message compelling.

## Midcourse Corrections

Imagine that you're in the middle of a presentation, and you suddenly make a mistake. You stutter, you say the wrong thing, you miss a point, or your mind simply goes blank.

If you let your internal critic take over and start berating you for this, you risk launching your fight-or-flight response. Your body would shut down "unnecessary" functions such as your brain's ability to think rationally—probably the last thing you'd want in that particular situation.

So what to do?

If you've luckily noticed the critical thoughts before the corresponding emotions fully blossomed, aim for a quick perspective shift (rewriting your reality). Just considering, even for a second, the mistake you made as a *good* thing can be enough to stop the fight-or-flight response in its tracks. Because the brain's first reaction to new concepts is to accept them as valid, in the extra second it takes disbelief to arise, you will already have moved on with renewed confidence.

You can tell yourself, for instance, that business moguls and entertainers make mistakes purposefully to make themselves more relatable to the audience. Sam Walton (the founder of Walmart) would drop his notes on his way to the lectern. Frank Sinatra would carefully mess up his shirt collar before stepping on stage. You're in good company.

If the negative emotions have already arisen, you're going to need to flood your body with oxytocin to turn off the fight-or-flight response. To do this, follow the instructions below:

## Putting It into Practice: Midcourse Corrections

♦ Check your body. Make sure that no tense posture is worsening your internal state.

♦ Take a deep breath and relax your body.

♦ Destigmatize and dedramatize. Remember that this happens to everyone, and it will pass.

♦ If any negative thoughts are present, remember that they're just thoughts, and not necessarily valid.

♦ Find little things to be grateful for: your ability to breathe, the fact that you will still be alive by the end of this.

♦ Imagine getting a great hug from someone you trust for twenty seconds (of course, you may not have twenty seconds, but if you do, this is remarkably effective).

Once your threat response is quieted down, to bring yourself back into a state of confidence remember a moment in your life when you felt absolute triumph. Thanks to your brain's inability to distinguish imagination from reality, your body will be filled with the same cocktail of chemicals (yes, we're helping you play chemist with your brain) as it was during that confidence-filled moment, thereby changing your body language into exactly what you need to be impressive, persuasive, and inspiring again.

Though this may seem like a lot of steps, the whole sequence can happen in less than two seconds. With practice, this becomes so natural, it happens at lightning speed and you're back in grounded confidence within seconds. The human mind is astonishingly quick and agile.

Practice this process with little crises as often as possible, so that when a big crisis hits, it's second nature. Use the go-to visualization you developed in chapter 5.

You could practice this during meetings. Imagine that you're not completely happy with an answer you gave and your inner critic is acting up. While the rest of the group converses, run through this midcourse correction before you speak up again.

## Speech Day: Getting into the Zone

The single most important guideline for a successful speech is simple: make it about them, not about you. As soon as you start worrying about yourself—wondering how you're doing, or if this or that sentence was good enough—self-criticism can easily arise. If, instead, you can make it all about your audience—wondering how they're doing—you take the focus off yourself, lift your self-consciousness, and get into a state of goodwill, which will be read and appreciated by the audience.

Use any of the tools you learned in chapters 4 and 5 either to get yourself into this state of goodwill and stay there or to get back there whenever you need to.

### Putting It into Practice:
### Speech Day Checklist

♦ Arrive early if you can; walk the stage to visualize and own the stage.

♦ Go into a quiet room nearby, and use internal tools such as visualization to get into a state of confidence and warmth.

♦ Pause before you start. Count three beats, facing the audience, before you begin to speak.

*(continued on next page)*

*(continued from previous page)*

♦ During the presentation, *expect* things to go wrong— whether an external disruption or your flubbing something.

♦ Use the midcourse corrections tools you've just learned. Take it with humanity and invite the audience into this mistake as a shared joke.

♦ Throughout your speech, remember to pause, breathe, and slow down.

♦ Don't run off stage; pause after your last words.

## KEY TAKEAWAYS

- Your presentation should have one main, simple, crystal-clear message, supported by three to five key points.
- Support each point with an entertaining story, interesting statistic, concrete example, or vivid metaphor.
- Make your presentation short and entertaining. Watch the value of each sentence.
- Arrive early if you can; walk the stage to visualize and own it.
- Use a wide, well-balanced stance and take up as much space as possible on stage. Limit superfluous gestures that distract the audience's attention.
- Speak as if you're sharing a secret with the audience, telling them something special and confidential.
- Use smiles and fluctuation to warm your voice.
- Keep eye contact for one to two seconds per person.
- Pause frequently and deliberately to show confidence and add drama as well as give yourself a chance to breathe.

# 12

# Charisma in a Crisis

CHARISMA IS PARTICULARLY effective during times of uncertainty, ambiguity, or crisis. "Leaders perceived as charismatic are rated higher when times are tough and anxiety is high," Omar Sultan Haque of Harvard's department of psychology told me.

It's easier to be perceived as charismatic during a crisis because people facing an emergency are more readily affected by a leader's magnetism;[1] they become "charisma hungry." Whether it was Churchill's ability to rouse England's spirits and inspire her people to stand while the rest of Europe fell, Napoleon taking France by storm as it was reeling from the French Revolution, or Gandhi voicing a clear path during India's identity crisis, people who respond to crisis with bold, decisive actions will be perceived as charismatic.

If you find yourself in a crisis, it's actually an opportunity to gain charisma—*if* you play your cards right. This chapter will show you how.

**First, retain at least a certain measure of equanimity.** Most charismatic leaders are known for their ability to remain (or appear) calm even in the midst of turbulent circumstances. As you know, anxiety impacts how you feel, how you perform, and how others perceive you and react to you. It's often immediately visible in your body language.

As a leader, your body language already has a ripple effect through the company in normal times. This effect is only magnified in times of crisis, because crises put leaders in the spotlight, with people anxiously watching their every move. Stress systems go on constant, low-grade alert; primal brains take over, leading people to react to your body language far more than to your words. Your body language will have an even greater emotional contagion effect than usual. It becomes critical for you to maintain the right internal state so that you can broadcast the right body language. To keep cool, use all the internal tools—this is where they really shine. I particularly recommend the following techniques:

- Check your physiology often, both for your own sake (it affects your psychology) and for that of others (it will be "caught" by them and will spread).
- Skillfully handle internal negativity: destigmatize, dedramatize, and neutralize the negative perceptions that may be crowding your mind.
- Rewrite reality to whatever degree is helpful. To get out of a pessimistic state, find a few different ways of viewing the situation positively.
- Use visualizations to keep yourself in the right state. For instance, a responsibility transfer could be useful for reducing anxiety.

Refer as often as necessary to the midcourse corrections checklist found on page 198, which walks you through handling critical moments step by step. Practice this with little crises as often as possible, so that when a big crisis hits, this flow is second nature.

**Second, express high expectations**. Sometimes, simply assigning to people the labels you want them to live up to is enough. After hearing that they were considered charitable, New Haven housewives gave far more money to a canvasser from the Multiple Sclerosis Association than they ever had before.[2] The mere knowledge that they were viewed as charitable caused these women to make their actions consistent with others' perception of them.

After analyzing more than three dozen studies of charismatic leadership, Wharton School professor Robert House concluded that "expressing high performance expectations" of people while "communicating a high degree of confidence" in their ability to meet those expectations was the hallmark of charismatic leadership.

Think of the people you want your charisma to impact. What standard would you like them to live up to or exceed? Express this expectation as if you have full confidence that they can live up to it. Better yet, act like you assume they already are meeting these standards.

**Third, articulate a vision.** A charismatic vision is what will give your charisma staying power when the crisis is over. Think of Nelson Mandela, whose vision of unity and modernism for South Africa was so powerful that even after the crisis of apartheid had passed and his service as president was over, he continued to be seen as a transnational leader for all of southern Africa and an influential voice in international politics.

On the other hand, President George H. W. Bush, who had enjoyed 90 percent approval ratings during the Gulf War, was voted out of office the very next year. His charisma had soared during the crisis, but he had (in his own words) neglected "the vision thing."

To be charismatic, your vision must vividly illustrate the difference between the way things are now and the way they could be. Charismatic leaders often point out deficiencies in the status quo, contrast this picture to a glorious future, and show how they intend to get there. Though this might sound complex, it's something many of us do already. Even salespeople seek the deficiency in their potential clients' present condition (which will be remedied, of course, through the purchase of their goods or services).

Having a vision isn't enough; you also must be able to communicate it. Use the tools you learned in the previous chapter to craft a message and deliver it in the most charismatic way.

**Once you have expressed your vision, be bold and decisive.**

By the winter of 1815, Napoleon, defeated and humiliated by the French Royal Army, had been condemned to a life of exile on the island of Elba. The man who had risen from humble beginnings to lead the French army and crown himself emperor of France was now alive only because his attempt at suicide failed. In the last few days of February, he escaped the island and landed on the shores of France with nothing. He had neither power nor money, and had last been seen in a humiliating defeat.

And yet the sheer force of his visionary charisma drew people to him once again. He conveyed complete confidence in his ability to sweep through the country and regain power. He gave people a compelling vision of a country free from the long-hated ruling class.

He had nothing but a vision and charisma, yet that was enough. The unthinkable was happening: with no money to pay soldiers' wages, without even enough food to feed them, Napoleon was somehow gathering troops and proclaiming his intention to reclaim the throne.

The French court was incensed. Marshal Ney was asked to lead the charge to quash the ruffian once and for all. On the day of his departure, Ney made a public commitment to the whole court that he would "bring back the usurper in a cage." He then set off from Paris, marching at the head of the royal armies even as Napoleon was leading his much smaller band of men to meet him. On the morning of March 7, the two armies met at dawn.

On one side stood the massive French regiment; on the other, Napoleon's scrawny army. Napoleon emerged, alone. He crossed the divide, and when he was within gunshot range, he planted himself in front of the opposing troops—the same army that he had once led. And he shouted: "Here I am. Do you want to kill your emperor? Go ahead."

The soldiers, overcome with emotion, responded with cries of "Long live the emperor!" and crossed the divide to stand by his side. Ney himself abjured his mission and joined Napoleon, and they all followed as he marched upon Paris to reclaim the throne.

Studies consistently show that in times of crisis, people instinctively turn to individuals who are bold, confident, and decisive. Crisis creates uncertainty, which creates angst, and people will cling to whatever they feel diminishes this angst. This is why faith, vision, and authority have such power in times of crisis.

## KEY TAKEAWAYS

- Charisma is particularly effective in crisis situations.
- Stay in a calm, confident internal state so that your emotional contagion effect is positive.
- Express high expectations of people, and communicate your complete confidence in their ability to rise to the occasion.
- Articulate a bold vision, show your confidence in your ability to realize that vision, and act decisively to achieve it.

# 13

## The Charismatic Life

### Rising to the Challenge

WHEN THEY HEAR what I do for a living, people often ask if I spend most of my time with brilliant nerds. I respond with, "Actually, many of my clients are highly successful, highly charismatic executives who come to me not just to raise their charisma level but to learn how to handle its consequences." That, generally, is when they give me a blank look.

Yes, it's great to have charisma. And yes, it will make you more influential, more persuasive, and more inspiring. People will like you, trust you, and want to be led by you. But charisma does have its downsides. All forms of charisma come at a cost; what the cost is depends on the charisma style you choose. In this final chapter you will learn a few potential side effects of charisma and how to best handle them.

## You Become a Magnet for Praise
## as Well as Envy

As you become increasingly magnetic, you may find yourself attracting praise, admiration, and envy. When the team succeeds, credit
will naturally flow to you. It's *your* name the higher-ups remember,
*your* contribution, and *your* face they put on the success. And that's
all great. Until, that is, others start resenting you for it. At best, their
envy will make them feel alienated. At worst, they will try to sabo-
tage you.

You're going to have to compensate for your charisma in order to
limit the jealousy and resentment others may feel. You have three
choices: you can refuse the glory, reflect the glory, or transfer the
glory.

Refusing the glory means trying to self-efface—to minimize the
praise you're getting. You can try to bring yourself back down through
self-deprecation, downplaying compliments and praise. But we've
seen how this can backfire, as you're essentially contradicting your
admirers and making them feel wrong.

Reflecting the glory means highlighting others' contributions.
This works well, and has the additional bonus of making you look
modest. Something as simple as "Thanks! We were really lucky to
have Susan checking the financials and Bill doing his graphic magic."
But sometimes, no matter how much you reflect, some people will
still become envious or resentful of your magnetism and your success.
You may need to go a step further, which is to transfer the glory.

The CEO of a large multinational bank had asked me to coach
his entire executive team. Nancy, one of the senior executives, was a
highly charismatic rising star running the bank's southwest region.
In fact, she was so successful that the CEO asked one of Nancy's
peers—Kevin, a veteran with the bank—to send his team to learn
how Nancy ran her group and adopt her best practices. Accordingly,
Kevin's team arrived for a one-week visit to Nancy's headquarters.
Nancy was honored, delighted, and determined to do a great job.
Until, that is, she learned from one of her visitors that Kevin had

been bad-mouthing her to his team ever since the CEO's request came in.

"How should I handle this?" she asked me. I asked Nancy to put herself in Kevin's position and really try to experience the situation as he might be living it right now. "Imagine that you're a veteran with the bank. And you've been told to send *your* team to go learn from a young whippersnapper with ten years' less experience than you. How would that make you feel?"

Perhaps Kevin felt that he was no longer seen as successful, or at least not as successful as this less experienced "upstart." He might well have been feeling insecure, no longer admired or respected, and he might have been focusing these negative feelings on Nancy's success in the form of resentment.

I told Nancy that the only way her success wouldn't make him feel envious or resentful was if he could see it as *his* success, too. I encouraged her to give Kevin this sense of ownership by finding some way he might have participated in her success. I asked Nancy to think of something she might have learned from him, or some way in which he could have inspired her. "Oh, for heaven's sake. Do I have to?" she grumbled. "It would really be worth it," I answered.

It took Nancy a couple of minutes, but she eventually did come up with something: "Well, there was this one time in the management meeting where Alan started complaining about how cumbersome the new systems were. Kevin found a great, upbeat way of encouraging Alan to accept that as a known parameter and move on. The way he phrased it was just the right tone of humorous chiding. I'll go with that."

I also reminded Nancy of the Ben Franklin Effect. She could periodically ask Kevin for his thoughts and opinions to show him that she values his opinion, helping him to feel respected again. She could then go back to him later to tell him the impact of these thoughts or opinions.

Giving people a sense of ownership for your success is a great way to prevent resentment and engender good feelings, such as pride and loyalty, instead. This technique is, in fact, known as a Clinton classic. During his tenure in the White House, Bill Clinton was known to go around asking everyone, from his chef to his janitor, for their opinion on foreign policy. He'd listen intently, and in subsequent conversations would refer back to the opinion they'd offered. When people feel that they've had a hand in "making" you, they feel a certain ownership of and identification with you, and therefore a certain responsibility for your success.

As you become increasingly successful and visible, it might be worth regularly launching a brief envy-prevention campaign. Warning: you *must* be sincere in whatever it is you choose to say. One of my clients, when learning the following sequence, exclaimed: "Great! A shortcut! From now on, I can give people the feeling I care about them without actually liking them in the least, right?" Wrong. First, as you now know, the vast majority of the time, if you don't mean what you say, people will intuitively know. They'll feel it on a gut level. Second, expressing something we don't believe leads to cognitive dissonance, which uses up our focus, diverts our attention, and thus impairs our performance. Insincerity just isn't worth the toll it takes.

With this said, think of a dozen people who could matter to your career. Then reach out to them by phone or e-mail with the following envy-prevention technique:

**Justification.** Create an excuse for contacting the person; it can't seem completely out of the blue: "I was talking to Sue and your name came up" or "Bob made me think of you and that time when . . ." When I'm coaching clients, I tell them to use our session as a justification. After all, I have indeed asked them to think of the people who matter to their career, so they can truthfully say, "I was working with my executive coach, and your name came up."

**Appreciation.** Thank the person for what they've done for you. You can thank someone for taking time to meet you, whether in person or by phone, especially if you spoke with them for the first time or for a long time. You can also acknowledge good advice or interesting information someone gave you.

(continued on next page)

(continued from previous page)

**Lay it all out.** Demonstrate exactly how the person helped you. Acknowledge their effort: "I know you didn't have to do . . ." or "I know you went out of your way to do . . ."

**Impact.** Let them know the positive impact they've had on you. What did they do or say or what example did they set that changed you for the better? What do you do or say differently because of what they did or said or because of the example they set for you? How is your life or your behavior different? Tell them the difference it made to you personally; make it dramatic. People love to feel important.

**Responsibility.** The Justification-Appreciation-Laying-out-the-Impact sequence creates a feeling of Responsibility (JALIR). It gives people a feeling of vested interest in your success. Give them as much credit as you can. Make them feel that they own your success and they will feel driven to help you continue to succeed.

Envy and resentment are challenges mostly experienced by individuals with "high power" styles of charisma, such as authority and visionary. So if you want to emanate those styles, it's worth doing the JALIR sequence regularly. Once a month put a reminder in your calendar to pick people to give the JALIR sequence to, or to ask for their opinions, or to follow up on those opinions and show the impact they had.

Here's a JALIR e-mail that a client of mine recently sent out:

Dan—

I was just thinking about you the other day when someone asked me who were the people who'd had an impact on my career. I don't know if I ever mentioned how much I learned from working with you on the finance project. I'll always remember the way you handled that one hostile phone call—how calm you remained throughout. It taught me one could stay even-keeled no matter what the client was saying. These days, when I feel I'm losing patience on a call, I often remind myself, "Hey, remember how Dan handled that hostile call?"

Oh, and the advice you gave me on strategic pricing? I've been following it ever since. In fact, it played a key role in the success of the department's largest proposal this year.

All in all, I guess I just want to say thanks. Though you may not realize it, you had a big impact on me, so please take some credit for whatever success you see me have!

Best,

Jim

## People Can Reveal Too Much

When I first started coaching business executives, I delivered value just by improving their communication skills. These were practical, targeted tools and techniques that they could practice, fine-tune, and make their own. During the process, a strong intellectual connection would form between us. This was comfortable for all involved and made the coaching process rewarding as well as highly successful.

But gradually, as I started experimenting with the internal skills you learned in the previous chapters, I found that in addition to the intellectual connection, a strong emotional connection would form during coaching sessions.

Sometimes, the emotional connection and the intellectual connection would combine into one superstrong connection. As one client described it, it was as if I were creating a force field around us, a cocoon, a container within which magic would often happen. And that's when I started to notice a strange phenomenon.

In the moment, the experience would feel magical, a real "high" for both my clients and myself. They'd do extraordinarily deep work, gaining profound insights and revelatory epiphanies. I'd often be surprised by how much they would reveal but thrilled that they progressed so much further than either of us had expected.

And yet repeatedly, the very clients who'd spontaneously shared such personal revelations and expressed their awe and wonder in gaining such insights would then disappear from the face of the

earth. I couldn't understand why. Having reached such extraordinary depth and having made so much progress in just one session, I
imagined they'd be eager to return. It wasn't until I described this
situation to a veteran executive coach that I understood where my
error lay.

My fellow coach, Eli, was a former Israeli Army officer with decades of experience. "Of course they disappear," he told me. "They're
recoiling in shame. During the session, you created such a strong
force field that it *does* feel like magic to them, and they're on a high—
almost inebriated. In that altered state, they share much more than
they normally would and go much further than they would if 'so-
ber.'"

My heart sank as I realized how well his explanation fit. Eli continued: "A few hours later, or the next morning, as they come out of
the trance, their ego wakes up, realizes how much they shared, how
far they went, and moans, 'Oh, what have you done?'"

He related this to the experience of waking up the morning after
a night of debauchery with the horrified shame of realizing what
you've done under the influence. And he concluded, "Never take
people deeper than they're ready to go. It's *your* job to not give in to
the high, to not let them reveal more than they're ready for."

Over the years I've realized that this feeling of a safe cocoon can
have other side effects. Sometimes, without realizing it, as people feel
so safe and strong, they'll venture too close to their own demons,
ones that they're not ready to face. This challenge is one of the few
downsides that can accompany kindness or focus charisma.

I remember one extraordinary session where I led my client from
epiphany to epiphany. Oh, it was a high. He saw so much of his potential, so much of himself, he told me the scales had fallen from his eyes.
He said he felt lifted, renewed, and reborn. I thought this was quite a
triumph, gave him a few guidelines, and sent him on his way.

I didn't hear from him for a month. I was a bit concerned, but assumed he was focusing on his "homework." When he finally called,
he told me what had happened: "You can't imagine the impact, the
effect, that half hour with you had. I holed up in my apartment for a
week. For a week it absorbed my whole world. Turned it upside down."

Yes, he had emerged, and, like a phoenix rising from the ashes, his steady ascent through the company since that week is something he thanks me for to this day. *But we were lucky.* I'd unknowingly walked him right into the deepest waters, and wasn't holding his hand as I left him to figure out how to sink or swim.

In the years since, under the guidance of wiser mentors, I've learned not to give in to the magical feeling that charisma can create and to put the brakes on so that my clients' comfort builds gradually, over a number of sessions.

It's not easy, however, to slow people down when they're in the middle of this kind of experience without leaving them feeling hurt and rejected. Here are a few "soft landing" approaches to try:

1. Pay attention. When they start sharing, ask yourself: Will they regret having said this tomorrow?
2. As soon as you hear them start to say something you think they may regret, interject a "me, too" story. This is the *one* case where interruption is warranted. Ideally, this would be something you've personally experienced, second best would be something that someone close to you has experienced, and third best would be something you've heard about. The "me, too" interjection accomplishes three things:

   First, this forces them to pause, interrupts their flow, and gives them a chance to slow down the stream of personal revelations.

   Second, they get to hear something similar to what they've just shared told by someone else, and with this switching of roles, a chance to hear how revelatory their own sharing was. They can then decide whether they feel comfortable continuing on that path.

   Last, this will help them when they come off the high. If their ego recoils in shame over having shared too much, they can cling to the fact that the person they shared so much with revealed something similar.

3. If it's too late and they've already gone too far, show them that you are placing their revelations in the whole-scope context of all you know about them—that whatever they are revealing is just one piece of a much bigger picture that contains many elements they can be proud of. Say something like, "Wow, I never would have guessed you had such a strong impostor syndrome, too, considering all your accomplishments."

4. You can also aim to make them feel admired for having shared and revealed so much. Remember, what you're trying to counteract is shame, and few things work better for this than admiration. For example: "You're showing some serious courage to be delving so deep. That's impressive."

Let's say you're meeting a client for the first time. The meeting starts off great—the client clearly likes you, and you turn on your focus or kindness charisma full blast. You can feel the comfort growing, and the client increasingly reveals his plans for the company and explains where he'd most like your help. So far, so good—very good.

But as the meeting progresses and the comfort level keeps growing, the client tells you how amazing it is that he feels so at ease with you. He starts revealing more about his own personal thoughts and views about how his company is doing, how *he's* doing, what his hopes and dreams and fears are—even his insecurities.

Your job is to listen attentively to each sentence and, using one of the techniques above, aim to break the flow when you think the potential backlash for these revelations would be too damaging.

When you turn on your charisma full blast, you create a kind of reality distortion field around you. It's a bit like hypnosis; people can go into an altered state in your presence. And just as a hypnotist must take care when leading people out of a trance, so must you. You're putting them under the spell of your presence, so help them ease out of the altered state as well.

## You're in the Spotlight and
## Held to Higher Standards

Celebrities and CEOs have at least one thing in common: they're always on display. Whether they know it or not, whether they like it or not, they're almost always under scrutiny. This is another possible side effect of high-power charisma styles such as authority and visionary.

Business book author Marshall Goldsmith told me that many CEOs worry about the pressure to always be on their best behavior. "For them, it's always 'showtime.' They have to demonstrate charisma even when listening to the most tedious PowerPoint presentation, because everyone in the room is looking at them, as well as (or even more than) at the presenter."

Because charismatic people seem endowed with extra powers, we expect more of them than we do of others. We expect greater results and will not be content, much less impressed, with good but not extraordinary performance.

If their performance is poor, the criticism can be much more severe than it would be for an "average person." When asked what becomes of the failed charismatics in the world of business, Harvard professor Rakesh Khurana says: "We do what we've always done to our failed messiahs: we crucify them."

J. R. Wurster, the CEO of a small Los Angeles–based film company, gives off such a laid-back vibe that he's the last person I'd have expected to feel pressured by the spotlight. And yet when I mentioned this issue, he knew exactly what I meant: "This pressure to always overperform can really burn out charismatic people. We no longer allow ourselves to be human, and no one can live like that."

The answer? Allow yourself to be human. This means both *accepting* humanity and *showing* your humanity. Which means both accepting vulnerability and (gasp!) showing vulnerability. I know, I know, even just considering this may feel highly uncomfortable. And yet I promise it's worth it. Hayes Barnard (the charismatic CEO of Paramount Equity) told me that "executives who are very transparent and vulnerable are very charismatic." Remember Frank Sinatra and Sam Walton playing up their flaws before facing an audience.

The idea that drawing attention to your vulnerabilities would ultimately enhance your power may seem counterintuitive. But showing vulnerability and humanity makes you more relatable and helps to avoid the feeling of alienation, which is a real risk when your charisma gives you a touch of the superhuman. If Superman didn't have the foibles of Clark Kent to humanize him, he would be much less likable. It would be impossible to relate to him.

When Michael Jordan moved from basketball to baseball, his popularity remained sky-high despite his pitiful performance. Reporters noted that most people, in fact, related even more personally to Jordan the baseball player, in part because he seemed less superhuman and more like one of them. Jordan himself said that baseball gave him a more humanistic side.

This is equally true in business. We need to be able to relate to our charismatic business leaders. Studies have shown that the perceived similarity between follower and leader is a key element in charismatic leadership, and that showing your vulnerabilities can give others something to relate to, something they feel you share in common.[1] In addition, as people get accustomed to seeing your human side, you'll be relieved of some of the expectations of always being "on."

The conscious decision to show vulnerability was a critical turning point in Bill Clinton's career. Just five months before the 1992 presidential election, Clinton's poll ratings were dismal, lagging well behind both George H. W. Bush and Ross Perot. Political commentators were so convinced of his upcoming humiliation in the election that they declared him "irrelevant." Realizing that voters weren't feeling a sense of connection with him, Clinton's advisers suggested a surprising move: rather than try to impress with his strengths, he should try to build rapport with his vulnerabilities.

Clinton's team launched an all-out vulnerability campaign they code-named "The Manhattan Project," booking him on talk shows to reveal his troubled childhood and difficult family situations. Despite the Bush team calling this move "weird" and even downright "wacky," the Clinton team persevered, and within just *one month* his approval ratings soared from 33 to 77 percent. The rest, of course, is history.

You'll want to be selective in choosing with whom, how, and in which context to show your humanity. Choose your setting well, and don't attempt vulnerability for the first time in a high-stakes moment. Instead, practice when the stakes are low.

## Putting It into Practice: Showing Vulnerability

Think of the next three or four conversations you're going to have. Pick one or two that have low stakes. Now find a small vulnerability you could share. This should *not* be something major. Any minor fear, hesitation, concern, or regret will do. You might share something you're worried about, something you think you did wrong, or something you wish you could have done better.

Before the conversation, do a compassion visualization and a responsibility transfer for the outcome of this exercise. This gets your body language right and prevents anxiety from overwhelming you, though you should *expect* discomfort—that's what vulnerability is all about.

During the conversation, here are a few good ways to ease into the sharing:

♦ "You know, I have to tell you . . ." or "I have to admit . . ." are good preambles.

♦ Prepare the terrain by saying "I'm feeling a bit nervous about saying this, but . . ."

♦ You can also ask them to keep this conversation confidential. Not only will this make you feel safer, it will make people treasure the moment more. People love secrets.

Do another quick responsibility transfer immediately after revealing the vulnerability. This helps your brain get comfortable with expressing vulnerabilities by linking to the process the good feelings that a transfer of responsibility often brings.

As with the advanced delving into discomfort exercise, vulnerability can be highly uncomfortable. But you now have all the tools you need to handle this discomfort, and it's worth doing, because you'll gain a wonderful skill. You may notice already how very "alive" vulnerability can make you feel. It can also make you feel very connected to others.

If you want to refine your practice of vulnerability, pay attention to the following: it's not just what you say and what you share but also *how you feel* while you're sharing. Some people manage to disclose highly personal, intimate, vulnerable information but don't feel a thing while doing so. It's as if they keep themselves at a distance from the vulnerability. They lay out the facts as they would a math problem and they keep their hearts well shielded behind a wall.

As your skills increase, try actually feeling a little vulnerability when you share a small disclosure. If you can manage this, your body language will be much more effective. A small dose of vulnerability is all you need to project it successfully, and the self-compassion tools from chapter 5 will make the overall experience much easier.

## It's Lonely at the Top

As you are seen increasingly as a "star," even those who want to like you may find it hard to relate to you. In addition, *you* may feel increasingly separated from them. When people start to put you on a pedestal and to see you as special, different, or superhuman, you might end up feeling isolated.

This, actually, is one of the reasons why CEOs and senior executives frequently reach out to me. They have charisma already, but they need the checks and balances, the trusted advice and honest feedback that they no longer get from others, or at least not as much as they would like. I've heard this most often from those whose main charisma style is authority, and to a lesser degree from visionary and focus charismatics.

When you're charismatic, you feel that you have great power and influence over people. It's hard to see them as peers, and it can be lonely to feel that you don't have peers.

## Sometimes It Works When It Shouldn't

Arthur is a good friend and a true alpha male who broadcasts authority charisma everywhere he goes. In fact, we were originally introduced by a mutual friend who knew I was researching charisma and told me, "You have got to meet this guy." He was right.

Over the course of many weeks, Arthur was kind enough to let me observe his alpha male charisma in action. We were sitting on the terrace of a restaurant one day having brunch—eggs Benedict for him, poached salmon for me. Suddenly, he leaned over and told me: "You know, charisma can have side effects."

For Arthur, charisma's greatest danger is that it gives you the power to convince people even when you're completely wrong. "I've realized that as long as I'm convinced that I'm right, and strongly care about it, I can convince people of *anything*. And I am no more likely to be right than they are, frankly. It's just that when I combine logical arguments with emotion, passion, and charisma, it suddenly just feels right for everyone to do what I say."

Arthur told me that he's learned to consciously restrain his charisma when he's with his own team. He tries to set up guardrails to prevent it from overpowering worthwhile arguments. As he told me, "I've been noticing how convincing I sound, how objective and fair I appear, when in reality, as I realize later, I was neither. With great power comes great responsibility. I second-guess my decisions now much more than I used to."

As you become increasingly charismatic and things start happening easily for you, there's also a risk of assuming that things happen just as easily and smoothly for other people. Try to remember that this isn't the case; others don't all have your new charismatic powers.

Being seen as superhuman can also impact your entire organization as people start to rely on your special qualities and begin to assume that things will always turn out right. On the one hand, they may feel that they no longer need to work as hard; they may feel absolved of responsibility and become complacent. On the other hand, they can also become overconfident, taking risks they wouldn't otherwise take, feeling that if anything goes wrong, you'll magically fix it.

## Warning: Charisma Is a Power Tool; Use It Responsibly

People often ask me whether the techniques they're learning could have dangerous consequences. And of course they could—this stuff is powerful. There is indeed a dark side. Many of those who have studied charisma closely have come to warn against it.

Until the 1980s, in fact, many highly influential leadership thinkers, such as Peter Drucker, vehemently opposed both the study and the teaching of charisma. Drucker frequently pointed out that the most charismatic leaders of the last century were Hitler, Stalin, Mao, and Mussolini.

Charisma is powerful because it increases one's ability to influence others. Any training that heightens this ability has the potential of being used in both helpful and harmful ways. In its aim, charisma training is no different from any other leadership skills training. Should we, then, discourage all training in leadership effectiveness?

Marshall Goldsmith told me that he sees charisma as an asset like any other, just like intelligence: "If you're going in the right direction, you'll get there faster. In the wrong direction, charisma will also help you get there faster. It's an asset, not an insurance policy. Do many charismatic leaders fail? Of course they do. Just like many very intelligent leaders. That doesn't mean that either charisma or intelligence is wrong."

A knife can be used both to heal and to hurt. Whether in the hands of a surgeon or the hands of a criminal it's the same instrument. Tools are seldom good or bad per se. What you've gained throughout this book is an array of tools—you get to decide how to use them. It's what you do with your charisma that matters.

## KEY TAKEAWAYS

- Charisma has a few possible downsides: you can become the target of envy and resentment, others can reveal too much during your interactions, you are held to a higher standard, it can be lonely at the top, and charisma may work even when it shouldn't.
- To mitigate envy and resentment, reflect or transfer praise and glory. Highlight others who deserve praise and give people ownership of your success.
- To stop people from oversharing, interject a "me, too" story, or help them destigmatize if it's too late to do so.
- Showing vulnerability will make you more likable and more relatable, and will prevent people from expecting you to be superhuman, all-powerful, all-knowing, and always right. Charisma is a powerful tool—use it responsibly.

# Conclusion

IF YOU HAD met James in January 2005, you would have seen a young man of medium height, slight build, and brown eyes floating in his loose suit, off-white shirt, and brown shoes. He might have walked up to you a bit hesitantly and given you a rather limp hand-shake. Throughout the conversation, James would have spoken in a quiet, flat voice, rarely maintaining eye contact for more than a second or two. Uncomfortable with his own presence, he would have come across as reserved and distant, even when he was actually truly interested.

James had everything going for him: he had a sharp mind, deep insights, a lot of talent, and he worked hard. With full charisma, he would have been a powerful force within his firm. As it was, James's skills, dedication, and accomplishments went unnoticed. He might have been described as "nice," but he was completely forgettable.

When I first met James, he did *not* make a good first impression. Despite his keen intelligence, he had no idea how to own the space around him. His great technical skills didn't help him make his presence felt. Nor did he understand the perception that his questioning tone and nervous nodding gave off. He came across as shy, awkward, and hesitant—the very opposite of a confident and charismatic leader.

Those who'd worked with him knew this wasn't an accurate reflection of James's worth. "Listen, we *know* he's got great potential, a brilliant mind, and quite a bit of expertise," his boss told me. "But somehow, he's consistently ignored in meetings, passed over for promotions, and altogether overlooked." James was doing outstanding work, yet he never received the full recognition he deserved. Why? The decidedly uncharismatic impressions he made were always dogging his heels.

James was skeptical about how much of a difference charisma training could make to his career. He was, however, willing to give it one wholehearted attempt. In our very first session, we identified which charisma styles would work best for him. James learned several power- and warmth-enhancing visualizations that he could start using immediately. He learned how to change his posture to get a confidence-boosting cycle going. He learned how to "get into his toes." After just one session, the difference was striking. Already he was walking differently, holding himself differently, and projecting far more confidence. This was still James, yet he carried new strength.

In the weeks that followed, we worked on unleashing more of his charisma potential as he gained both verbal and nonverbal tools to increase his presence, power, and warmth. James continued adjusting and improving his posture, voice, conversation, and presentation skills. He could now take up space with his body language, finally comfortable being the big gorilla. He could fluctuate his voice with warmth and power and he spoke with a richer, more resonant tone.

Within just a few weeks of our working together, James had achieved an astounding transformation. His peers watched in awe and his superiors in amazement as their colleague's performance rating soared. As one of them told me later, it was "a complete metamorphosis."

Three months after our coaching began, James reflected on how profound this change had been: "The business star you see today did not exist ninety days ago." Nowadays, when James walks into a room, people *notice*. When he speaks at meetings, people listen. And he wrote me recently: "These practices have now become second nature."

Yet it's obvious to me that the charismatic presence he has now was always there, buried deep. It simply just took the right insights and the right skills to get him to where he is now, easily infusing his business dealings with more personal magnetism. Just like a rough diamond needs polishing to reveal its brilliance, it took a little skill and practice to bring James's inner superstar to the surface.

Now you know what charisma is: behaviors that project presence, power, and warmth. You know these behaviors can be learned, and you've been given an entire toolkit to do so. You've been absorbing a host of new practices, mindset shifts, and ways of being. From here onward, it's going to be a delicate balance between being true to your nature and stretching out of your traditional comfort zones. As you practice them, these techniques will gradually become a part of who you are rather than a set of skills you're learning. Remember, it's really a question of *accessing* different parts of you, learning to more fully express qualities that you already have. We all have the capacity for presence, power, and warmth.

Stretch the boundaries of your comfort zone in low-stakes situations. On the other hand, when you're in high-stakes situations, don't take the risk of coming across as uncomfortable or inauthentic. While you're learning, in difficult or important situations, stick with the charismatic behaviors and styles that are easiest for you.

You're embarking on an expedition. Expect ups and downs, detours, and obstacles along the way. But your interactions will soon start to feel increasingly positive, sometimes even magical. Remember to *enjoy* this progression. Sit back and appreciate how well the interaction is going, how well you're doing. Drink it in.

Your life is about to change. Enjoy the journey.

# Recommended Resources

## Books

Brach, Tara. *Radical Acceptance: Embracing Your Life with the Heart of a Buddha*. New York: Bantam, 2004. A great resource for emotional training; I've often called this one "graduate school for the heart."

Cialdini, Robert B. *Influence: The Psychology of Persuasion*. Rev. ed. New York: Harper Paperbacks, 2006. Considered the "bible" of influence, Cialdini's book is required reading in most MBA programs.

Frankl, Viktor E. *Man's Search for Meaning*. Rev. ed. New York: Pocket Books, 1997. A great help in gaining equanimity, this is a worthwhile read for anyone facing a crisis. Few books can give you perspective like this one (and in so few pages).

Germer, Christopher K. *The Mindful Path to Self-Compassion*. New York: Guilford Press, 2009. A great resource if you'd like to focus on self-compassion.

Haidt, Jonathan. *The Happiness Hypothesis*. New York: Basic Books, 2006. Best science I've found on the scientific study of happiness. Fascinating.

Hayes, Steven C. *Get Out of Your Mind and Into Your Life*. Oakland, CA: New Harbinger Publications, 2005. The best book I've found on how to handle your own mind.

Kabat-Zinn, Jon. *Wherever You Go, There You Are*. 10th anniv. ed. New York: Hyperion, 2005. The best introduction to mindfulness

I've ever found. Just the introduction and first two chapters are all you need.

Stone, Douglas, Bruce Patton, Sheila Heen, and Roger Fisher. *Difficult Conversations: How to Discuss What Matters Most*. New York: Penguin Non-Classics, 2000. The best framework I've found on difficult conversations.

Stone, Hal, and Sidra Stone. *Embracing Your Inner Critic*. New York: HarperOne, 1993. A great first start on getting to know the inner critic, and an easy read.

Williams, Mark, John Teasdale, Zindel Segal, and Jon Kabat-Zinn. *The Mindful Way through Depression*. New York: Guilford Press, 2007. The best of the best on this difficult topic. A must-read for anyone who has experienced depression or whose loved ones have suffered from it. I would also recommend it to anyone in a position of leadership; you would be amazed at the proportion of people in corporate America who experience depression.

### Online Resources

Visit http://www.CharismaMyth.com to access dozens of free articles packed with practical tools and tips. You'll find lots of free downloadable resources, such as a PDF workbook, audio recordings of all the visualization exercises, and many more resources to help you get the most out of this book.

### Speaking Engagements

Olivia is a frequently requested keynote speaker, seminar leader, and facilitator for executive leadership retreats. To book Olivia for a speaking engagement, you can view highlights of her live keynote speeches and find more information on her topics of expertise at http://www.AskOlivia.com. You can also contact her via e-mail at Olivia@AskOlivia.com.

## Coaching and Consulting

For a more intensive or in-depth experience tailored to you or your organization's specific needs, you may also want to explore Olivia's extensive coaching and consulting practice, which has attracted clients such as Google, Harvard, and Northern Trust. You can find more information at http://www.AskOlivia.com.

# Chapter Summaries

### 1. Charisma Demystified

Becoming more charismatic involves simple tweaks to your behavior. Charisma doesn't require you to be outgoing or attractive, or for you to change your personality. It's a skill, a discipline, like playing a sport or an instrument. It takes work, practice, and the right set of tools. This book gives you the tools you need—which come from many disciplines, from neuroscience to athletic conditioning. And because you're interacting with other people every day, you get countless opportunities to practice these skills.

### 2. The Charismatic Behaviors: Presence, Power, and Warmth

Increasing your charisma involves behaviors that project more of three core charismatic qualities: presence, power, and warmth. All three are communicated mostly through body language, which isn't under your conscious control. Instead, your internal (emotional and mental) state determines your body language. By choosing what you imagine, and by learning how to adjust your mental state, you can ensure that body language projects more presence, power, and warmth, and thus charisma. In terms of achieving charisma, your internal state is critical. Get the internal state right, and the right charismatic behaviors and body language will pour forth automatically. Being present—paying attention to what's going on rather than being caught up in your thoughts—can yield immense rewards. When you exhibit presence, those around you feel listened to, respected, and valued.

### 3. The Obstacles to Presence, Power, and Warmth

Discomfort affects your mental state and prevents you from projecting presence, power, and warmth. It impacts how you feel, how you perform, and how others perceive you. This applies to both physical discomfort and mental discomfort, such as anxiety, dissatisfaction, self-criticism, and self-doubt. Aim to prevent discomfort by planning ahead to ensure comfort in clothing, location, and timing. If discomfort arises, you can either address it (for instance, with a mental technique such as the responsibility transfer) or explain it so that it's not misperceived. In all cases, being aware of the discomfort is the first step in being able to address it.

### 4. Overcoming the Obstacles

There is a simple three-step process for addressing internal discomfort so that your charisma can shine through. First, destigmatize it by recognizing that we all experience the same kinds of internal discomfort, that they're completely normal and nothing to be ashamed of. Think of others who've gone through this before—especially people you admire—and see yourself as part of a community of human beings experiencing the same feeling at the same moment. Second, neutralize the negativity attached to the experience by reminding yourself that the negative thoughts are not necessarily accurate. Third, rewrite reality by designing and adopting an interpretation of the situation that gives you a more charismatic state.

## 5. Creating Charismatic Mental States

Once you've addressed the obstacles, the next step is to consciously create mental states that help you project charisma. Visualization, used commonly by professional athletes, is a remarkably versatile and powerful tool for accessing the right mental state. Practicing gratitude, goodwill, and compassion puts you in a mental state that projects warmth. And compassion for yourself, surprisingly, helps you access all aspects of charisma. You can also use those elements of body language you do control, such as posture and facial expressions, to impact your mental state, which then feeds back into the rest of your body language, initiating a positive cycle. Just as professional athletes and performers do, plan a gradual warm-up to your peak charismatic performance. Before important events, avoid experiences that would impair your warmth and plan confidence-boosting activities instead.

## 6. Different Charisma Styles

Different styles of charisma are appropriate for different people and different situations. We look at four that are both practical and accessible. Focus charisma is achieved primarily through presence and good listening, and makes people feel heard, understood, and respected. Visionary charisma requires a bold vision that is delivered with complete conviction; it inspires people to believe in and want to be a part of this vision. Kindness charisma primarily involves warmth and acceptance, and creates an emotional connection. Authority charisma is achieved primarily through the projection of power and status, and leads people to listen or obey. You can alternate among different charisma styles or even blend them together. To decide which charisma style to use, consider your personality, your goals, and the specific situation at hand.

## 7. Charismatic First Impressions

First impressions matter. Within minutes or even seconds, people form an impression of your status, your personality, and much else about you, and this evaluation filters their future perceptions of you. The first impression you make starts with your appearance, and typically continues with your handshake and the start of your conversation. People feel most comfortable with those who are similar to them in some way, including appearance and behavior. Good first impressions can weigh heavily in your favor, just as bad ones can take significant work to undo. Great conversationalists keep the spotlight on the other person and make them feel good about themselves, because people will associate you with whatever feelings you produce in them.

## 8. Speaking—and Listening—with Charisma

There are specific verbal and vocal techniques for projecting each of the three elements of charisma. Presence is communicated by listening well, not interrupting, and pausing before you speak. Warmth is projected by creating positive associations, avoiding negative associations, and making other people feel valued and important. Power is projected when you speak concisely, using metaphors and providing high value. The pitch, tone, and tempo of your speech are as important as what you say in determining what you project.

## 9. Charismatic Body Language

Your verbal communication—*what* you say—primarily reaches people's logical side. Your nonverbal communication—*how* you say it—primarily reaches people's emotional side. Nonverbal communication creates stronger reactions and moves people to action. Through emotional contagion, your emotions can spread to other people. Nonverbal warmth can be projected by managing physical and personal space to make the other person feel comfortable, by mirroring their body language, and by making the right kind of eye contact. Nonverbal power can be projected by using "big gorilla" body language and avoiding unnecessary movements.

## 10. Difficult Situations

Difficult situations may challenge your charisma skills, but they also present opportunities. Charismatically handling a difficult situation can make the difference between making an enemy and making a friend. Preparation and approach are important: choose the timing and location to maximize their comfort and your charisma, and be prepared with ways to be both appreciative and empathetic. When you need to win someone over, asking them for their opinion and expressing gratitude for things they've done for you in the past are ways to encourage them to rationalize in your favor. When delivering positive information, make it specific and personal; when delivering negative information, make it specific but depersonalize it. All of the charisma tools you've learned are useful here, especially the ones to manage your own internal state.

## 11. Presenting with Charisma

Public speaking can have a major influence on how you are perceived. Craft your message clearly and simply, use vivid stories, metaphors, and analogies, and focus on things the audience can relate to. Make your presentation short and entertaining. Watch the value of each sentence. Choose your clothing to create a specific image and feeling, but also to be comfortable. Practice extensively (including in front of real audiences), and weed out unnecessary sounds and motions. During the speech itself, put your focus on your audience rather than on yourself, and don't forget to pause and breathe. Use body language and intonation to express the types of power and warmth you want to project. Limit superfluous gestures that distract the audience's attention. Pause frequently and deliberately to show confidence and add drama as well as to give yourself a chance to breathe.

## 12. Charisma in a Crisis

In times of crisis, charismatic leadership is especially important. Others are often more open to charismatic leadership, but they are also more sensitive to the mood and emotions of the leader. Retain equanimity, regularly check your physiology, and use the tools for managing your mental state. Express high expectations and articulate a vision that both addresses the crisis and has relevance beyond it. Articulate a bold vision, show your confidence in your ability to realize that vision, and act decisively to achieve it.

## 13. The Charismatic Life: Rising to the Challenge

Charisma changes the way people relate to you, and challenges come along with the benefits. You become more of a magnet for praise, but also for envy, and you may be held to higher standards than others. And at the highest levels, being charismatic may set you apart enough for it to be a lonely experience. Sharing credit, expressing praise for others, and showing vulnerability can help mitigate these possible side effects. People may also feel more comfortable with you in the moment, and open up in ways they regret or feel ashamed of later.

Charisma can also be powerful in the wrong ways. People may want to follow you even when you're wrong, rely on you too much, or take unjustified risks because of their faith in your ability to fix anything. Charisma is a powerful tool that you need to use responsibly.

# Charisma Exercises

The following quick summaries bring together key exercises detailed throughout this book.

## Presence (page 15)

Set a timer for one minute. Close your eyes and try to focus on one of three things:

1. Sounds: Scan your environment for sound. Imagine your ears are satellite dishes, passively registering sounds.
2. Your breath: Focus on your breath and the sensations it creates in your nostrils or stomach as it goes in and out.
3. Your toes: Focus your attention on the sensations in your toes.

## Responsibility Transfer (pages 34–35)

Whenever you feel your brain rehashing possible outcomes to a situation, try a transfer of responsibility to alleviate the anxiety.

1. Sit comfortably or lie down, relax, and close your eyes.
2. Take two or three deep breaths. As you inhale, imagine drawing clean air toward the top of your head. As you exhale, let it whoosh out, washing all your worries away.
3. Imagine lifting the weight of *everything* you're concerned about off your shoulders and placing it in the hands of whichever benevolent entity you'd like to put in charge.

Now that everything is taken care of, you can sit back, relax, and enjoy whatever good you can find along the way.

## Destigmatizing Discomfort (page 46)

The next time an uncomfortable emotion is hindering you, try this step-by-step guide to destigmatizing:

1. Remind yourself that this is normal and that we all experience it from time to time.

2. Think of others who have gone through this, especially people you admire.

3. Remember that right now, in this very moment, many others are going through this very same experience.

## Neutralizing Negativity (pages 50–51)

Use these techniques anytime you're having persistent negative thoughts and you'd like to lessen their effects.

♦ Remember that these thoughts may be inaccurate.
♦ See your thoughts as graffiti on a wall or as little electrical impulses.
♦ Depersonalize the experience. Observe it as a scientist might: "How interesting, there are self-critical thoughts arising."
♦ Imagine yourself from afar. Zoom out to see planet Earth hanging in space. Zoom back in to see your tiny self having a particular experience at this particular moment.
♦ Imagine your mental chatter as coming from a radio; turn the volume down or put the radio to the side.

## Rewriting Reality (page 56)

If a persistent mental annoyance is causing irritation, use one of these techniques to imagine an alternative reality in order to regain a calm internal state:

- Ask yourself a few times, "What if this experience is, in fact, a good thing for me?" and watch how creative your mind can get with its answers.
- When you're dealing with more serious situations, write down your new realities by hand. Write: "The presentation is going well . . ." Or, better yet, use past tense: "The presentation was a complete success . . ."

## Getting Satisfaction (page 57)

- Think of someone who has aggrieved you.
- Take a blank page and write them a letter saying everything you wish you had ever told them. Make sure you write it out by hand.
- When you've gotten absolutely everything off your mind, put the letter aside.
- Now write their answer, apologizing for everything they've done and taking responsibility for all their hurtful actions.
- For maximum effect, reread their apology a few times over the course of a week

## Delving into Sensations (pages 62–63)

To practice your endurance in uncomfortable situations, find a quiet, comfortable spot to sit with a partner, and set a timer for thirty seconds.

- Look into your partner's eyes. As soon as you become aware of discomfort, notice where the feelings are located in your body.
- Delve into each sensation as much as you can; feel its texture. Describe each as if you were a chef describing a featured dish.
- Let the discomfort build. Observe and name the sensations you feel: hot, cold, tightness in your jaw, a knot in your stomach.
- Resist the urge to laugh, talk, or relieve the discomfort.
- Try the same practice again, this time giving yourself continuous encouragement. Remind yourself that your efforts will reap rewards and that the discomfort *will* pass.

## Stretching Your Comfort Zone (pages 64–65)

Strike up a conversation with a complete stranger. When you're standing or sitting near someone, see if there's something they're looking at that could give you something with which to start the conversation.

Let's say you're in a coffee shop waiting in line. You could make any small comment about the pastries, and follow with an open-ended question (one that cannot be answered with a yes or no). Say something like: "I'm trying to decide which is most sinful: the muffin, the brownie, or the coffee cake. How would you rank them?"

## Visualization (pages 69–70)

Close your eyes and relax. Employ your senses as you focus on a moment in your life when you felt triumphant:

♦ *Hear* the sounds in the room: the murmurs of approval, the swell of applause.
♦ *See* people's smiles and expressions of warmth and admiration.
♦ *Feel* your feet on the ground and the congratulatory handshakes.
♦ Above all, *experience* your feelings, the warm glow of confidence rising within you.

## Gratitude (pages 77–79)

For quick gratitude access, find three things you can approve of right now. Scan your body and your environment for little, tangible things you could be grateful for.

1. _____

2. _____

3. _____

## Compassion (page 83)

Follow the three steps below to practice compassion for someone:

1. Imagine their past. What was it like growing up in their family and experiencing their childhood?
2. Imagine their present. Put yourself in their place. See through their eyes. Imagine what they might be feeling right now.
3. Imagine delivering their eulogy.

## Self-Compassion (page 87)

Keep a self-compassion list. Jot down five ways that you already care for yourself when you're having a hard time. If you're on a roll, go for ten. Star those that are particularly effective.

1. _____

2. _____

3. _____

4. _____

5. _____

## Metta (pages 88–89)

The visualization below will guide you through Metta step by step. If you'd prefer to hear me guide you through this exercise, you'll find a recording online at http://CharismaMyth.com/metta.

♦ Sit comfortably, close your eyes, and take two or three deep breaths, letting them wash all your worries away.
♦ Think of any occasion in your life when you performed a good deed, however great or small.
♦ Now think of a being—present, past, mythical, or actual; person, pet, or even stuffed animal—that you can imagine having warm affection for you.
♦ Picture this being in your mind, and see their warmth, kindness, and compassion. Imagine their affection and let it envelop you.

♦ Feel them give you complete forgiveness for everything your inner critic says isn't good enough about you or your life.

♦ Feel them giving you complete acceptance as you are right now, with all your imperfections, at this stage of your progression.

## Using Your Body to Change Your Mind
## (pages 91–92)

Try out the following postures to see for yourself just how powerfully the position of your body can affect your mind and your feelings:

♦ Adopt the body language of someone who's depressed. Let your shoulders slump, head hang, and face sag. *Without moving a muscle,* try to feel really, truly excited. It's nearly impossible.

♦ Now do the opposite. Physically spring into excitement. Jump up and down, smile the biggest smile you can, wave your arms in the air, and while doing all this, try to feel depressed. Again, it's nearly impossible.

## The Perfect Handshake (pages 121–22)

Follow the recommendations below to perform a gold-star handshake:

1. Keep your right hand free.
2. Use plenty of eye contact, and smile warmly but briefly.
3. Keep your head straight and face the other person.
4. Keep your hand perpendicular, thumb pointing straight to the ceiling.
5. Get full palm contact by draping your hand diagonally downward.
6. Wrap your fingers around your counterpart's hand.
7. Once you make full contact, squeeze to their level of firmness.
8. Shake from the elbow, step back, and then let go.

## Great Listening (page 128)

In your next conversation, see if you can practice not interrupting. Let the other person interrupt, and from time to time wait a second or two before you answer while letting your face show the impact of what they've just said.

## Voice Fluctuation (page 140)

You can gain great insights into your own voice fluctuation by practicing sentences with a tape recorder. Repeat a sentence several times with as wide a variation in styles as you can. Say it with authority, with anger, with sorrow, with empathetic care and concern, with warmth, and with enthusiasm.

## Vocal Power (page 141)

The guidelines below will help you broadcast power through your voice.

1. Speak slowly. Visualize the contrast between a nervous, squeaky-voiced teenager speaking at high speed and the slow, emphatic tone of a judge delivering a verdict.
2. Pause. People who broadcast confidence often pause while speaking. They will pause for a second or two between sentences or even in the middle of a sentence. This conveys the feeling that they're so confident in their power, they trust that people won't interrupt.
3. Drop intonation. You know how a voice rises at the end of a question? Just reread the last sentence and hear your voice go up at the end. Now imagine an assertion: a judge saying "This case is closed." Feel how the intonation of the word *closed* drops. Lowering the intonation of your voice at the end of a sentence broadcasts power. When you want to sound superconfident, you can even lower your intonation midsentence.
4. Check your breathing. Make sure you're breathing deeply into your belly and inhale and exhale through your nose rather

than your mouth. Breathing through your mouth can make you sound breathless and anxious.

## Charismatic Seating Choices (page 152)

The next time you want to establish warm rapport with someone, avoid a confrontational seating arrangement and instead sit either next to or at a 90-degree angle from them. These are the positions in which we feel most comfortable. In fact, this is an exercise you can try out with a partner.

- Start a conversation at a 90-degree angle.
- After five minutes, change positions so that you're sitting across from each other. You'll likely feel a clear difference in comfort level.
- After another five minutes, move back to a 90-degree angle, and feel the difference.
- Finally, come back to your original position sitting next to each other.

Pay close attention to the rise and fall of feelings of trust and comfort throughout the exercise.

## Being the Big Gorilla (pages 159–60)

Use this exercise when you want to both feel and broadcast confidence—for instance, before a key meeting, or with someone who's a bit intimidating.

1. Make sure you can breathe. Loosen any clothing if need be.
2. Stand up and shake up your body.
3. Take a wide stance and plant your feet firmly on the ground.
4. Stretch your arms to the ceiling.
5. Stretch your arms to the walls on either side of you.
6. INFLATE. Try to take up as much space as possible.
7. Roll your shoulders up and then back.
8. Imagine yourself as a four-star general reviewing his troops. Puff up your chest, broaden your shoulders, and put your arms behind your back.

## Midcourse Corrections (page 198)

♦ Check your body. Make sure no tense posture is worsening your internal state.
♦ Take a deep breath, relax your body.
♦ Destigmatize and dedramatize. This happens to everyone, and it will pass.
♦ If any negative thoughts are present, remember that they're just thoughts, and not necessarily valid.
♦ Find little things to be grateful for: your ability to breathe, the fact that you will still be alive by the end of this.
♦ Imagine getting a great hug from someone you trust for twenty seconds (of course, you may not have twenty seconds, but if you do, this is remarkably effective).

Once your threat response is quieted down, to bring yourself back into a state of confidence, remember a moment in your life when you felt absolute triumph. Thanks to your brain's inability to distinguish imagination from reality, your body will be filled with the same cocktail of chemicals as it was during that confidence-filled moment, thereby changing your body language into exactly what you need to be impressive, persuasive, and inspiring again.

## Showing Vulnerability (page 217)

Think of the next low-stakes conversation you're going to have and follow the steps below to show a little vulnerability:

♦ Select a small vulnerability you could share.
♦ To prepare, perform a responsibility transfer for the outcome of this exercise.
♦ During the conversation, ease into the sharing by saying, "You know, I have to tell you . . ." Or prepare the terrain with, "I'm feeling a bit nervous about saying this, but . . ."
♦ Ask for their confidentiality. Not only will this make you feel safer, it will make people treasure the moment. People love secrets.
♦ Perform a quick responsibility transfer immediately after sharing the vulnerability.

# Acknowledgments

DUE TO A version error in the first edition of this book, two people did not receive proper thanks, and I'm grateful for the opportunity to rectify this error: First, David Arkless provided guidance during our initial interviews as well as impressive support and patronage in the high business and political spheres in which he moves. And second, Professor Catalina Stefanescu-Cuntze, whose structural insights for the introduction and conclusion shaped them into readability.

I was blessed with the extraordinary privilege to have some of the best minds I know involved throughout this process.

Thanks, above and beyond, to Daniel Lieberman—pedagogical expert, content maestro, structure wizard—for his extraordinarily keen insights, clear thinking, and awe-inspiring generosity.

A number of people dedicated time, insights, and valuable brain-power to this endeavor: Barney Pell, Mark Herschberg, Artem Boys-tov, Joshua Keay, Natalie Philips, and Zachary Burt.

William Bosl at the Harvard-MIT Health Sciences and Technology program, Stephen Kosslyn of Stanford's Center for Advanced Study in the Behavioral Sciences, and Maxine Rodenthuis at the UC Berkeley Haas School of Business provided fantastic research work.

Many of these great business minds were so kind as to contribute insights: Chris Ashenden, Gilles August, Sunny Bates, Steve Bell, Charles Best, Michael Feuer, Tim Flynn, Scott Freidheim, Matt Furman, Carl Guardino, Catherine Dumait Harper, Ira Jackson, Ken Jacobs, Randy Komisar, Jack Leslie, Maurice Levy, Dan'l Lewin, Angel Martinez, Jeff Mirich, Peter Moore, Elon Musk, Tom

Schiro, Nina Simosko, Kevin Surace, Peter Thiel, Duncan Wardle, Bill Whitmore, and Bill Wohl.

With great skill, dedication, patience, kindness, and generosity, Courtney Young led Penguin's impressive team effort. Adrienne Schultz worked wonders, making the writing clearer and more concise, and greatly improving the flow. Rebecca Gradinger at Fletcher & Company took a chance on a first-time author.

Marissa Mayer and Zack Bogue kindly took this author under their wing, and their patronage brought the book's launch to soaring heights. Thank you both.

I was blessed to have wonderful help, comments, and encouragement from William Bachman, Silvia Console Battiliana, Clark Bernier, Devon and Pablo Cohn, Malcolm Collins, Fabian Cuntze, Robin Faramanfarian, Daniel Ford, Darius Golkar, Joe Greenstein, Jaden Hastings, Rich Hecker, Chris Hill, Samantha Holdsworth, Jesse Jacobs, Dina Kaplan, Alex Kehl, Eric Keller, Emma Berntman Kraft, Jessamyn Lau, Greg Levin, Greg Lory, Ana Rowena McCullough, Patrick McKenna, Shauna Mei, Xavier Morelle, Earl Pinto, Judah Pollack, Semira Rahemtulla, Dom Ricci, Professor John Paul Rollert and his Harvard class, Jean Yves SantaMaria, Katharina Schmitt, Jon Teo, J. R. Wurster, Justyna Zander, and Roni Zeiger.

I would also like to dedicate this book to my clients, as together we've shared discoveries, confessions, laughter, struggles, triumphs, pride, and joy. I'm looking forward to continuing our journey together.

To the teachers whose wisdom guided me along the path: Tara Brach, David and Shoshana Cooper, Michele McDonald, Linda McDonald, and Victoria Moran.

To my family and extended family: Bernard Cabane and Celie Fox Cabane, Guillaume Cabane and Marine Aubry, Gerard Cabane, David and Doris Schoenfarber, Barney Pell and Nadya Direkova, Deepak and Nalini Bradoo, Ruth Owades, Anusheel Bhushan, and Ana and Michael McCullough.

And always, to Privahini Bradoo, Fabian Cuntze, Joe Greenstein, Joshua Keay, Judah Pollack, Seena Rejal, Natalie Phillips, David Dayan Rosenman, and Torsten Rode. You have made me who I am today. You keep me grounded. You own a piece of my heart.

# Notes

## Introduction

1. Recounted by *Redbook* editor Robert Stein, who followed Marilyn throughout this episode (*American Heritage* magazine, November/December 2005).
2. B. J. Avolio, D. A. Waldman, and W. O. Einstein, "Transformational Leadership in a Management Game Simulation," *Journal of Management, Group and Organizational Studies* 13 (1988): 59–80; B. J. Avolio and B. M. Bass, "Transformational Leadership, Charisma, and Beyond," in *Emerging Leadership Vistas*, eds. J. G. Hunt, B. R. Baliga, H. P. Dachler, and C. A. Schriesheim (Lexington, MA: Lexington Books, 1988), 29–49; Hater and Bass, "Superiors' Evaluation and Subordinates' Perceptions of Transformational and Transactional Leadership," *Journal of Applied Psychology* (1988): 695–702; G. A. Yukl and D. D. Van Fleet, "Cross-Situational Multimethod Research on Military Leader Effectiveness," *Organizational Behavior and Human Performance* 30 (1982): 87–108.
3. B. Shamir, M. Arthur, and R. House, "The Rhetoric of Charismatic Leadership: A Theoretical Extension, a Case Study, and Implications for Research," *Leadership Quarterly* 5 (1994): 25–42.
4. Robert J. House, *The Rise and Decline of Charismatic Leadership*, The Wharton School at the University of Pennsylvania, rev. January 26, 1999, http://leadership.wharton.upenn.edu/l_change/publications/House/Rise%20and%20Decline%20of%20Charismatic%20Leadership%20-%20House.doc; R. J. House and B. Shamir, "Toward the Integration of Charismatic, Transformational, Inspirational and Visionary Theories of Leadership," in *Leadership Theory and Research Perspecties and Directions*, ed. M. Chemmers and R. Ayman (New York: Academic Press, 1993): 81–107; R. J. House and J. M. Howell,

"Personality and Charismatic Leadership," *Leadership Quarterly* 3, no. 2 (1992): 81–108.

5. A. Erez, V. F. Misangyi, D. E. Johnson, M. A. LePine, and K. C. Halverson, "Stirring the Hearts of Charismatic Leadership as the Transferral of Affect," *Journal of Applied Psychology* 93, no. 3 (2008): 602–16; C. G. Brooks Jr., "Leadership, Leadership, Wherefore Art Thou Leadership?" *Respiratory Care Clinics of North America* 10, no. 2 (2004): 157–71.

## 1. Charisma Demystified

1. A group of enterprising behavioral scientists demonstrated the feasibility of increasing people's level of charisma in a controlled laboratory setting through a series of multiple controlled experiments. They analyzed which verbal and nonverbal behaviors could be used to increase or decrease charisma. Their test subjects' levels of charisma rose and fell depending on which behaviors they were instructed to demonstrate. As long as you know how to exhibit the correct body language and behaviors, you will be seen as charismatic. J. M. Howell and P. J. Frost, "A Lab Study of Charismatic Leadership," *Organizational Behavior and Human Decision Processes* 43 (1989): 243–69.

2. R. E. Riggio, "Charisma," in *Encyclopedia of Leadership*, eds. J. M. Burns, W. Goethals, and G. Sorenson (Great Barrington, MA: Berkshire Publishing, 2004), 1:158–62.

## 2. The Charismatic Behaviors

1. Li, W., R. E. Zinbarg, S. G. Boehm, and K. A. Paller. "Neural and Behavioral Evidence for Affective Priming from Unconsciously Perceived Emotional Facial Expressions and the Influence of Trait Anxiety," *Journal of Cognitive Neuroscience* 20 (2003): 95–107.

2. Daniel Gilbert has done some fascinating research on happiness. Daniel Todd Gilbert, *Stumbling on Happiness* (New York: Alfred A. Knopf, 2006).

3. S. T. Fiske, A. J. C. Cuddy, and P. Glick, "Universal Dimensions of Social Cognition: Warmth and Competence,"*Trends in Cognitive Sciences* 11, no. 2 (February 1, 2007): 77–83.

4. Alex (Sandy) Pentland, *Honest Signals—How They Shape Our World* (Cambridge, MA: The MIT Press, 2008).

5. J. I. Davis, J. J. Gross, and K. N. Ochsner, "Psychological Distance and Emotional Experience: What You See Is What You Get," *Emo-*

*tion* 11, no. 2 (2011): 438–44. J. J. Gross, G. Sheppes, and H. L. Urry, "Emotion Generation and Emotion Regulation: A Distinction We Should Make (Carefully)," *Cognition and Emotion* 25, no. 5 (2011): 765–81. doi:10.1080/02699931.2011.555753.

6. P. Ekman, R. J. Davidson, and W. V. Friesen, "The Duchenne Smile: Emotional Expression and Brain Physiology: II," *Journal of Personality and Social Psychology* 58, no. 2 (1990): 342–53.

7. R. A. Hahn, "The Nocebo Phenomenon: Concept, Evidence, and Implications for Public Health," *Preventive Medicine* 26, no. 5, part 1 (September–October 1997): 607–11.

## 3. The Obstacles to Presence, Power, and Warmth

1. M. T. Gailliot, R. F. Baumeister, C. N. DeWall, J. K. Maner, E. A. Plant, D. M. Tice, et al., "Self-Control Relies on Glucose as a Limited Energy Source: Willpower Is More Than a Metaphor," *Journal of Personality and Social Psychology* 92, no. 2 (2007): 325-36.

2. See Jeff Bell, *When in Doubt, Make Belief* (Novato, CA: New World Library, 2009).

3. S. Harris, S. A. Sheth, and M. S. Cohen, "Functional Neuroimaging of Belief, Disbelief, and Uncertainty," *Annals of Neurology* 63 (2008): 14.

4. Image generation has a powerful impact on emotions and physiological states and a high impact on brain function. See A. Hackmann, "Working with Images in Clinical Psychology," in *Comprehensive Clinical Psychology*, eds. A. Bellack and M. Hersen (London: Pergamon, 1998), 301–17.

5. T. J. Kaptchuk, E. Friedlander, J. M. Kelley, et al., "Placebos without Deception: A Randomized Controlled Trial in Irritable Bowel Syndrome" (2010), http://www.plosone.org/article/info:doi/10.1371/journal.pone.0015591.

6. I highly recommend Robert Sapolsky's fascinating—and free— Stanford University lecture "Why Zebras Don't Get Ulcers" on iTunes.

7. David Rock, "SCARF: A Brain-Based Model for Collaborating with and Influencing Others," *NeuroLeadership Journal* 1 (2008).

8. P. R. Clance and S. A. Imes, "The Imposter Phenomenon in High Achieving Women: Dynamics and Therapeutic Intervention," *Psychotherapy: Theory, Research and Practice* 15, no. 3 (1978): 241–47.

## 4. Overcoming the Obstacles

1. David Rock, *Your Brain at Work* (New York: HarperBusiness, 2009).
2. D. J. Simons and C. F. Chabris, "Gorillas in Our Midst: Sustained Inattentional Blindness for Dynamic Events," *Perception* 28, no. 9 (1999): 1059–74, http://en.wikipedia.org/wiki/Digital_object_identifier.
3. James J. Gross, "Emotion Regulation: Affective, Cognitive, and Social Consequences," *Psychophysiology* 39, no. 3 (May 2002): 281–89.
4. Ibid., 289.
5. T. J. Kaptchuk, E. Friedlander, J. M. Kelley, et al., "Placebos without Deception: A Randomized Controlled Trial in Irritable Bowel Syndrome" (2010), http://www.plosone.org/article/info:doi/10.1371/journal.pone.0015591.
6. Andrew Hunt, *Pragmatic Thinking and Learning: Refactor Your Wetware,* rev. ed. (Raleigh, NC: Pragmatic Bookshelf, 2010).
7. Robert B. Cialdini, *Influence: The Psychology of Persuasion,* rev. ed. (New York: Harper Paperbacks, 2006); and B. J. Sagarin, R. B. Cialdini, W. E. Rice, and S. B. Serna, "Dispelling the Illusion of Invulnerability: The Motivations and Mechanisms of Resistance to Persuasion," *Journal of Personality and Social Psychology* 83, no. 3 (2002): 526–41
8. Hunt, *Pragmatic Thinking and Learning.*

## 5. Creating Charismatic Mental States

1. David Rock, *Your Brain at Work* (New York: HarperBusiness, 2009)
2. Ibid., and Jeff Hawkins, *On Intelligence,* adapted ed. (New York: Times Books, 2004).
3. On a scale of suicides per 100,000 since 1990, MIT had a rate of 10.2, compared to Harvard with a rate of 7.4, and Johns Hopkins, the third-place school, with a rate of 6.9.
4. R. A. Emmons and A. Mishra, "Why Gratitude Enhances Well-Being: What We Know, What We Need to Know," in *Designing Positive Psychology: Taking Stock and Moving Forward,* eds. K. Sheldon, T. Kashdan, and M. F. Steger (New York: Oxford University Press, 2011); R. A. Emmons, "Gratitude," in *Encyclopedia of Positive Psychology,* eds. S. J. Lopez and A. Beauchamp (New York: Oxford University Press, 2009), 442–47.
5. Martin E. P. Seligman, *Authentic Happiness: Using the New Positive Psychology to Realize Your Potential for Lasting Fulfillment* (New York: Free Press, 2002).

6. K. D. Neff, "Self-Compassion," in *Handbook of Individual Differences in Social Behavior*, eds. M. R. Leary and R. H. Hoyle (New York: Guilford Press, 2009), 561–73.

7. K. D. Neff, "Self-Compassion, Self-Esteem, and Well-Being," *Social and Personality Compass* 5 (2011): 1–12; K. D. Neff and P. McGeehee, "Self-Compassion and Psychological Resilience among Adolescents and Young Adults," *Self and Identity* 9 (2010): 225–40; K. D. Neff, K. Kirkpatrick, and S. S. Rude, "Self-Compassion and Its Link to Adaptive Psychological Functioning," *Journal of Research in Personality* 41 (2007): 139–54.

8. K. D. Neff, "Self-Compassion," in *Handbook of Individual Differences*.

9. Ibid. Self-compassion deactivates the threat system (which generates feelings of fear, insecurity, and defensiveness) and activates the soothing system instead.

10. T. Barnhofer, T. Chittka, H. Nightingale, C. Visser, and C. Crane, "State Effects of Two Forms of Meditation on Prefrontal EEG Asymmetry in Previously Depressed Individuals," *Mindfulness* 1, no. 1 (2010): 21–27; T. Barnhofer, D. Duggan, C. Crane, S. Hepburn, M. J. Fennell, and J. M. Williams, "Effects of Meditation on Frontal Alpha-Asymmetry in Previously Suicidal Individuals," *NeuroReport* 18, no. 7 (2007): 709–12; B. R. Cahn and J. Polich, "Meditation States and Traits: EEG, ERP, and Neuroimaging Studies," *Psychological Bulletin* 132, no. 2 (2006): 180–211; G. Feldman, J. Greeson, and J. Senville, "Differential Effects of Mindful Breathing, Progressive Muscle Relaxation, and Loving-Kindness Meditation on Decentering and Negative Reactions to Repetitive Thoughts," *Behaviour Research and Therapy* 48, no. 10 (2010): 1002–11; A. Manna, A. Raffone, M. G. Perrucci, D. Nardo, A. Ferretti, A. Tartaro, et al., "Neural Correlates of Focused Attention and Cognitive Monitoring in Meditation," *Brain Research Bulletin* 82, nos. 1–2 (2010): 46–56.

11. Paul Gilbert, Mark W. Baldwin, Chris Irons, Jodene R. Baccus, and Michelle Palmer, "Self-Criticism and Self-Warmth: An Imagery Study Exploring Their Relation to Depression," *Journal of Cognitive Psychotherapy* 20, no. 2 (2006): 183–200.

12. D. R. Carney, A. J. C. Cuddy, and A. J. Yap, "Power Posing: Brief Nonverbal Displays Affect Neuroendocrine Levels and Risk Tolerance," *Psychological Science OnlineFirst*, September 21, 2010, http://www.people.hbs.edu/acuddy/in%20press,%20carney,%20cuddy,%20&%20yap,%20psych%20science.pdf.

13. R. F. Baumeister, "Ego Depletion and Self-Regulation Failure: A

Resource Model of Self-Control," *Alcoholism: Clinical and Experimental Research* 27, no. 2 (2003): 281–84.

14. M. T. Gailliot, R. F. Baumeister, C. N. DeWall, J. K. Maner, E. A. Plant, D. M. Tice, et al., "Self-Control Relies on Glucose as a Limited Energy Source: Willpower Is More Than a Metaphor," *Journal of Personality and Social Psychology* 92, no. 2 (2007): 325–36.

## 6. Different Charisma Styles

1. S. Milgram, *Obedience to Authority: An Experimental View* (New York: Harper & Row, 1975); N. J. Russell, "Milgram's Obedience to Authority Experiments: Origins and Early Evolution," *British Journal of Social Psychology* 50, part 1 (2011): 140–62.

2. A. Freed, P. Chandler, J. Mouton, and R. Blake, "Stimulus and Background Factors in Sign Violation," *Journal of Personality* 23 (1955): 499.

3. R. M. A. Nelisson and M. H. C. Meijers, "Social Benefits of Luxury Brands as Costly Signals of Wealth and Status," *Evolution & Human Behavior* 32, no. 5 (2011): 343–55.

4. From Halpin in 1954 to Pillai in 1991.

## 7. Charismatic First Impressions

1. John Kenneth Galbraith, *Economics, Peace and Laughter* (New York: New American Library, 1971), 50.

2. Dr. Nalini Ambady, *First Impressions* (New York: Guilford Press, 2008).

3. L. P. Naumann, S. Vazire, P. J. Rentfrow, and S. D. Gosling, "Personality Judgments Based on Physical Appearance," *Personality and Social Psychology Bulletin* 35, no. 12 (2009): 1661–71.

4. P. Borkenau, S. Brecke, C. Mottig, and M. Paelecke, "Extraversion Is Accurately Perceived After a 50-Ms Exposure to a Face," *Journal of Research in Personality* 43 (2009): 703–6; P. Borkenau and A. Liebler, "Trait Inferences: Sources of Validity at Zero Acquaintance, *Journal of Personality and Social Psychology* 62 (1992): 645–57; S. D. Gosling, S. J. Ko, T. Mannarelli, and M. E. Morris, "A Room with a Cue: Personality Judgments Based on Offices and Bedrooms, *Journal of Personality and Social Psychology* 82 (2002): 379–98; M. J. Levesque and D. A. Kenny, "Accuracy of Behavioral Predictions at Zero Acquaintance: A Social Relations Analysis, *Journal of Personality and Social Psychology* 65 (1993): 1178–87.

5. N. Ambady and R. Rosenthal, "Half a Minute: Predicting Teacher Evaluations from Thin Slices of Nonverbal Behavior and Physical Attractiveness," *Journal of Personality and Social Psychology* 64, no. 3 (1993): 431–41.

6. T. Emswiller, K. Deaux, and J. E. Willits, "Similarity, Sex, and Requests for Small Favors," *Journal of Applied Social Psychology* 1 (1971): 284–91.

7. G. L. Stewart, S. L. Dustin, M. R. Barrick, and T. C. Darnold, "Exploring the Handshake in Employment Interviews," *Journal of Applied Psychology* 93, no. 5 (September 2008): 1139–46.

## 8. Speaking—and Listening—with Charisma

1. Ronald E. Riggio, *The Charisma Quotient: What It Is, How to Get It, How to Use It* (New York: Dodd Mead: 1988), 76.

2. Artur Schnabel, in *Chicago Daily News*, June 11, 1958.

3. Robert B. Cialdini, *Influence: The Psychology of Persuasion*, rev. ed. (New York: Harper Paperbacks, 2006).

4. Ibid.

5. Dale Carnegie, *How to Win Friends and Influence People* (New York: Simon & Schuster, 1936).

6. A. Hackmann, "Working with Images in Clinical Psychology," in *Comprehensive Clinical Psychology*, eds. A. Bellack and M. Hersen (London: Pergamon, 1998), 301–17.

7. Riggio, *Charisma Quotient*.

8. R. P. Perry, P. C. Abrami, and L. Leventhal, "Educational Seduction: The Effect of Instructor Expressiveness and Lecture Content on Student Ratings and Achievement," *Journal of Educational Psychology* 71 (1979): 107–16.

9. A. Drahota, A. Costall, and V. Reddy, "The Vocal Communication of Different Kinds of Smile," *Speech Communication* 50, no. 4 (2008): 278.

## 9. Charismatic Body Language

1. D. Goleman, "What Makes a Leader?" *Harvard Business Review* (January 2004).

2. Ronald E. Riggio, *The Charisma Quotient: What It Is, How to Get It, How to Use It* (New York: Dodd Mead, 1988).

3. J. E. Bono and R. Ilies, "Charisma, Positive Emotions and Mood Contagion," *The Leadership Quarterly* 17, no. 4 (2006): 317–34.

4. Ker Than, "Why Some Old Lovers Look Alike," *LiveScience*, February 14, 2006.

5. D. Goleman and R. Boyatzi, "Social Intelligence and the Biology of Leadership," *Harvard Business Review* (September 2008).

6. N. Gueguen, C. Jacob, and A. Martin, "Mimicry in Social Interaction: Its Effect on Human Judgment and Behavior," *European Journal of Social Sciences* 8, no. 2 (2009).

7. Heini Hediger, *The Psychology and Behaviour of Animals in Zoos and Circuses* (New York: Dover Publications, 1955).

8. Allan and Barbara Pease, *The Definitive Book of Body Language* (New York: Bantam, 2006).

9. Ibid.

10. J. Kellerman, J. Lewis, and J. D. Laird, "Looking and Loving: The Effects of Mutual Gaze on Feelings of Romantic Love," *Journal of Research in Personality* 23 (1989): 145–61.

11. Les Fehmi and Jim Robbins, *The Open-Focus Brain: Harnessing the Power of Attention to Heal Mind and Body* (Boston: Trumpeter, 2007).

## 10. Difficult Situations

1. E. Aronson, R. D. Akert, and T. D. Wilson, *Social Psychology*, 6th ed. (Upper Saddle River, NJ: Pearson Prentice Hall, 2006).

2. K. Izuma, D. N. Saito, and N. Sadato, "Processing of Social and Monetary Rewards in the Human Striatum," *Neuron* 58, no. 2 (2008): 284–94.

3. D. A. Redelmeier, J. Katz, and D. Kahneman, "Memories of Colonoscopy: A Randomized Trial," *Pain* 104, nos. 1–2 (2003): 187–94.

## 11. Presenting with Charisma

1. "What's with the Newspapers?" *Plain Language at Work Newsletter* (May 15, 2005), http://www.impact-information.com/impactinfo/newsletter/plwork15.htm; S. L. Mailloux, M. E. Johnson, D. G. Fisher, and T. J. Pettibone, "How Reliable Is Computerized Assessment of Readability?" *Computers in Nursing* 13, no. 5 (1995): 221–25; Joe Kimble, "Writing for Dollars, Writing to Please," *Scribes Journal of Legal Writing*, 1996–97, http://www.plainlanguagenetwork.org/kimble/dollars.htm.

2. P. Valdez and A. Mehrabian, "Effects of Color on Emotions," *Journal of Experimental Psychology: General* 123, no. 4 (1994): 394–409; T. W. Whitfield and T. J. Wiltshire, "Color Psychology: A Critical Re-

view," *Genetic, Social, and General Psychology Monographs* 116, no. 4 (1990): 385–411.

## 12. Charisma in a Crisis

1. G. Devereux, "Charismatic Leadership and Crisis," in *Psychoanalysis and the Social Sciences*, vol. 4, eds. W. Muensterberger and S. Axelrod (New York: Dutton, 1955): 145–57.
2. Robert B. Cialdini, *Influence: The Psychology of Persuasion*, rev. ed. (New York: Harper Paperback, 2006).

## 13. The Charismatic Life: Rising to the Challenge

1. Jay A. Conger and Rabindra N. Kanungo, "Toward a Behavioral Theory of Charismatic Leadership in Organizational Settings," Academy of Management. *The Academy of Management Review* 12, no. 4 (1987).

# Index